Ambrose Macaulay

20 September 1998

PROTESTANT, CATHOLIC AND DISSENTER

Edited by Liam Swords

Protestant, Catholic and Dissenter

THE CLERGY AND 1798

the columba press

First published in 1997 by
the columba press
55A Spruce Avenue, Stillorgan Industrial Park, Blackrock, Co Dublin

Cover by Bill Bolger
Origination by The Columba Press
Printed in Ireland by Colour Books Ltd, Dublin

ISBN 1 85607 209 6

Contents

List of Abbreviations

A.A.E.	Archives des Affaires Etrangères, Paris
A.N.	Archives Nationale, Paris
Anal. Hib.	*Analecta Hibernica*
A.P.	Archives de la police judiciare, Paris
Arch. Hib.	*Archivium Hibernicum*
A.S.P.	Archives de la Seine, Paris
A.V.	Archives de Versailles
B.N.L.	*Belfast Newsletter*
Brit. Mus.	British Museum
D.D.A.	Dublin Diocesan Archives
D.E.P.	*Dublin Evening Post*
D.N.B.	Dictionary of National Bibliography
D.O.D.	Papers on the United Irishmen in P.R.O.N.I.
F.D.J.	*Faulkner's Dublin Journal*
I.C.P.	Irish College, Paris
I.S.P.O.	Irish State Papers Office
L.C.S.	London Corresponding Society
Nat. Arch.	National Archives, Dublin
P.R.O.	Public Record Office, London
P.R.O.N.I.	Public Record Office, Belfast
R.C.B.	Representative Church Body, Dublin
R.G.S.U.	Records of the General Synod of Ulster

Christian Citizens: The Catholic Church and Radical Politics 1790-1800[1]

Daire Keogh

The French Revolution cast a long shadow over Ireland in the 1790s: throughout the decade the country fell increasingly under the Gallic spell. The revolution quickly became the test of political opinions; while for Tone and the reformers it represented the morning star of liberty, the great majority of the Catholic clergy saw it as the incarnation of all that was contrary to Christianity. Thomas Hussey, chaplain to the Spanish Ambassador in London, summed up these sentiments in August 1790 when he attributed the changing temper of Irish Catholics to what he called 'the French disease'.[2] The progress of this contagion brought about novel relationships in Ireland and in this intense political atmosphere the 'race for the Catholic' took on a greater urgency.[3]

I

The last quarter of the eighteenth century witnessed the re-emergence of the Catholic Church from the isolation and dislocation it had suffered under the penal laws. Debate remains as to whether the laws were a draconian code, or merely 'reasonable inconveniences', as has been suggested by Connolly.[4] Nevertheless, it is increasingly clear that the story of the Catholic community in the eighteenth century is more one of 'endurance and emergence' than of subjugation, as was previously accepted.[5]

By the outbreak of the French Revolution in 1789, the Catholic revival was well under way. The Relief Acts of 1778 and 1782 removed most of the penal restrictions regarding religious practice, and through the efforts of reforming bishops, especially James Butler II of Cashel, John Troy of Dublin and Patrick Plunket of Meath, steps had been taken to re-establish discipline within the church.

Regular meetings of the four Metropolitans were resumed in 1787. The younger bishops engaged in frequent visitations of their dioceses, correcting abuses and bringing practice into line with the Roman ritual. Clerical conferences became increasingly common and the emphasis placed on catechesis is reflected in the revival of the confraternities, particularly the Confraternity of Christian Doctrine, and in the impressive amount of religious and devotional material printed. Hugh Fenning's recent work on Catholic print-ings in Cork alone forces a rethink of the so-called 'devotional revolution' of the mid-nineteenth-century.[6]

Further evidence of the Catholic revival may be seen in the spate of chapel building which characterised the last quarter of the eighteenth century. There were by then 1,800 priests in the country and the renewed vigour of the church gave them a heightened role in the community. The bishops, too, were enjoying increased status. They were fortunate in having men of the calibre of John Troy amongst their number. It is perhaps both a reflection of his ability and of the renewed authority of the episcopacy (or indeed the ab-sence of effective lay agitation) that Troy was consulted by Luke Gardiner prior to the framing of the relief bills of 1778 and 1782. While divisions within the parliamentary reform movement for most of the 1780s forced the Catholic question to the background, the revolutionary events in France quickly reopened the debate.

The progress of 'the French disease' had serious implications for the hierarchy. In France, the Catholic Church had been abolished under the terms of the Civil Constitution, and throughout Europe the spread of the revolution made serious inroads into institutional religion. The bishops were well aware of European events since the Irish mission depended on the continental colleges for the supply of priests.

The Revolution and its associated Irish radicalism created a nightmarish scenario for the Irish bishops. Under French influence, it quickly became the consensus that the Catholic 'Church seemed to represent all the illiberal forces of arbitrary despotism, privilege, and tradition, and the ignorance and superstition which retarded the progress of rational and virtuous government'.[7] In Ireland, however, it is fair to argue that the bishops' opposition to the radicalism of the 1790s was as much pragmatic as principled.

Troy's celebrated pastoral of 1793, *On the Duties of Christian Citizens*, reflects this, since his claim that Catholics were fit to enjoy the benefits of a free constitution, exposed him to the charge of advocating republican government.[8] Catholic loyalty had been their trump card since the late 1770s. The relief measures of 1778 and 1782 had arguably been made in an attempt to recall the patriots to their senses, but those concessions had come from the benevolence of the crown and not from a sense of justice or right. In the 1790s the bishops feared that these concessions would be repealed, or that future relief would be restricted by imprudent agitation. Apart from these concerns, the bishops were haunted by the images of the devastated church in France; it was the excesses of the French rather than radical principles *per se* which inspired their pastorals throughout the 1790s.

Along with this, the crisis brought a novel convergence of interests between the British government and the Catholic Church and their mutual concern created a new atmosphere of trust and dialogue. The Catholic Church, with its renewed institutions, became the perceived bulwark against Jacobinism in Ireland, while British arms offered the only hope of salvation for the continental church. As the decade progressed, and the revolutionary armies threatened the Papal States, the Irish bishops came under intense pressure from Propaganda Fide to urge loyalty and obedience to the British crown. Underlying both the appeal from the administration and Rome was the assumption that the hierarchy was in a position to control their people, but the Catholic community had been transformed and the bishops were at best only able to motivate a *willing* flock.

Within the Catholic Committee, the 1780s had seen the emergence of confident middle class rivals to the traditional aristocratic leadership. French revolutionary influence accelerated this transformation and in December 1791 Lord Kenmare and the old guard withdrew, relinquishing the leadership to John Keogh, Thomas Braughall and the other advanced radicals. This renewed leadership demanded redress for Catholic grievances as a right, rather than as a reward to be sought with deference.

The schism within the Committee was a bitter one and the episcopal decision to side with Kenmare resulted in their humiliation. Throughout the country their attempts to gain signatures to the loyal address resulted in a paltry response and it became increasingly clear that either the clergy joined with the people or the people would go it alone. A resolution of the General Committee of the Catholics in January 1792 spoke of the divide in the Catholic body, the attempts of the seceders to 'seduce the ... clergy from the laity' and the conversion of 'the ministers of the gospel into instruments of oppression'.[9]

The lessons of the Kenmare episode were not lost on the radicals who, throughout 1792 and 1793, exploited episcopal weakness to the limit. The bishops were now in an unenviable position with both the radicals and the Castle administration vying for their support. The bitter debate on Hercules Langrishe's relief bill of 1792 incensed sensitivities on the Catholic Committee and they particularly resented the 'shopkeeper and shoplifter' jibes hurled in their direction. Their immediate decision was to present a declaration of their civil and religious principles, but more significantly they called a convention in an attempt to display once and for all their truly representative nature.

The Committee decided to muster the assistance of the Catholic clergy to secure maximum support for the declaration. Troy at once rallied to their side and this prompt response was inspired by his desire to bring his isolation from the Committee to an end. No doubt he was also aware of criticism that the bishops appeared more concerned with government approval than with the sufferings of their people.[10] The Committee's success in obtaining so many signatures to the declaration was largely due to their effective marshalling of the clergy through the country. There is, however, little doubt that the clergy were in some cases intimidated into supporting the venture against their own judgement; in Wexford Bishop Caulfield was threatened with a revival of the Rightboy tactics of withholding dues, while John Keogh confirmed that 'the people seem well inclined to give them [the non-co-operating clergy] the French cure'.[11]

In the same way, it was the Committee's exploitation of the renewed institutions of the church which made the convention possible. The reform congress of 1784 had failed because the High Sheriffs in the counties were unwilling to co-operate in the election of delegates, but the Catholic Convention of 1792 had been a success precisely because the Committee had used parish structures and the clergy in building a broadly democratic and representative convention.

The appearance of Archbishop Troy and Bishop Francis Moylan at the Back Lane Parliament, and their promise to rise or fall with the Committee, seemed to place the hierarchy inextricably at the head of this great swell, but this was misleading since the bishops were following the lead of the people. Nevertheless, the reality was lost on the administration and ultra-loyalists and they retained the memories of the parish meetings which gave the impression of a powerful church, one capable of exerting real influence over its members. As Leighton has observed, if the convention was proof of Catholic ability to organise in support of their publicly declared aims, their ability to plot rebellion could also be assumed.[12] However, the reverse of this was that if the institutions of the church could be harnessed by the administration, rebellion could be prevented.

In this way the church became the object of attention for both radicals and loyalists. The Convention Act of 1793 made overt political activity impossible, but the United Irishmen found a surrogate for their meetings in the large number of debating societies and political clubs spread through the country. In a similar way, the radicals turned their attention to the church and took advantage of the many proselytising opportunities offered by its structures. Chapel meetings were a constant feature of both urban and rural radicalism in the 1790s and the level of reports reaching Dublin Castle reflects the anxiety which the meetings generated. Leonard McNally, the United Irish lawyer and informer, claimed that the Defenders had originated in these parochial meetings, but his information as usual was vague and tended towards sensationalism.[13] The notorious spy,

Francis Higgins, claimed that the Dublin charitable societies were entirely composed of United Irishmen and that they were formed for no other purpose than to carry out sedition.[14] The large chapel congregations also provided the radicals with opportunities to disseminate their propaganda; broadsheets were frequently posted to chapel doors and handbills passed out among Mass goers.

The confraternities, which had formed an essential part of the Catholic revival, provided ideal opportunities for covert association. From Rush, in north Dublin, came warnings of meetings which supposedly met for religious purposes but 'too frequently to disseminate their traitorous principles and to form plans for outrage'.[15]

Scapulars, too, became symbols of identification and badges of sedition. James Little, the rector of Lacken, in his diary recording the events of 1798 in Mayo, pointed to the use made of scapulars and confraternities by the radicals in mobilising the people: 'after undergoing the cookery of scapularism,' he declared, the people were enticed to feast upon 'the dishes of athestical libertinism'.[16] In Edenderry, the behaviour of a prisoner was attributed to his enthusiasm for the 'popish mania' of the 'rosary or scapular of the Blessed Lady' which had spread amongst the lower classes, particularly in the Defenders.[17] Significantly, Fr James McCary, the United Irish emissary and later government spy in the Ards peninsula, described himself as organiser of the White Scapular Confraternity in the diocese of Down and Connor. Amongst the subscribers to his devotional 1797 tract, *The Sure Way to Heaven*, were the Teelings and the Dublin United Irishman Hugh MacVeagh.[18] In the wake of the rebellion, Richard Musgrave devoted considerable hostile attention to the use made of scapulars by the United Irishmen and in 1799 the Archbishop of Tuam published a pastoral against scapulars which he believed had become not only the objects of superstition, but had been used as banners by the rebels.[19]

Religious processions and funerals also became transformed into United Irish rallies and displays. The initial symptoms of this were seen at a funeral of a freemason in Dungannon in November 1796. The first of the Dublin United Irish funerals took place in April 1797 when five thousand, including the 'Marats of Pill Lane', marched in procession behind the remains of Edward Dunn.[20] There were also incidents of mock funerals, but these high profile funerals attracted adverse attention from the Castle authorities and much of the cover which the confraternities and clubs had provided for the United Irishmen was now gone. The government prohibited such political displays, but the *Northern Star* humourously reported on the repressive regulations concerning funerals, declaring that in future people must literally follow the Lord's instructions and 'let the dead bury the dead'.[21]

Clerical involvement in the United Irish cause was significant, even though the numbers of priests involved was very limited. The Armagh man, Fr James Coigly, discussed elsewhere in this volume, remains the most celebrated of these priests, but in a similar way Frs John Martin OSA of Drogheda and the Dominican James McCary of Carrickfergus exploited the opportunities their priesthood provided in propagating the United Irish gospel.[22]

Loyalists, too, alarmed at the often bizzarely exaggerated accounts from informers, attempted to tap the potential of the church. On one level there was a fear in government circles that the financial dependence of the clergy on their people was bound to expose them to contagion. It was this consideration which had made a state provision for the clergy so attractive since the notion was first mooted by the Viceroy's private secretary, Thomas Lewis O'Beirne, in 1782, but even in the crisis of the 1790s the Catholic hierarchy successfully resisted this and the proposal to establish a Royal veto on episcopal nominations.

The foundation of the Royal College in Maynooth with government support in 1795, however, successfully detached the episcopacy from any further flirtation with Catholic out-of-doors politics. The foundation of the college deepened the divide between the bishops and their people, since the latter regarded it as a sop for the failure of Grattan's emancipation bill.[23] The bishops, however, were undeterred and continued to urge their flocks to loyalty and passive obedience in the growing crisis.

In spite of these divisions, the chapel meetings and petitioning of the 1790s presented a powerful, if mistaken, image of Catholic unity to outsiders. Thus, prior to the rebellion many magistrates emulated the radicals and attempted to exploit the potential of the church in an effort to instill loyalty. Just as the radicals raised petitions, so the magistrates orchestrated loyal resolutions, often choosing a chapel in which to administer oaths of allegiance. Andrew Newton of Coagh, Co Tyrone, claimed to have been the first magistrate to encourage Catholics to enter into these resolutions. Newton began his campaign at Ardboe where the priest and 678 parishioners signed a loyal declaration. He repeated this through much of mid-Ulster and was confident that his efforts had made a 'split between them [the Catholics] and the Presbyterians'.[24]

Newton's example was adopted elsewhere, and published resolutions provide an interesting barometer of regional tensions in late 1797 and early 1798.[25] The earliest addresses are mainly from Antrim, Down and other parts of Ulster, but from early 1798 they appear in the south, with the Catholics of Richard Musgrave's parish of Cappoquin, Co Waterford, being amongst the first to publish a declaration.[26] Petitioning reached a peak in March 1798 and it generally formed part of a wider campaign, as was the case of Bishop Caulfield's pastoral, delivered in the context of Lord Mountnorris' drive against the United Irishmen in Wexford.

Such resolutions were viewed with scepticism in some loyal quarters; it was suggested that they provided a cover for the true sentiments of the people, but while the Marquis of Downshire had little faith in them, he believed they 'did no harm' and might at least be useful in separating 'some of these poor deluded fools from the general conspiracy'.[27] Arthur O'Connor's radical *Press* condemned the petitioning, as 'the most thoroughly abominable' scheme ever employed by the 'abandoned administration', claiming that the resolution from Rathlin Island had been misrepresented to the people there as a petition to bring the Armagh magistrates to justice for their treatment of Catholics.[28]

Many priests joined with local magistrates in urging their people to surrender arms. Some, like Fr Patrick Ryan, pastor of Coolock, Co Dublin and subsequently Bishop of Ferns, were more than willing to lend their support to the loyal effort, but in other instances the magistrates and militia, like the radicals, intimidated the clergy. Immediately prior to the rebellion, the loyalist *Dublin Journal* praised the efforts of Captain Swayne of the City of Cork Militia who had addressed the congregation of Fr John Lynch of Ballysax, near Kilcullen. So successful was his exhortation that five hundred pikes and vast quantities of arms were 'voluntarily surrendered' over the next two days.[29]

While the *Dublin Journal* carried the sanitised official account of the proceedings, William Farrell, a Co Carlow United Irishman, recalled a more brutal, if equally embellished, memory of Swayne's visit to the chapel of Fr Higgins at Prosperous, Co Kildare. According to this account, the captain interrupted Mass and ordered the people to bring in their arms. Then, turning to the old priest who later became a target of the United Irishmen, Swayne warned, 'If you don't have it done I'll pour boiling lead down your throat.' Farrell recalled that the congregation dispersed 'in sullen and silent indignation, whispering their wrongs and insults and breathing vengeance at any hazard'.[30] In Higgins' case, then, we see a concrete example of the 'battle for affection' as the curate was subject to alternative loyalist and United Irish intimidation.

Similarly, the hierarchy were subjected to pressure from both parties. In the spring of 1798 Troy, described by Patrick Duigenan as 'a steady loyalist', was criticised by the Lord Lieutenant Camden for his timidity in failing to call the people to their senses.[31] The radical press, on the other hand, lampooned the hierarchy for their supine support of the administration. At Christmas 1797 *The Press* carried a seasonal reflection with striking parallels between Judaea and Ireland:

> The PRIESTHOOD and the Government of the province where he [Jesus] had his birth, found his doctrines incompatible with the foreign yoke which their tyranny imposed.[32]

In a measure of the success of this campaign, the bishops were forced to address these specific criticisms in their pastorals.

Such was the 'battle for affection' or the race for the support of the Catholic clergy run between the radicals and the administration in the 1790s. Once the rebellion burst out in May 1798, the great majority of the clergy remained steadfastly loyal, with only seventy of their number joining the rebel cause. But in the bitter post-rebellion polemic, there was a sense in which both sides were justified in their criticism of the clergy. On the one hand, Richard Musgrave believed that the rebellion sprang from 'the envenomed hatred with which the popish multitude ... [were] inspired from their earliest age by their clergy' towards the Protestant state and British connection. On the other, Miles Byrne railed against the clergy for their 'pious assiduity and earnest endeavours' to keep the Irish in thraldom. It was only this, he believed, which saved 'the infamous English government in Ireland from destruction'.[33] These shared conservative and radical assessments of the political potential of the church gave urgency and sense to the propaganda battle of the 1790s.

Notes:

1   A version of this paper was first published in *Bullán; an Irish studies journal*, vol. 2, no. 2 (Summer 1995), pp. 35-45.
2   Thomas Hussey to Richard Burke, 28 August 1790, *Burke Corr.*, iv, p. 134.
3   Bartlett, T., *The fall and rise of the Irish nation; the Catholic question 1690-1830* (Dublin, 1992).
4   Connolly, SJ, *Religion, Law and Power; the making of Protestant Ireland 1660-1760* (Oxford, 1992), pp. 263-314.
5   See T. Power and K. Whelan (eds), *Endurance and Emergence; the Catholic Community in eighteenth century Ireland* (Dublin, 1990).
6   Fenning, Hugh, 'Catholics in "A purely Protestant town": a catalogue of Cork imprints from 1723 to 1830' in *Cork Arch. Jn.*, vol. 100 (1995), pp. 129-148.
7   Curtin, N.J., *The United Irishmen: popular politics in Ulster and Dublin 1791-98* (Oxford, 1994), p. 36.
8   Troy, J., *Pastoral Instructions on the duties of Christian Citizens* (Dublin, 1793).
9   Edwards, R.D., (ed.), 'The minute book of the Catholic Association, 1791-93' in *Arch. Hib.*, XL (1942), p. 157. See D. Keogh, 'Archbishop Troy, the Catholic Church and Irish Radicalism, 1791-3' in D. Dickson, D. Keogh and K. Whelan (eds.), *The United Irishmen; Republicanism, Radicalism and Rebellion* (Dublin, 1993) pp. 124-34.
10   Troy to Brancadero, 18 May 1792, Dublin Diocesan Archives.
11   J. Keogh to T. Hussey, 29 March 1792, P.R.O. H.O. 100/38/243.
12   Leighton, C.D.A., *Catholicism in a Protestant State: a study of the Irish Ancien Regime* (Dublin, 1994) p. 65.
13   J.W. to 24 July 1796, Nat. Arch. Reb. Papers, 620/36/227.
14   F.H. to 26 February 1798, Nat. Arch. Reb. Papers, 620/18/14.

15 T. Roche to E. Cooke, 12 May 1798, Nat. Arch. Reb. Papers, 620/37/61.
16 Little, J., Diary, in *Anal. Hib.*, II, p. 67.
17 Mrs Brownrigg to E. Cooke, 27 August 1797, Nat. Arch. Reb. Papers, 620/32/77
18 McCary, J., *The Sure Way to Heaven* (Belfast, 1797).
19 Circular letter of Dr Dillon of Tuam, 27 March 1799, D.D.A.
20 *Morning Post*, 8 December 1796; *The Times*, 12 April 1797, cited in J. Smyth, *The Men of No Property* (Dublin, 1992) p. 155.
21 *Northern Star*, reported in the *Morning Post*, 8 December 1796.
22 See D. Keogh, "The most dangerous villain in society'; Fr John Martin's mission to the United Irishmen of Wicklow in 1798' in *Eighteenth Century Ireland* (1992) pp. 115-35; J. Gray, 'A loyal sermon of 1798' in *Linen Hall Review*, 1990.
23 Corish, P.J., *Maynooth College, 1795-1995* (Dublin, 1995), pp. 1-19.
24 *Dublin Evening Post*, 24 June 1797; Andrew Newton to 1 February 1798, Nat. Arch. Reb. Papers 620/35/102. For a recent study of radical politics in Ulster, see L.M. Cullen, 'The United Irishmen: problems and issues of the 1790s' in *Ulster Local Studies*, vol 18., no. 2 (Spring, 1997), pp. 7-27.
25 See D. Keogh, *The French Disease: The Catholic Church and Radicalism in Ireland 1790-1800* (Dublin, 1993) pp. 258-61.
26 Address of the Catholics of Cappoquin, *D.E.P.*, 17 March 1798.
27 Downshire, 14 January 1798, Nat. Arch. Reb. Papers, 620/35/34.
28 *Press*, 21 December 1797; 8 February 1798.
29 *F.D.J.*, 22 May 1798.
30 McHugh, R., (ed), *Carlow in '98*, p. 227.
31 Duignan cited in J. D'Alton, *The Memoirs of the Archbishops of Dublin* (Dublin, 1888), p. 486; Camden to Portland, April 1798, H. O. 100/76/91-4.
32 *The Press*, 26 December 1797.
33 Musgrave, R., *Memoirs of the Different Rebellions in Ireland* (Dublin, 1800) p. 67; M. Byrne, *Memoirs*, 1, p. 54.

Irish Priests and Students in Revolutionary France

Liam Swords

When Wolfe Tone arrived in Paris from Philadelphia on 1 February 1796, he quickly became aware of the existence of a network of Irish revolutionaries there. One of them, Nicholas Madgett 1,[1] was then the head of the translation department in the Ministry of Foreign Affairs. Delacroix, the minister, left Irish affairs, and particularly Tone's mission, largely in the care of Madgett. Nicholas Madgett 1 was the nephew of the Bishop of Kerry, also of the same name. He had been educated and ordained at the Irish College, Toulouse, where he later became prefect of studies. At the outbreak of the revolution he was serving as a *curé* in the provinces. In the summer of 1790 the National Assembly adopted the Civil Constitution of the Clergy and subsequently imposed an oath on all clergy to support it. Pope Pius VI condemned it and threatened all those who took the oath with excommunication. Many of the French clergy chose to go underground or join the growing numbers of royalist *émigrés*. Others, including some Irish priests like Madgett, as well as Henry O'Kane, an Irish *curé* in Nantes, chose to abandon the priesthood and opt for a secular career. He made his way to Paris, where he became politically active.

The main concentration of the Irish in Paris was in the two Irish colleges in the city, Collège des Lombards and Collège des Irlandais. The former was reserved exclusively for priest-students, while the latter catered solely for non-ordained students and seminarians. A group of the latter became involved in a fracas with the National Guard at the Champ de Mars on 6 December 1790.[2] An 'altar of the fatherland' had been erected there to commemorate the fall of the Bastille on 14 July 1789. The Irish students, on a day out from Collège des Irlandais, indulged in some horseplay in the vicinity of the altar, which incensed the guards on duty there. In the ensuing encounter six Irish students, among them Thomas McKenna, were arrested. They were frog-marched across Paris, escorted by Lafayette, to Hotel de Ville, where they were tried and subsequently imprisoned for a couple of weeks. The incident provoked a rash of pamphlets, mainly condemning the Irish as the enemy of the people. It also made the two Irish colleges targets for the revolutionary mobs. The first riot against Collège des Irlandais took place on the evening of the incident, when the superior, Charles Kearney, had to be rescued by the National Guard, but riots continued to erupt outside both colleges on and off through 1791 and early 1792.

Irish priest-students from Collège des Lombards, where a Killaloe priest, John Baptist Walsh, was superior, had been leaving Paris from shortly after the outbreak of the revolution. One of the first to escape with difficulty in October 1789 was James Coigly. By early summer 1791 the remaining priest-students were preparing to leave. A number of Irish students continued to reside in Collège des Irlandais. It was invaded by the mob on 10 August 1792 and the students were forced to flee and found temporary accommodation in the neighbourhood. The superior, Charles Kearney, was also forced to go into hiding. The palace of the Tuilleries had been invaded on the same day and the King was put under arrest. It emerged later that, during this time, Kearney had been sent on a royal mission to London where he spent three weeks. He was back in Paris, though not in the Irish College, by 2 September.

For the next four days, the September massacres took place, during which one hundred and sixty priests, who were prisoners in the Carmelite church in rue Vaugirard, were killed. One of those fortunate enough to escape on that occasion was an Ardagh priest, Peter Flood. Flood, who had been procurator of the prestigious Collège de Navarre, refused to take the oath but remained on in Paris. He was rescued 'from the sword of the armed mob' by one of the commissioners of the Commune and presented the following day at the bar of the National Assembly as proof to the English people 'of fraternity and generosity'. He was voted the means of returning to Ireland where he later became president of Maynooth.[3]

While Kearney was absent from Collège des Irlandais, a number of students complained about his administration of the college to the commissioners of the Commune. But their main complaint was directed at John Baptist Walsh. As superior of Collège des Lombards, Walsh was the supremo of both colleges. He had been appointed in 1787, replacing four superiors, one from each province. A royal decree of 1728 had given the students of each province the right to elect their superior. The students now claimed that Walsh's appointment violated the students' right of election.[4] The commisssioners made their report and the municipality decided to dismiss Kearney and Walsh and authorised the election by the students of new superiors, under the supervision of two of the municipality.

The election took place on 29 October. Only nine voters participated. There were then from twenty to twenty-five students in the college, what remained of some seventy who were there in 1789. The election was won by William Duckett from Killarney by a single vote and he thus became superior to replace Kearney. Duckett had completed his studies and left Collège des Irlandais in July 1789. A second ballot was then held to find a replacement for Walsh as over-all administrator of the Irish properties. Here the successful candidate was Nicholas Madgett 1.[5]

Of the nine voters, a number were later to become active in Irish affairs, such as William Duckett himself, Bernard MacSheehy, Edward Ferris, Jeremy Curtayne, and Bartholomew Blackwell. These were probably the five who voted for Duckett. Another, Thomas MacKenna, who later took part in an expedition to Ireland, on this occasion, with characteristic independence, signed a protest a few days later 'against all that had taken place at the request of the above citizens'.[6] The keys of the college were duly handed over to Duckett. Kearney, still in hiding, wrote immediately to Lebrun, Minister of Foreign Affairs, protesting against the election. He was prepared to return if his safety was guaranteed. Lebrun, himself a former priest of obscure origins, was surprisingly sympathetic. Kearney may have known him in pre-revolutionary days as Lebrun had been a student in the nearby Collège de Montaigu.

Lebrun wrote immediately to Roland, Minister of the Interior. Referring to 'the special affection we have for the Irish nation', he requested his colleague to intervene promptly and secure Kearney's restoration.[7] Shortly afterwards Kearney was re-instated.

The students were becoming increasingly politicised. Even prior to the revolution, Irish students were street-wise. As Collège des Irlandais was not a teaching college, the students there mixed with other Paris students in some of the many other colleges in the University of Paris, and were thus *au courant* with all the exciting ideas then sweeping through these institutions. For some time they had been attending the meetings of the Society of the Friends of the Rights of Man which were held on Thursdays and Sundays at White's Hotel, in 7 passage des Petits Pères. They attended the banquet given there by the English-speaking residents of Paris on 18 November. These were heady times in Paris, especially for Irish college students just cuttting their first political teeth. Here they mixed with the emerging Irish patriots, Lord Edward FitzGerald, and the Sheares brothers, John and Henry, as well as pro-revolution officers like Colonel Arthur Dillon, fresh from his triumphs on the eastern front. At the banquet toasts were drunk to the new young republic. Dillon proposed a toast to 'the people of Ireland', offering to place his own sword at its service. Lord Edward FitzGerald proposed 'the abolition of hereditary titles' and publicly renounced his own, adopting in its place the now fashionable 'citoyen'.

The French army had just won a decisive victory over the Austrians at the battle of Jemappes and made clear their intentions of carrying their revolution abroad. The banquet in White's hotel drew up a congratulatory address to be presented to the National Convention. The address, which was presented by a large deputation at the bar of the Convention on 28 November, concluded: 'Soon, there will only remain a shameful memory of all those would-be governments, fraudulent creations of priests and tyrants combined.'[8] It was greeted with prolonged applause. Following the signature of Lord Edward FitzGerald came those of William Duckett and the Irish students, John O'Neill, Edward Ferris, Bartholomew Murry, and a little further on those of Bernard MacSheehy and

Jeremy Curtayne. It was also signed by Nicholas Madgett 1. Madgett later informed the Minister for Foreign Affairs that 'within four days the English minister had received an exact copy of the address presented to the National Convention by British citizens, with a list of all the signatories.'[9] Madgett accused Walsh and Kearney of being the informers. The informer was in fact a Jamaican-born priest, Charles Somers, who was a paid English spy in Paris.

At the end of 1792 the King was put on trial and in January of the following year was found guilty and sentenced to be executed. Louis XVI was guillotined on 21 January 1793, attended on the gallows by the Longford priest, Abbé Edgeworth. In March four of the Irish students were sent on a mission to Ireland to desseminate propaganda there on the French Revolution. William Duckett acted as leader.[10] They went via England and were arrested in London shortly after they arrived. It was in fact Charles Somers who had informed Bland Burges on 4 March about 'a parcel of young fellows just escaped from an Irish seminary here'. Detained for a while in London, they were eventually released, possibly because as Somers had observed 'they were not at all qualified for such a mission' and represented no threat to British security.[11] One of the four, Edward Ferris, made his way to his native Tralee, where he remained active in republican circles.

On 1 February France declared war on England and the position of many of the Irish in France changed dramatically. The war was now going against the French and a wave of xenophobia swept France. Madgett had denounced Walsh and Kearney as spies. Later that year they were again denounced by the Irish students. The students' denunciation was signed by Bernard MacSheehy. On 5 September, terror became officially the order of the day and the Convention decreed that 'all foreigners, born in the territories of powers with whom the Republic was at war' should be arrested. Kearney was arrested almost immediately and detained at first in the Irish College. Shortly afterwards he was transferred to the Luxembourg Palace, where another Irishman, Arthur Dillon, was incarcerated on the same day.

Thirteen Irish students, including Thomas McKenna, presented a petition to the National Convention expressing their 'deep anxiety' at the decree issued against British subjects. 'We declare before this august assembly,' their petition concluded, 'that we yeild to no citizen whatever in our republican sentiments.'[12] Their plea fell on deaf ears. The Irish students were detained in Collège des Irlandais, which by now had been converted into a *maison d'arret.*

One of the very few Irish priests to escape arrest was Richard Ferris and ironically his republicanism was more than suspect. Ferris from Kerry was procurator of the Collège de Montaigu at the outbreak of the revolution. 'Abbé de Ferris', as he then styled himself, refused to take the oath imposed by the Civil Constitution of the Clergy. When the war of the first coalition against France began in April 1792, Ferris exchanged his cassock for a military uniform and joined Berwick's Regiment, where he was quickly promoted to captain and aide-de-camp to Duc de FitzJames.[13] Ferris was stationed at Bingen on the Rhine, where Count Bartholomew O'Mahony was the brigadier-general of the regiment, which was assigned as bodyguard to the Bourbon princes, including Monsieur, brother of the King and the future Louis XVIII.

When the war turned against the coalition, with French victories at Valmy and Jemappes at the end of 1792, Ferris decided to abandon his captaincy and try his luck once more in France, this time posing as an ardent republican. He crossed the border and went into hiding in Triel, a little town about twenty miles west of Paris, close to the home of one of his married sisters. From there in July 1793 he sent a *mémoire* to Lebrun, Minister of Foreign Affairs, on the subject of Ireland and the prospects of a French invasion. He was particularly disdainful of the failed Irish student mission in March. 'Is it with such feeble means,' he asked, 'that the French ministry believes that entire nations are to be conquered?'[14] Unfortunately for Ferris, Lebrun, who had been a student of Ferris at Collège de Montaigu, had been dismissed and placed under house arrest. Ferris continued to write to Foreign Affairs seeking an exemption from the decree against foreigners and asking for a passport to come to Paris and explain himself. By now the police in Triel began to take an unhealthy interest in Ferris.

Finally his persistence paid off. Foreign Affairs wrote to the Committee of Public Safety asking them to extricate Ferris as quickly as possible from the dangerous situation he was in. They pointed out that Ferris had presented a very interesting *mémoire* on Ireland and that 'he had given several other proofs of his ardent zeal for liberty and his attachment to the French Republic.'[15] It was decided to send Ferris on a secret mission to England, 'a mission that required a certain latitude if it was to produce results'.[16] For this purpose he was given 900 *louis d'or* and 1,200 *livres,* and left Paris for London in October, with money, passport and secret code, just as most of his compatriots in Paris – and many of them with much better republican credentials than his – were about to begin their prison sentences.

Once in England, Ferris tried to make contact with the Foreign Secretary, Lord Grenville, with the intention of offering his services to the British intelligence. Grenville referred him to Bland Burges, the under-secretary. The two met in London on 13 October and Burges made a detailed and lengthy minute of their meeting. Ferris told Burges that he had been sent to infiltrate the English ministry and gather information about armaments and prepare the way 'for introducing people to assassinate the king and some of the ministers.'[17] Ferris then produced the French secret code and offered it to Burges who believed it was the same as that used by other French agents in Germany and elsewhere. Ferris told Burges that the French had told him that that they had somebody in the Foreign Office working for them but were not prepared to reveal his name to Ferris. Possibly here, Ferris over-played his hand as Burges quickly pointed out that it was strange that the French Foreign Affairs trusted him with such an important mission and yet withheld such a vital piece of information. Burges cross-examined Ferris on his connections with Somers. Ferris was closely linked to Somers who had advised him to accept the French mission 'as a sure way of aborting the plans of the Jacobins'.

After their meeting Burges wrote to Lord Grenville summarising his interview with Ferris. He advised him that one item deserved special attention, Ferris' commission 'to prepare things for the safe reception of certain persons who might be sent over to assassinate the king and those of his servants, who are more particularly obnoxious to the Jacobin party'. Regarding Ferris himself, Burges observed: 'He appears to be a very sensible discreet man, and to know fully the importance of keeping the secret; and I therefore think it will be safe in his hand.'[18]

On the following day Ferris himself wrote to Grenville, making a number of propositions to the Foreign Secretary.[19] He should be mandated to acquire all public news from newspapers or taverns. The minister should have communicated to Ferris all inconsequential news relative to the movements of troops, etc. which would enable him to continue to enjoy the confidence of the French government. Ferris concluded his letter by offering to provide in England 'persons of the highest distinction who would answer for his honour and his principles'. He gave the names of the Duke and Duchess of Harcourt, Duc and Duchesse de Montmartre and the two Princesses de Craon, among 'a host of other people of quality'. Ferris had made many important connections while he was administrator of Collège de Montaigu. He had been tutor to Prince de Craon, who was now living in England with his cousin, Lord Harcourt.

On 17 October, Grenville replied to Burges saying that his seeing Ferris was out of the question.[20] However, he suggested that Ferris' statement be shown to Pitt, the Prime Minister, and insisted that Ferris be shadowed constantly. M. Duban, whom the Foreign Office believed to be a French gentleman, was given the assignment. London in late 1793 was teeming with French émigrés, among whom were more than five thousand priest-refugees. Among them was Abbé Germain, a former colleague of Ferris in Collège de Montaigu and now teaching French to the children of a rich Englishman. Ferris called on him and Germain later described Ferris to Duban as 'a respectable priest, an excellent royalist and a brave soldier during his campaign'. Ferris was visited by the Bishop of Périgueux and also saw the Bishop of Limoges.

He had several meetings with 'M. Ozée' (Hussey), chaplain at the Spanish embassy.[21] This was Thomas Hussey who later became president of Maynooth College and Bishop of Waterford. Hussey was a friend of Edmund Burke and suggested that Ferris write to him as he carried considerable weight with the English government. He did so but Grenville replied to Burke about the 'necessity of caution and reserve, in such times and on such an occasion'.[22] In London Ferris also sought out some of his old army comrades. Moves were then afoot to form a new Irish brigade in the British army from the royalist remnants of the Irish regiments in France, and a scheme devised by Count Charles Daniel O'Connell was submitted to Pitt. O'Connell was among a group of senior army officers, headed by Duc de FitzJames, who signed an attestation for Ferris declaring 'that in all cicumstances he has given unequivocal proof of the most steadfast conduct and zeal and attachment to the royal cause'.[23] In spite of all his friends' protestations in his favour, the English government continued to keep Ferris at arm's length. He offered to join Lord Moira's expedition to La Vendée where the royalists had rebelled against the French revolutionary government, but Grenville had him detained at Portsmouth until the expedition had departed. From there he wrote to Edmund Burke: 'I fear neither the sea nor the French, and I will not refuse ... to embark on the smallest cutter in a cause such as ours.'[24] By July 1794 Ferris had almost exhausted his French funds and appealed to Grenville to grant him a gratuity. He believed that English suspicions of him originated from a confusion in British intelligence circles between himself and his cousin, Edward Ferris of Tralee. 'Someone must have mistaken me for a disloyal subject of the same name sent to spread sedition in Ireland,' he protested to Grenville.[25]

Be that has it may, Burges had already informed Grenville that he had received reliable information that Ferris was 'a dangerous agent of the Jacobins'. Another Irish priest, Nicholas Madgett II, had continuously informed the Foreign Office that Richard Ferris was 'the secret agent of Charles Delacroix, French Minister of Foreign Affairs and in his pay'.[26] Madgett II, like his cousin, Madgett I, was also a priest but at the opposite end of the political spectrum. He was educated for the priesthood at Collège de Ste Barbe in Paris, where his uncle of the same name was then superior and later Bishop of Kerry. Later he served as *curé* of Blaignon in the diocese of Bordeaux. He refused to take the oath required by the Civil Constitution of the Clergy and had to quit his parish. However, he remained a priest and intransigently opposed to the revolution. He later claimed that he was in Ireland from the beginning of the revolution until January 1794. He was certainly there in June 1793 when he was employed in the English secret service. The Chief Secretary at Dublin Castle wrote to Whitehall: 'A Mr Madgett, a French clergyman of a Kerry family, has been employed by the government here privately.' He went on to add, 'Madgett might be of use if anything is on foot.'[27]

The following August Madgett II left London on *The Belmont* bound for Jamaica. The vessel was captured off the coast of France by three French frigates and Madgett was taken as a prisoner-of-war to Brest, where for four weeks he was detained in a ship at anchor in the bay. In January 1795 he was transferred to a hospital in Brest, from where he escaped with four other English detainees and made his way back to England. By May he was preparing to return to France when Huskisson, who dispensed the secret service funds, gave him £100 sterling 'for a journey to Paris'.[28] By the end of May he had acquired a passport made out in the name of William S. Burns, an American businessman, and signed by the US chargé d'affaires in London.[29] On 23 June he had his passport signed by the municipality of Calais with an attestation by the mayor who was US vice-consul. Four days later he arrived in Paris where he tried to get his passport visaed. He was told to return the following day with a witness to identify him. The next day he was recognised as 'a dangerous intriguer' and immediately arrested and detained at Quatre Nations prison.[30]

Early in July Citizen Delaunay raised the activities of Madgett II on the floor of the Convention.[31] Recounting the history of Madgett from his arrival in Paris in 1770 as a student of Collège de Ste Barbe until he left France, he went on to describe his activities in Ireland: 'Sold to the English ministry, Madgett went to Ireland, spied and persecuted the patriots in Dublin who, jealous of our revolution, wish also to become free.' He proposed to the Convention that it should make an example of Madgett and he introduced a decree which was adopted, that Madgett, *alias* William S. Burns, American businessman, be charged with espionage and tried by a military commission. The trial took place in public on 22 July. Here Madgett II was subjected to a rigorous examination and surprisingly found not guilty on the charge of espionage. However, he admitted under cross-examination that he had previously escaped from prison and he was returned to prison until the government decided on appropriate measures.

Madgett II was released on 25 November 1795. Though he had protested, 'I would blush to eat a morsel that contained either shame or remorse,' once safely back in London, Madgett promptly put in a bill for £100 'to repay the expenses of his trial and escape from prison in Paris'.[32] The English government decided that Madgett II would be more efficient and less expensive if he stayed out of France and out of prison for the future. He was posted to Ireland in 1796 to report on the activities of the United Irishmen and French emissaries there.

In one of his reports he referred to the 'traitorous correspondence' carried on by William Duckett. 'It was no secret in my relation's (Madgett I) house that Mr Duckett was a violent republican and that the object of his mission was to prepare the minds of the people for insurrection.' Duckett did in fact preach revolution in Ireland, writing articles for the *Morning Chronicle* and the *Northern Star*, attacking the British government, under the pseudonym 'Junius Redivivus'. Madgett II also stated that Duckett had been sent to Ireland by the French government with 14,000 *livres* to assist the defence of William Jackson.[33] Jackson, a Protestant clergyman from Dublin, was one of those who signed the congratulatory address from White's Hotel in 1792. Early in 1794 the French government sent him to Ireland to sound out opinion on the feasability of a French invasion but, betrayed by a friend who shadowed him all the way, he was arrested. Jackson had sent a memoir from Tone on the subject through the open post which was intercepted, forcing Tone to flee the country.

Meanwhile, back in *prison des Irlandais* in the Irish college, the students continued in detention. Another Irish priest was also detained among a host of French prisoners.[34] Dominick Fitzsimons, an English language teacher, had been the guardian of the Irish Capuchin monastery at Bar-sur-Aube. On 25 April 1794 the National Convention issued a decree ordering the national treasury to pay 500 *livres* to each of the ten Irish students in the Irish College to enable them to return home.[35] Their release was ordered within twenty-four hours. Early in May, armed with certificates of civism, the Irish students set out for Dunkirk, where they hoped to take a neutral ship bound for Hamburg. While they were waiting for a boat at Dunkirk, the Committee of Public Safety ordered the suspension of the decree authorising their departure, giving as the reason recent despatches from the war front.[36] The students were to be transferred to Arras and imprisoned there.

The ten students, including Thomas MacKenna and Bernard MacSheehy, were to remain there until September. Then the representative of the north wrote to the Committee of Public Safety seeking instructions as the students were in need and demanding their release and the matter required prompt attention. They were subsequently released and returned to Paris and the Irish College. Most of the prisoners there were released in the winter of 1794-5. The ex-Capuchin, Dominick Fitzsimons, was released from there on 24 September 1794. The winter of 1794-5 was particularly harsh and with the collapse of the *assignats* and a steep rise in prices, many Parisians were threatened with famine. The Irish students were reported to be dying of hunger. In April 1795 there were food riots in Paris. Walsh, who had been released from prison in late 1794, petitioned the Committee of Public Assistance for help on behalf of twenty-two persons who now made up the Irish community.[37] The matter was raised on the floor of the Convention and their petition was successful.[38]

On 26 February 1795 Wolfe Tone had a meeting with Delacroix, the Minister of Foreign Affairs. While waiting in the minister's ante-chamber he had a casual encounter with a man reading an English newspaper. Delacroix informed Tone that the person in question was an Irish patriot, named Duckett, 'who was persecuted into exile for some writing under the signature of Junius Redivivus', and that he had presented several memorials on the state of Ireland. 'Who the devil is Junius Redivivus?', Tone wondered. 'I must talk a little to Madgett of this resurrection of Junius, of which, to speak the truth, I have no good opinion.'[39] By now Madgett I had been appointed head of translation in the Ministry of Foreign Affairs and Delacroix left the Irish affairs largely in his hands. Later Delacroix mentioned Duckett again to Tone in the context of sending suitable people to Ireland to give notice of French intentions.[40]

Tone had already met Carnot, Minister of War, at the Luxembourg Palace, where he was holding one of his public audiences. Carnot referred Tone to General Clarke who questioned him on the influence of the Catholic clergy in Ireland. Clarke was descended on both sides from a long line of military men who served in the Irish regiments and began his own career as a lieutenant in Berwick's regiment. Tone believed Clarke's view of Ireland was thirty years out of date. In a later interview Clarke was preoccupied with finding somebody suitable to send to Ireland. He sought Tone's views on the Irish priests still remaining in France. Tone informed him that the priests in Ireland 'hated the very name of the French revolution'. If one was sent from France he would immediately 'get in with his brethren in Ireland, who would misrepresent everything to him; and, of course, that any information which he might collect would not be worth a farthing'.[41] Tone was equally dismissive of Irish soldiers in France, and tactlessly so, given Clarke's own background. When Clarke suggested General Kilmaine as a possible leader of the French expeditionary force, Tone replied 'that in Ireland we had no great confidence in the officers of the old Irish brigade'.[42]

Delacroix had first suggested to Tone that Dominick Fitzsimons, the ex-Capuchin priest, might be the right man to send to Ireland but Tone protested that he 'had strong objection to letting priests into the business at all'.[43] He finally met Fitzsimons in the flesh in Madgett's office where Madgett spoke to Fitzsimons 'without reserve'. 'I never was more provoked in my life,' he wrote in his diary. He had become obsessed by Fitzsimons after one casual meeting. 'I objected all along to priests as the worst of all possible agents,' he wrote, 'and here is one who is the worst of all possible priests.'[44] The following day Tone called on Delacroix and informed him that Fitzsimons 'was absolutely unfit for the mission'.[45]

With Fitzsimons disposed of, Tone's paranoia switched to Duckett. Madgett I informed Tone that he heard from Duckett that two French expeditions were planned, one from Flushing commanded by General MacDonald, the other from Brest under General Hoche. Tone thought 'it is most terribly provoking to have the subject bandied about as table-talk by such a fellow as this Duckett'.[46] When Clarke once more raised the 'boring' matter of Duckett, Tone said that he did not know him or wish to know him and that he was informed that 'he was a blackguard'. Clarke, somewhat taken aback, remarked, 'Ay, but he is clever.'[47] When Tone arrived at Rennes in September to join the army of the west preparing for the invasion of Ireland, Hoche asked him about Duckett, who was also in Rennes. Tone said that he neither knew or intended to know Duckett but mentioned 'his prating at Paris to all his acquaintance, about his influence with General Clarke and Hoche himself'.[48] Two days later Duckett's name came up again in conversation with Clarke's uncle, Colonel Henry Shee. Tone reiterated that 'he believed him to be a blackguard'. Shee informed Tone that Duckett had told several people that he had been sent from Ireland by the committee of nine, who managed the affairs of Catholics, as their plenipotentiary. Tone was furious. 'I'll Duckett him, the scoundrel,' he wrote in his diary, 'if I can catch him fairly in my grip.'[49]

When Tone arrived at Rennes he was given as adjutant Bernard MacSheehy, who had finally left the Irish College in Paris some time after April 1795. Tone was not impressed by MacSheehy, whom he referred to as a 'blockhead'.[50] On 1 November 1796 Tone and MacSheehy arrived at Brest where the preparations for the expeditionary force to Ireland were in an advanced state. A week later Colonel Shee informed Tone that Hoche wished to have last minute information on the state of Ireland and wanted somebody to go there 'as he had a safe American who would sail at a minute's notice'. Tone suggested MacSheehy. Hoche sent for MacSheehy and gave him instructions. He should contact the persons named by Tone, 'and learn from them as much as he could on the actual state of the country at this moment, the temper of the people, the number and disposition of the troops, whether the French were expected or desired, and if so, in what part particularly.'[51] It was a daunting task for a twenty-two year old former student. Tone gave him two addresses, those of Oliver Bond and Richard McCormick, secretary of the Catholic Committee.

MacSheehy boarded the waiting ship, the *Washington*, at 8pm. 'I hope MacSheehy will acquit himself well,' Tone wrote in his diary that night, 'he has not much to do.'[52] It was a gross understatement. They were scarcely clear of Brest when they were intercepted by an English squadron of four frigates and later encountered two other English fleets. 'During these examinations,' MacSheehy later wrote in his report, 'I always took great care to remain hidden in a corner, having someone to cover me with some of the sailors' old clothes.'[53] Eventually they reached the Isle of Wight and were piloted into Cowes. From there MacSheehy made his way via Portsmouth to London where he spent three or four days 'as much to await a place in the mail coach as to throw off the government spies in the event of their having learnt of my arrival'.

The English government had in fact learnt about MacSheehy's arrival. The only other passenger on the mail coach to Holyhead was a king's messenger with whom MacSheehy quickly developed a relationship. He told MacSheehy that he was bringing instructions from the English government to the Irish Viceroy to take immediate measures to arrest 'one Bryan, aged about twenty years, who had come from Brest to Portsmouth on the American ship, *Washington*.'[54] The only other two passengers on the Dublin packet, were Major-General Lake, who was about to take command of the army of the north in Ireland, and his aide-de-camp. Lake was not very happy with his appointment, fearing 'the wrath of an embittered and exasperated people'. They reached Dublin at midnight on 26 November, where the king's messenger actually offered MacSheehy accommodation in Dublin Castle, which MacSheehy declined. He stayed instead at the Marine Hotel on Rogerson's Quay.

Next day he tried to get in touch with his contacts. Eventually a rendezvous was arranged outside the Post Office in College Green and a signal agreed. As the clock finished striking, MacSheehy emerged from the shadow and gave the agreed sign to William James MacNeven, while two others stood away at some distance. They all walked towards Parliament House, informing MacSheehy of the state of the forces in the country. They met again the following day outside the Marine Hotel, where they strolled and exchanged information for about an hour. An emissary was sent north and returned two days later with the information that there were 50,000 men ready to welcome the French. With his mission completed MacSheehy left Dublin for London which he reached on 4 December and from there via Guernsey to France. He arrived at Brest on 18 December only to discover that the Hoche expedition had set sail for Ireland two days earlier. General Hédouville forwarded MacSheehy's report to the Directory, adding that 'this intelligent and educated Irishman seems to have fulfilled his mission perfectly'.[55]

Hoche's expedition, consisting of 43 sail, had left Brest on 16 December with Wolfe Tone on board among the 14,450 troops. Also on board was a former Irish College student, James Bartholomew Blackwell from Ennis. He had already seen service in the early revolutionary campaigns and held the rank of colonel on this expedition. There was a more recent recruit from the Irish College on board, Thomas MacKenna. Thick fog dispersed the fleet on the first night and Hoche's frigate became separated from the main fleet. They arrived in Bantry Bay during a snowstorm on 21 December, with still no sign of their commander. Ravaged by storms and indecision, they finally cut their cables on the day after Christmas and sailed back to Brest.

Later Tone had a brief interview with Hoche in Paris when the latter requested a copy of MacSheehy's report. A week later Hoche sent a letter of thanks to MacSheehy, expressing the government's appreciation of all he had achieved. 'I am very grateful,' he wrote, 'for all the trouble and care you took to carry out the mission entrusted to you.'[56] However, Tone remained unimpressed by Mac

Sheehy. Hoche had transferred his interest to the Rhine and kept Tone on his staff. Much to Tone's dissatisfaction MacSheehy was reassigned to him as his adjutant. Referring to MacSheehy as a 'sad blockhead', he went on to complain that he,

> 'latterly is turning out the most insufferable coxcomb I ever saw – he pesters my life out; he is the neat pattern of a vulgar, impudent, Irish dunce, with great pretensions. I will move heaven and earth to get rid of him; – confound him! I wish he was up to the neck in the Rhine with all my heart.'[57]

They parted company a year later, MacSheehy making his way to Toulon where he joined Bonaparte's expedition to Egypt in May 1798. He served at the siege of Cairo and had a sword of honour conferred on him by General Kléber for his part in the recapture of Suez.

In December 1796 Léonard Bourdon was appointed French agent in Hamburg and William Duckett became his private secretary. Hamburg, a neutral port, was an important transit centre for *émigrés* and soon became the preferred route for Irish republicans entering and leaving France. It was an obvious centre for British and French espionage networks. Bourdon and Duckett concentrated on establishing an intelligence network in England and Ireland and especially on infiltrating the British navy with United Irishmen. In numerous memoranda to the French government Duckett emphasised, and at times exaggerated, the numbers of Irish seamen serving on British ships.[58] His main argument for a French invasion of Ireland was that it would cut off an important source of supplies, both of men and provisions, to British shipping. In the early months of 1797 he worked energetically at inciting mutinies among Irish sailors in British ports.[59]

As the news of the rebellion in Ireland in the summer of 1798 began to trickle back to France, the Directory's enthusiasm for a French invasion began to revive. Duckett was sent on a mission directed mainly at the Irish in the British armed forces in the hope of getting them to come out in sympathy with the rebellion.[60] He was arrested by mistake at Hanover when he produced his French passport with the result that Hanover's neutrality was violated. As a result of the rumpus he created, and as neither England nor France wished to compromise Hanover's neutrality, Duckett was released and returned to Hamburg.

Preparations were made to send three expeditions to Ireland, one under General Rey from Dunkirk, another under General Humbert from Rochefort and the third under General Hardy from Brest. Wolfe Tone joined the latter, while his brother, Matthew, and Bartholomew Teeling joined Humbert, and Napper Tandy went to Dunkirk. Humbert's three frigates were the first to arrive, reaching Killala on 22 August. One of the first to reach the shore was a former priest, Captain Henry O'Kane. He had been a *curé* near Nantes at the outbreak of the revolution 'when he was reduced by poverty to enlist in the French armies'.[61] Poverty may not have been the sole motive as O'Kane had been a member of a revolutionary club, *L'Irlandaise du soleil levant*, composed of Irish priests and medical students in 1776.[62] Also travelling on the Humbert expedition was Sullivan, a nephew of Madgett 1. Among those who volunteered their services to the French in Ireland was a 36-year-old priest, Michael Gannon from Castlebar, who had been educated in France and had returned to Ireland at the beginning of the revolution.

After an initial success at Castlebar, Humbert and his Irish-French contigent were annihilated at Ballinamuck some two weeks later. He and his French officers were taken to Dublin where they were treated more as guests than as prisoners of war but Matthew Tone and Bartholomew Teeling were court-martialled and executed. Henry O'Kane escaped the gallows, pleading that he was a naturalised French citizen, had eight years service in the French army prior to the expedition and had lived in France for fourteen years. He was also given a favourable attestation of his conduct during the rebellion by Joseph Stock, Protestant Bishop of Killala and Achonry.[63] Sullivan, the nephew of Madgett 1, appears to have escaped detection, probably by successfully masquerading as a French soldier. Gannon went on the run, hiding in Connemara. Later he escaped to Portugal and finally made his way to France where he became a *curé* in the diocese of Versailles in January 1803.[64]

The second French expedition reached Rutland Bay in Donegal on 17 September. It consisted of one fast-sailing frigate, the *Anacréon*, with 200 officers on board, some of whom were Irish. Among the latter was James Napper Tandy. His adjutant was the Irish College student, Thomas MacKenna. Originally from Maghera, Co Down, MacKenna had spent ten to twelve years in Collège des Irlandais. George Orr, who was also on board and became an English spy, gave a description of MacKenna to the government. 'He has very much the air and demeanour of a Frenchman and speaks French as well as any Parisian; he is about five feet seven inches high, has a black beard and is strongly built.'[65] Another former Irish College student, Bartholomew Blackwell, was also on board. In a secret report to Dublin, he was described as thin and smart, about five feet ten high and 'wearing long whiskers of a light sandy colour and also mustachios of the same colour'. He took a lot of snuff and spoke French like a Frenchman. Orr described Tandy as marching about on deck in the foppish finery of a general, looking more like a decadent politician than a rebel leader, and added that 'This Blackwell had Tandy like a child in leading strings.'[66]

In Rutland Bay the French expedition heard of the defeat and surrender of Humbert. Many of those on board were eager to march into the hills and continue the struggle but Tandy and Rey felt the situation was hopeless and decided to withdraw. They sailed away the day after they arrived on 18 September. The *Anacréon* reached Bergen in Norway where it disembarked its passengers. Tandy and Blackwell decided to make their way back to Paris via Hamburg. In Hamburg the English ambassador persuaded the city magistrate to arrest them as British subjects and requested their extradition to England. France declared that the extradition of the prisoners would violate the neutrality of Hamburg.

In spite of the international tug-of-war that followed through the spring and summer of 1799, the Hamburg senate handed the prisoners over in September to be transported to England. It was decided to convey them directly to Ireland where they were interned in Kilmainham. The French Directory reacted swiftly, denouncing the action of Hamburg to all allied and neutral governments, withdrawing her diplomatic and consular agents from the city and placing an embargo on all Hamburg ships in French ports.[67] Blackwell's wife, Sophie, wrote to the French Minister of the Marine, pointing out that her husband was a naturalised French citizen who had given 17 years military service to France and whose case should not be confused with that of Napper Tandy who had only recently come to France. She addressed a similar letter to the Irish Attorney General.[68] In spite of her efforts both Blackwell and Tandy had to wait for their release until March 1802, when France signed the Treaty of Amiens with England.

The third and last of the French expeditions arrived in Lough Swilly on 12 October 1798. It consisted of one sail of the line and eight frigates under Admiral Bompart with 3,000 soldiers under the command of General Hardy. Wolfe Tone sailed with the expedition. In Lough Swilly they were engaged in action with a superior force commanded by Admiral Warren and decisively defeated. Tone was arrested and taken to Dublin where he was tried and condemned to death. He cheated the gallows by cutting his own throat and died a week later on 19 November. When word reached Paris of the complete failure of all three expeditions, the French became thoroughly disillusioned with the exaggerated claims of Irish patriots, particularly those of Napper Tandy. William Duckett advised the Minister of the Marine to be wary in future of the views of upper class United Irishmen who were out of touch with the mass of ordinary Irish people.[69]

William Duckett continued to furnish the French government with valuable reports on Ireland until interest in that cause finally petered out. While in Hamburg he married a lady from a prominent Danish family. On returning to Paris, he was appointed professor in Collège de Ste Barbe and later published an English grammar and a book of poems. He died in Paris in 1841 at the age of seventy-four, 'quoting his favourite Horace on his death-bed and receiving extreme unction', according to his son who wrote his biography. A former pupil and notable literary figure, Charles Durozoir, wrote an appreciation of him which was published in Le Moniteur Universel.[70] Another Irishman, Nicholas Madgett II, who worked for the English secret service, later resumed his ministry as a *curé* in the diocese of Bordeaux, which he had left almost a quarter of a century earlier.[71]

Richard Ferris carved out a successful and prosperous career in post-revolutionary France. When he returned from England in 1799 he was arrested and imprisoned in the Temple accused of 'passing intelligence to enemies of the state'.[72] He was described in the prison register as a '45-year old native of Ireland, without profession, one metre 74cms tall, fair hair, low forehead, blue eyes, long sharp nose, average mouth, round chin and oval pockmarked face'. He was released on 15 April 1800. He busied himself renewing old acquaintances among the returned *emigrés* and cultivating new ones among the rising stars of the Napoleonic administration. As a result he was co-opted in 1808 on to the *bureau de surveillance* of the Irish colleges. In 1813, much to the chagrin of the Irish bishops, the ex-priest Ferris was appointed administrator-general of all the Irish colleges, properties and revenues in the French empire, a well as of all English and Scots establishments. He remained in this position, with a brief intermission, until 1822. From then on he concentrated on his legal practice, in which he was very much in demand among British subjects claiming compensation for losses sustained during the revolution. It was apparently highly remunerative for he purchased a handsome country house near Soissons which he named *La Maison Blanche*, where he died in June 1827 in his seventy-fifth year.

Nicholas Madgett 1, who was Wolfe Tone's chief mentor in Paris, continued to live there where he developed a close relationship with the ex-double-agent, Ferris. He was also co-opted with Ferris on the *bureau de surveillance* of the Irish colleges and both of them conspired successfully to have John Baptist Walsh removed from his post as administrator-general of the Irish properties. In 1812 he named Ferris executor of his will 'because of our long and sincere friendship'. He died on 9 March 1813.[73]

Irish soldiers, as might be expected, enjoyed shorter prospects. Bernard MacSheehy was the first to die, killed by a cannon ball at the snow-driven battle of Eylau, while serving as a colonel on

Napoleon's staff. He was described as 'a brave officer with military talents of the first order, a vast erudition, and capable of speaking and writing several languages.'[74] Major James Bartholomew Blackwell quit the Irish Legion in its early days. He rejoined the main French army and served in the cavalry corps in the Prussian and Austrian campaigns of Napoleon. Ill-health forced him to retire as a colonel on half-pay to Paris where he died in 1812.[75]

Henry O'Kane resumed his miltary career on returning to France after the defeat of the Humbert expedition. Miles Byrne recalled meeting him in Paris in 1803. He met him again in Portugal in 1810-11, where the Irish Legion was on active service and where O'Kane frequently entertained Irish officers. 'He was good-humoured and generous to a degree. He would never let the Irish officers pass his quarters or bivouac without entertaining them to the best of his means.' He was among the first to be awarded the Legion of Honour. He retired on pension in 1815 after the restoration of the Bourbons.[76]

Fr Michael Gannon was transferred from parish to parish almost annually until finally quitting the pastoral life on account of a drink problem. He taught for a while in the Irish College, Paris. Later he became a military chaplain but was suspended in September 1819. He was last mentioned in April 1820, unemployed in Paris and in 'urgent need of help'. The Ministry of the Interior granted him 100 francs to enable him to take up a position offered to him in the diocese of Autun.[77]

Thomas MacKenna abandoned the army soon after his return to France and reverted to civilian life. In 1807 he was a wealthy ship-owning merchant, had married a widow and was living in style. Miles Byrne met him for the last time that year when the Irish Legion were stationed at Boulogne-sur-Mer, prior to their departure for the Spanish campaign. MacKenna was always eager to render a service to any of his former comrades-in-arms. One of the Irish officers (possibly Henry O'Kane or Sullivan, nephew of Madgett 1) was court-martialled for insulting a superior officer, a Prussian. MacKenna, who had a superb command of French, prepared a written brief for the defending officer and as a result the court-martial found in his favour. To celebrate, MacKenna put on a splendid breakfast with bumpers of sparkling champagne for his French and Irish friends, which lasted until evening when the Irish officers returned to their camp 'in high spirits'.[78]

Notes

1   He is so described here to distinguish him from his cousin of the same name, another priest who will be designated as Nicholas Madgett II.

2   For detailed account see Swords, *The Green Cockade*, pp. 31-9.

3   A.N.C 163, f. 6624v; A.Tuetey, *Répertoire général des sources manuscrites de l'histoire de Paris pendant la Révolution*, vol. 5, p. 30.

4   This was not in fact true. Since 1737 superiors were appointed by the Archbishop of Paris.

5   I.C.P. 14 A., *Mémoire pour Walsh*, pp. 27-8. A certain confusion existed about the identitiy of this Nicholas Madgett, as there was another priest of the same name, a *curé* in Bordeaux. In my book *The Green Cockade*, p. 64, I wrongly concluded that it was the latter who was elected on this occasion, though I added, 'His role in this affair seems completely inconsistent with the rest of his life.'

6   A.S.P. D.13. U.I., 5 Nov 1792.

7   A.A.E. Corr. Pol. Angl., 583, ff. 106-7, 110-111.

8   *Moniteur*, XIV, pp. 592-3, 29 Nov 1792.

9   A.A.E. Corr. Pol. Angl., 587, f. 20, 13 Mar 1793.

10 A.A.E. Corr. Pol. Angl., 587, f. 45, 22 Mar 1793.

11 P.R.O. London, FO 27, 4 Mar 1793.

12 A.N. C. 271. 666, 8 Sept 1793.

13 P.R.O. London, FO. 27, 43. Purcell, 'Richard Ferris 1754-1828' in *Journal of the Kerry Archaeological and Historical Society*, 18 (1985), p. 34.

14 A.A.E. Corr. Pol. Angl. 587 ff. 296-300, July 1793.

15 A.A.E. Corr. Pol. Angl. 587, ff. 319rv, 325, 326, 19, 21, 26 Aug 1793.

16 A.A.E. 587, f. 14, 2 Oct 1793.

17 Bodleian Library Oxford, Bland Burges Papers, 13 Oct 1793.

18 Dropmore Papers, II, 445 qtd Purcell, op. cit., p. 29.

19 Ferris to Grenville, 4 Oct 1793, Bland Burges Papers, pp. 183-7.

20 ibid., Grenville to Burges, 17 Oct 1793, p. 188.

21 ibid., 26 Oct 1793, pp. 188-92.

22 *Corrispondence of Edmund Burke*, VII, pp. 464-5, qtd Purcell, op. cit., p. 31.

23 P.R.O. FO. 27, 43; qtd Purcell, op. cit., p. 34.

24 Qtd Purcell, op. cit., pp. 34-7.

25 P.R.O. FO. 27, 45 ERD: 2354, qtd. Purcell, op. cit., pp. 39-40.

26 ibid.

27 P.RO. FO. 43, June 1793; qtd Hayes, *Ireland and Irishmen during the French Revolution*, p. 206n.

28 Brit. Mus. Huskisson Ms. 38769, qtd Hayes, op. cit., p. 207n.

29 *Moniteur*, p. 187, *Séance* of July 1795.

30 ibid.

2   UB/19038   STOCK   HB   UB/28038

0.00   25.00

PROTESTANT, CATHOLIC & DISSENTER   SWORDS

@COL 0026   1856072096   I41215   20/03/98   HIRH

2 0   2 0   0 0   0 0   6 0   0 0   0 0   0 0   0 0   0 0

NUMBER IN STOCK

8   RE-ORDER QUANTITY

31 *Moniteur,* p. 187-8, 8 July 1795.
32 Brit. Mus. Huskisson Ms. 38769; qtd Hayes, op. cit., p. 207n.
33 ibid., pp. 285-6.
34 A.P. Register, 19 & 25 Oct 1793.
35 *Procès-verbaux de la Convention Nationale,* p. 141, 25 April 1794.
36 Aulard, *Recueil des actes du Comité de Salut Public,* XIII, p. 586.
37 A.N. F 17 14764, 4 April 1795.
38 *Moniteur,* XXIV, p. 148, 4 April 1795.
39 Tone, *Memoirs,* vol. 1, p. 250.
40 ibid., vol. 1, p. 269.
41 ibid., vol. 1, p. 306.
42 ibid., vol. 1, pp. 309-10.
43 ibid., vol. 1, p. 271.
44 ibid., vol. 1, pp. 330-1.
45 ibid., vol. 1, p. 333.
46 ibid., vol. 1, p. 421.
47 ibid., vol. 2, p. 14.
48 ibid., vol. 2, p. 56.
49 ibid., vol. 2, p. 59. R.R. Madden, *The United Irishmen,* vol. 3, p.59, accepted Tone's judgement of Madgett, whom he described as 'the *soi-disant* agent of the United Irishmen in Paris, whom there is good reason to believe was not employed by the Irish Directory, but by the British minister, Mr Pitt.' W.J. Fitzpatrick, *Secret Service under Pitt,* p. 106, rejected this: 'I cannot endorse this imputation.'
50 ibid., vol. 2, pp. 76-7.
51 ibid., vol. 2, pp. 94-5.
52 ibid., vol. 2, p. 97.
53 A.N. F III 186b. See F. W. Van Brock, 'Captain MacSheehy's Mission' in *Irish Sword,* vol. x, pp. 215-28; C. J. Woods, 'The secret mission of Captain Bernard MacSheehy, an Irishman in French service, 1796' in *Journal of the Cork Hist. & Arch. Society,* LXXVIII, pp. 92-108.
54 This suggests the presence of an English spy in Tone's entourage at Brest.
55 A.N. F III 186b, doss. 860, qtd Van Brock, op. cit., p. 223.
56 A.N. AF IV, carton 1671, f. 129v, qtd Woods, op. cit., p. 105.
57 Tone's *Journal,* 13 April 1797. Passage suppressed from *Memoirs,* qtd Woods, op. cit., p. 107.
58 See A.A.E. Corr. Pol. Ham. III, ff. 311-12; Corr. Pol. Angl. 592, ff. 80, 84-5, 129-130.
59 Marianne Elliot, *Partners in Revolution,* pp. 140-2.
60 A.N. BB4 123, ff. 193-8; AF III 149, doss. 701, ff. 67, 71; see Elliot, op. cit., pp. 218-9.
61 Hayes, *Last Invasion of Ireland,* p. 206.
62 A.N. FM²18
63 *Narrative,* p. 48.
64 A.V. 35F 11.
65 Qtd Hayes, *Biographical Dictionary of Irishmen in France,* p. 183.
66 Hayes, *Ireland and Irishmen in the French Revolution,* pp. 31-2.
67 *Moniteur,* XXIX, p. 856, 19 Oct 1799.
68 A.A.E. 592, f. 288r; 593, ff. 451rv, 452rv.
69 Marianne Elliot, *Partners in Revolution,* p. 235.

70 *Life of William Duckett,* N.L.I. microfilm, pos. 210.
71 Hayes, *Biographical Dictionary of Irishmen in France,* p. 196.
72 A.P. A B / 334 f. 25, 15 April 1800.
73 A.N. MC et/1/733
74 De la Ponce Ms., qtd Hayes, op. cit., p. 192.
75 Hayes, *Biographical Dictionary,* pp. 13-14.
76 Byrne, *Memoirs,* ii (1907 ed.), pp. 206-208; Hayes, *Last Invasion,* pp. 205-7.
77 A.N. F 17 14764, *Etat de Situation,* 19 Feb 1808; F 19 1223; MC et/xlvii/564; A.V. 35F 11.
78 Byrne, op. cit., iii, pp. 165-8.

William Steel Dickson

W. D. Bailie

I

Dr William Steel Dickson was the eldest son of John Dickson and Jane Steel of the Old Kiln, Ballycraigy, in the parish of Carnmoney, Co Antrim. He was born on 25 December 1744 and baptised on the thirtieth of the same month by the Rev John Thompson, minister of Carnmoney.[1] The name 'Steel' is not entered on the baptismal register, but it was adopted by Dickson some time after the death of his uncle, William Steel, his mother's brother, who died on 13 May 1747.[2]

Little is known of his early education. In his *Narrative* Dickson writes 'my boyish years were spent in the usual, and I am sorry to add, almost useless routine of Irish country schools'. He states that it was due to the 'paternal attention and valuable instructions of the Rev Robert White', then Presbyterian minister of Templepatrick that he 'gained a knowledge ... of Latin, Greek ... logic, metaphysics, morals and natural theology'.[3] In 1763 Dickson matriculated at Glasgow College.[4] His professors were Mr Moorhead in Latin; the celebrated economist Dr Adam Smith; Dr Leechman, the principal of the university; and Mr John Millar in Law.[5] Dickson kept up a friendship with Principal Leechman and Mr Moorhead who honoured him 'with their correspondence as long as they lived'.[6]

At first Dickson's thoughts turned towards the law and politics, but after his return from college, where he did not take a degree, he was persuaded by 'the flattering solicitations of my early and venerated friend Mr White to become a candidate for the office of a preacher of the gospel, much sooner than I intended, or ought to have done'.[7] He was recommended to the presbytery of Templepatrick by the Rev John Wright, minister of Donegore, as 'a student

in Divinity as well entitled to the notice of this Pby' on 20 January
1766.[8] The presbytery minutes report that the brethren 'willing to
encourage him appointed him to deliver a specimen [sermon] to
Messrs White and Wright and they are to report their opinion of
his performance, at the next meeting'.[9] This was the first piece of
'trial', as these exercises were called, and in the course of the next
fourteen months Dickson had to prepare and deliver sermons and
lectures in the presence of the presbytery on six separate occasions,
defend a thesis on a controversial theological subject, and be examined on two occasions in 'the Languages, Philosophy and Theology'.[10] In all these he acquitted himself to the entire satisfaction of
the presbytery and on 8 April 1767 the Moderator, in the name of
the presbytery, licensed him to preach the gospel.[11] Dickson was
not required to sign the *Westminster Confession of Faith* as the presbytery, a few years before his reception as a student for the ministry,
had abolished 'the requiring of Subscription to any human confession, or insisting on any other confession of faith than that the
Sacred Scriptes [sic] are the only rule of faith and practice'.[12]

Unlike licentiates today, who are generally employed as assistant
ministers while awaiting a call to a vacant congregation, licentiates
in eighteenth-century Irish Presbyterianism usually took up positions as school teachers or tutors to well-to-do families, preaching
occasionally on Sundays in vacant congregations under the care of
the local presbytery. Dickson's period as licentiate lasted from April
1767 till his ordination in March 1771. In the course of these four
years Dickson, at the direction of his presbytery, preached occasionally on supply in the congregations of Carrickfergus and
Islandmagee, for which he received three half crowns per Sunday.
He was invited to be a candidate for the vacancy at Islandmagee in
May-June 1768, but the congregation did not issue him with a call.
In November 1769, at the request of the presbytery of Bangor, he
preached for a period on trial for Dunmurry but another was preferred before him. He also preached on trial for Killead[13] before
finally receiving a call to the congregation of Ballyhalbert in the
Ards peninsula.

Dr W. T. Latimer suggests that Dickson, at this stage in his career, was either not a particularly powerful preacher or unfortunate as a candidate as he had to wait for four years before being settled in a charge.[14] The reason, however, would seem to lie with the congregational practice of those days: congregations often took anything from one to two years to meet the requirements of presbytery regarding payment of arrears to the last minister or his family; to agree the stipend to be paid to his successor; and then to arrange the hearing of a number of candidates, each one for four Sundays at least, before deciding whether to issue a call or not.

II

Referring to this period in his life Dickson says:

> the frequent excursions which I was obliged to make to vacant congregations, some of which were many miles distant, not only extended my connexions, but gave me access to many families of rank and respectability, in the counties of Down and Antrim, of whose kind attentions I shall ever cherish a pleasing and grateful remembrance. Among these I have the honour of mentioning that of the late Alexander Stewart, Esq., father of the present Earl of Londonderry, and grandfather to Lord Viscount Castlereagh.[15]

Dickson was ordained by the presbytery of Killyleagh on 6 March 1771 at Ballyhalbert (now Glastry). As the presbytery was one of the non-subscribing presbyteries it is most unlikely that the ordinand was required to sign the *Westminster Confession*. Of his settlement at Ballyhalbert in 1771 Dickson records, 'I ... became an husband and a farmer'.[16]

His wife was Isabella McMinn, a young lady whom he describes as being of a 'genteel family, brought up in affluence and liberally educated'.[17] Dwelling in the midst of fishermen, agricultural labourers and farmers, Dickson devoted the opening years of his ministry to his parochial and domestic duties and to general studies. His non-subscribing principles came to the fore when he joined with the majority of the Bangor presbytery in the ordination of S. M. Stephenson at Greyabbey on 20 June 1774, following Stephenson's refusal to subscribe the *Westminster Confession of Faith*.[18]

The American War of Independence which broke out in 1775

was to Dickson 'unnatural, impolitic and unprincipled'.[19] Feeling
as he did, he did not attempt to hide his ideas or sentiments on the
war. His comments gave offence to the landed gentry and others in
the district, an offence which was intensified by reports of the contents of the sermons he preached on the two fast days proclaimed
by the government in the course of the American conflict. A general
outcry was raised against the Ballyhalbert pastor and he was labelled
'traitor', 'rebel', and 'trumpeter of sedition'.[20] Those who had not
heard the sermons were loudest in their condemnation. In order to
vindicate himself Dickson published the two sermons. The first
was entitled *On the Advantages of National Repentance* [21] and the
second *On the Ruinous Effects of Civil War*.[22] The sermons, according to Dickson, were read with avidity, and found to be 'less pesti-
lential than they had been represented'.[23]

In the course of his first sermon Dickson is careful to point out
that he has no intention of discussing the political questions involved
in the American struggle against the British government. He says:

I do not mean, that we should begin to discuss the political
questions so much agitated, concerning the omnipotence of
Parliament, the rights of America, etc. etc., or to determine
whether the Americans were forced into the present opposition
by illegal extensions of prerogative, and claims of power – or
have rushed into rebellion against Law, without a cause. These
are enquiries for the solution of which I frankly confess, I have
neither taste nor inclination. They are, in many circumstances,
by me unfathomable; as many of the facts, on which their solution
depends, are yet veiled in thick darkness.

What is more; such inquiries would be to us, totally unprof-
itable. We are so far removed from power, that it cannot be supposed that our opinions can ever enter a Council-chamber, or
ascend a Throne – or if they could, they must there be light as
the down which skims along the deep.

He continues:

Further, from whatever cause the present distraction and blood-
shed originated, the effects are the same. Nor are we to charge
these effects, wholly, either upon destructive counsels at home,

or rebellious dispositions abroad. Moderation will readily admit
that there may be, and indeed have been, errors on both sides.
How vain, then, for us to indulge our rancour, or expose our
ignorance, by forming uncharitable, indigested opinions; or
venting torrents of scurrility and abusive language either against
the Administration or its opponents?[24]

The cause, he avers, goes back further than people were generally
willing to look. God requires a national repentance, a return from
wickedness. Let us, he says, apply this to ourselves:

And, as we desire that a stop may be put to the effusion of
Protestant blood – that civil discord may cease, and peace be restored, with all its blessings, to every member of this far-extended
Empire – As we desire that tyranny, oppression, and arbitrary
power, should be banished from our land, and that rebellion
should be extinguished for ever – And, as we desire to be preserved from foreign invasion, and maintained in the peaceable
possession of our lives, liberties, and religion – as we desire these
things, let us, from this day, be employed in examining our
hearts, rooting out vicious affections, and resolving that we will
henceforth walk as it becometh rational beings, and Christians
– That we will be humble and devout, and turn from every
wicked way, animated with the pleasing hope, that God will,
then, hear our prayers from Heaven, heal our land in its present
distractions, and preserve it from all such disorders in time to
come.[25]

In his second sermon on the American War Dickson is much more
outspoken and critical in his denunciations of the evils of the conflict. Preaching about the time that news of the defeat of General
Burgoyne's army had been received in Britain, he states:

Had the first repulses of our troops been thus attended to, and
the consequences, to which they pointed, duly weighed, counsels of peace would have prevailed with us also; and, even now,
we would have been rejoicing in their influence. However different measures were preferred and the effects are notorious to
all ... Our troops, which, so lately, spread the terror of the
British Arms over half the globe, are partly surrounded by the

power of the enemy, partly confined in dungeons, and partly numbered with the dead; While the Army, which was to lay America at the feet of the Ministry, is, at this day, returning to Europe in chains.[26]

He asks:

Does not every real friend of his country look forward with earnest desire to the happy day when the sword shall cease to devour? Is it not the first prayer of his heart that the wisdom of Britain may yet stretch forth the peaceful Olive to the western world; and the second that she may not stretch it forth in vain?'[27]

He concludes by praising the Presbyterians for their moderation:

We must receive a peculiar satisfaction from a review of the conduct of the Irish Presbyterians, on this trying occasion. Our enemies if any such we have, can scarcely deny that as a body, we have been guided by the spirit of moderation. We have neither attempted to clog the wheels of Government by frantic opposition; nor to encourage measures of violence by sanguinary addresses. If we have, in any instance, censured the principle or conduct of the war, our censures have been justified by the general feelings of humanity, and a zealous concern for the common interests of Britain and America ... And as we have, thus, cherished a love of peace, and followed its path in time past, let us persevere in it, in time to come.[28]

It was at this time that France espoused the cause of the American colonists; and the British government, declaring its inability to defend Ireland from foreign attack, caused the Protestant populace to band together to form the Volunteers. Physicians, surgeons, lawyers and even 'the Presbyterian ministers were so fully inspired with the patriotism of the day, that, in several places, the rusty black was exchanged for the glowing scarlet, and the title of "Reverend" for that of "Captain"'.[29]

Catholics offered themselves in great numbers for enrolment in the ranks of the Volunteers, but throughout the greater part of Ulster their offers were rejected. This naturally caused distrust and excited alarm in the community. The Upper Ards was also affected and Dickson deplored the non-inclusion of Catholics, not only in his private conversation, but also in his meeting-house, for when the opportunity came to preach to the Echlinville Volunteers in March 1779, he expressed his strong disapproval.[30] The effect of his words was 'to offend all the Protestant and Presbyterian bigots in the country'.[31] Once more the cry of rebellion was raised against him and he was described as a Papist in his heart. The general content of his sermon pleased the Volunteers and he was persuaded to publish it 'with a modification of the part respecting the admission of Catholics to the Volunteer ranks'.[32] To this Dickson agreed with great reluctance 'and merely from respect to, what I then thought, superior judgement, and, at least, an equal zeal in public cause'.[33]

Dickson's participation in political affairs did not prevent him from attending to his farming. In Dickson's day it was customary for ministers to farm as well as to preach and Dickson himself seems to have been quite a successful farmer. For some time the wheat crop in the district had been subject to damage by smut, a small fungus which attacks growing crops, also called blacks because of its numerous black spores. In a letter dated 4 September to the *Belfast News Letter*, Dickson observes that the 'grain has been much damaged, in this country, for some years past', and notes that he had seen 'many fields this season in which every fourth stalk, at least, is black'.[34] Having experienced this damage to his own crops in 1775, Dickson carried out experiments to reduce the amount of smut damage on his own farm in the townland of Moab, midway between Glastry and the village of Ballyhalbert.

> For this reason I steeped my seed-wheat in pickle, made of salt and water, so strong that an egg could swim in it: then I spread it upon a floor, and mixed it with dry slacked lime, till the whole was covered over.[35]

He sowed five acres with the prepared seed and when the harvest came there was 'not one-fortieth part of my crop black ... whereas my neighbours have a third, fourth, fifth' so affected.[36] So successful was his method that he was in a position to advertise that he had Red Lammas wheat, quite free from all Mixture, Goose-corn, Sturdy, Papple and Blacks for sale.[37] The following year he again wrote to the *Belfast News Letter* describing further experiments which he had carried out for the prevention of smut in wheat seed. As well as making use of the pickle-wheat, he had treated some seed by exposing it in a room where he had lit sulphur candles, but his conclusion, after having sown the seed, from which not one grain ever grew, was that 'the smoke of sulphur is as fatal to vegetables as to animal life'.[38] However, by the month of July 1779, Dickson had grown tired of farming, for he offered to let two farms consisting of 33 acres for 'years, lives or lives renewable, as soon as the present crop is removed'.[39]

During Dickson's ministry a new meeting-house was erected by the congregation at Glastry, about one and a half miles inland from the village of Ballyhalbert where the site of the first meeting-house had been. This occurred at the time that a section of the congregation withdrew to build its own meeting-house at Kircubbin, in defiance of the rules of the General Synod of Ulster. It has been suggested that it was due to Dickson's political beliefs that the Kircubbin faction took this action.[40] However, the dispute had begun at least four years previously, in 1773, before Dickson's involvement in politics over the American war, when the local church authorities in Ballyhalbert had refused to build a new meeting-house at Glastry. It was when the Kircubbin dissidents were already decided on secession that the authorities agreed to build at Glastry but the concession came too late to effect a change of attitude on the part of the seceders. Additional evidence that Dickson's political actions were not the cause of the division in the congregation is contained in a Remonstrance presented to the General Synod by the neighbouring congregations of Greyabbey and Portaferry which declared 'that the party in Kircubbin had not separated from their brethren on acct. of any religious concern, matter of, or objection against the conduct or the ministry of Mr Dixon [*sic*].[41]

III

William Steel Dickson resigned the charge of Ballyhalbert on 1 February 1780 and was installed as minister of Portaferry by the presbytery of Killyleagh on 6 March.[42] Dickson had been invited by the Portaferry congregation to preach a sermon in memory of the late pastor of Portaferry, the Reverend James Armstrong, on 14

November 1779 and his address had been so much appreciated by the congregation that he was invited to become its minister.[43] Dickson states that his stipend at Portaferry was £100 per annum from the congregation, but the Church Committee book shows that he was in fact paid £70 annually from 1780 till 1788 and £80 from then onwards.[44] The explanation for the discrepancy is that he received the extra £20 to £30 in kind from members of the congregation.[45] Shortly after his settlement in Portaferry he opened an academy for boys from which he derived about £100 per annum. The *Belfast News Letter* carried a number of weekly advertisements in April and May 1781 publicising the formation and curricula of the new school as follows:

> Portaferry School – the Revd William Steel Dickson will open a public school on the 15th day of May next in which will be taught, under his inspection, the English, Latin and Greek tongues, grammatically; geometry, trigonometry, Euclid's elements and all the lower branches of mathematics necessary for genteel business or a college education. And, if requisite, a class will be instituted in which a sketch of Logic, Metaphysics and Morals will be given. A master of approved character and abilities is engaged to teach writing and the common Rules of Arithmetic, at such hour in the evenings as may be convenient; and, an assistant, who has taken the degree of Master of Arts; which will enable Mr Dickson to pay complete attention to his pupils, and, he hopes, to give full satisfaction to gentlemen who may put their sons under his care. The situation of Portaferry is remarkably favourable for an institution of this kind. The town and neighbourhood possess a clean air, and dry soil; the outlets, for amusement, are excellent; all the benefits of salt-water may be enjoyed in full perfection, the inhabitants are remarkable for sobriety, and, as yet, total strangers to those vices which generally corrupt the minds of youth. These circumstances, equally friendly to health and good morals, are too important to be overlooked; and Mr Dickson is determined to make both the objects of his strictest care and attention. Board and tuition, three guineas entrance, and eighteen guineas per annum. Single beds, twenty

guineas per ann. Tuition alone, half a guinea entrance, and three guineas per ann. Writing and Arithmetic, one guinea per ann. additional. As Mr Dickson's plan is extensive, and in some measure new, any gentleman desirous of further information, may be furnished with a sketch of the whole by applying to him, at Portaferry. April 4th, 1781.

This income from the school, together with his share of the *Regium Donum*, a small private income and a farm, enabled him to live tolerably well.

Dickson continued to preach and to publish occasional sermons. In June 1781 he preached to the clerics and elders of the General Synod met in annual conference; and at Portaferry on 25 December 1792 and 13 January 1793, he gave two discourses which, together with the synodical sermon were afterwards published under the title of *Three Sermons on the subject of Scripture Politics*, in which a case is made justifying the need for and enforcement of reform and emancipation on the basis of biblical theology. Another product from his pen published in 1792 was a pamphlet entitled *Psalmody, an address to the Presbyterian congregations of the Synod of Ulster* in which he makes a plea for members of congregations to become acquainted with a larger number of psalm tunes than was in common use at that time. This work carries within its pages the approbation of nine presbyteries in the Synod.[46]

IV

Dickson does not appear to have been appointed as a delegate to the great Volunteer conventions in Dungannon in 1782 and 1783, which called for legislative and parliamentary reform, and repudiated the stricture that Volunteers should not express opinions on political subjects or on the conduct of parliament or public men. Nevertheless, Dickson was politically active in 1783, playing a large part in the election in Co Down between the Hills of Hillsborough and the Stewarts of Mount Stewart. Despite his zeal and influence in gathering in supporters for the Stewart cause, his friend was not returned to parliament.[47] However, he continued to display an interest in parliamentary affairs for early in 1785 he appended his signature to an appeal, made by some 500 freeholders in Co Down, for a meeting to be held at Downpatrick for the purpose of selecting five delegates to attend a national convention in Dublin, to call for a 'reform in the representation of the people in parliament as indispensably necessary'.[48]

It was at this period, 1784, that Dickson was awarded a Doctorate in Divinity from Glasgow University.[49]

In the 1790 election, Robert Stewart Junior, later Viscount Castlereagh, was elected, Robert Stewart Senior having been ennobled in 1789 as Lord Londonderry. Dickson played a large part in his success: to report the event in Dickson's own words:

> For several weeks previous to the election, and the three months during which it continued, I was on horseback almost every day, and seldom slept in my own house at night. In fact, I rode one horse nearly to death, reduced another to half his value, and expended above £50, part of which I was obliged to borrow; nor, can I now say, whether I was most actuated by affectionate esteem for the youthful candidate, confidence in his professions, or zeal for the interests of my country, in my quixotical excursions. Under the joint influence of the whole, I canvassed, far and wide, regardless of interest, influence, and connexions, and succeeded so far as to provoke some of my best friends, by voting their tenants for Mr Stewart, contrary to their orders, and in their presence.[50]

At first Robert Stewart and the Whig party with which he was associated appeared to be following the path of parliamentary reform but bolder spirits in the Belfast area, seeing no hope of any radical reform under the Whigs, founded the Society of United Irishmen in Belfast in October 1791, with the avowed intent of uniting all Irishmen in support of parliamentary reform and Catholic emancipation.

Dickson, whose advocacy of Catholic emancipation went back to 1778,[51] took the test of the Belfast Society in December 1791. He maintains that he was never present at any succeeding meetings of the Society, in Belfast or elsewhere, although he admits that he was often in the company of United Irishmen.[52] In 1792 Dickson was

present at the great Volunteer gathering in Belfast on 14 July to celebrate the third anniversary of the taking of the Bastille, the outbreak of the French Revolution. Among the resolutions was one
which, without using the actual words, clearly referred to Catholic
emancipation. It reads as follows:

> But while we thus state our sentiments on the subject of reform,
> we feel it incumbent upon us to declare, as we now do, that no
> reform, were even such attainable, would answer our ideas of
> utility or justice, which should not equally include all sects and
> denominations of Irishmen. We reprobate and abhor the idea
> that political inequality should result from religious opinions;
> and we should be ashamed, at the moment when we are seeking
> for liberty ourselves, to acquiesce in any system founded on the
> slavery of others.[53]

An amendment was proposed calling for the gradual emancipation
of Catholics, to which, among others, the Revs Sinclare Kelburn, T.
Ledlie Birch and W. S. Dickson voiced their opposition. Having reported the debate, the *Northern Star* said of Dickson's speech:

> It is but justice to the Doctor to assure our readers that we have
> been able to give but a very imperfect sketch of his able and cap-
> tivating speech, which being delivered with an air of ease and
> good humour, did not fail to draw from the audience the
> strongest expressions of pleasure and approbation, particularly
> for the varied and happy strokes of irony which abounded in it,
> and which throw the most ludicrous shade upon the arguments
> of his adversaries.[54]

Following Dickson's address the vote was taken and the original resolution overwhelmingly adopted.

A meeting of the townsfolk of Belfast was held on 26 December
1792, and a committee of 21, which included six United Irishmen,
was formed to correspond with fellow citizens in all parts of the
country and to concert with them measures to procure county
meetings and provincial assemblies, leading to a National Assembly
to demand reform and Catholic emancipation.[55] Dickson states
that:

> with a view to this reform I used every exertion, of which I was

capable, both in public and private, to convince all with whom I was conversant of its necessity to restore our paralysed constitution, conciliate the public mind, and establish his Majesty's throne in the affections of the people, and the equal necessity of union among Irishmen.[56]

He was active in meetings held for these purposes in many parts of Co Down and, as a delegate from the Barony of Ards, was the leading spirit at the provincial convention in Dungannon on 15 and 16 February 1793 at which he took 'no inconsiderable share in proposing and modifying the resolutions'.[57]

There was some opposition to one of the resolutions which expressed abhorrence of revolutionary principles in general, and of republicanism as applied to Ireland in particular. When Dickson strongly supported the resolution, explaining that he was not 'utterly opposed to republican forms of government, as improper in themselves ... but because he thought them by no means proper applied' to Ireland; that there would be those who would seek to 'misinterpret the sentiments of the Convention'; and that the resolution would 'prevent them further falsifying an oppressed people', the opposition was withdrawn, and the resolution passed.[58]

So great an impression did Dickson make on the members and people assembled at Dungannon that a request was made to him to preach in the local Presbyterian meeting-house on the Sunday after the convention at the hour of five 'in the evening at which hour all religious denominations would have it in their power to attend'.[59] According to the *Northern Star*, the meeting-house was crowded with the principal people of the place including the established and Catholic clergy. Dickson took for his text Joseph's advice to his brethren, 'See that ye fall not out by the way.' 'Had there been a want of unanimity here on the subjects now in agitation,' wrote the *Northern Star*, 'the Doctor's arguments would certainly have united us. United as we are, he has strengthened our union, and done much good.'[60]

The government, now thoroughly alarmed by the activities of the northern patriots, issued a proclamation forbidding all further assemblies of armed men and charging magistrates to disperse all such assemblies and to arrest those leaders who did not obey the order. This proclamation was followed by the Convention Act which put an end to the existence of the Volunteers as a political force: those who were not willing to submit to the government's edict took their places in the ranks of the United Irishmen.

Dickson's championing of Catholic emancipation and parliamentary reform, and his preaching of 'Scripture Politics' from his pulpit in the early part of 1793, brought a sharp reaction from members of his Portaferry congregation:

> Many families withdrew from my ministry, for a season; and an attempt was made to have a new meeting-house erected ... These things only enlivened my sense of duty, and roused me to increased exertion. To public addresses from the pulpit, I added local visitations of the districts into which my parish was divided, and even domiciliary calls on the disaffected. Thank God, my efforts succeeded. The wanderers returned to my fold.[61]

Later the same year the Church Committee resolved that a balance in the hands of the church treasurer of £38.6.0½ be given to Dr Dickson as a present 'for the services he has rendered to this Congregation'.[62]

It was in 1793 that Dickson was elected to the chair of the General Synod which met at Lurgan in June. This was the meeting of Synod which passed a declaration calling for a reform in the representation of the House of Commons, and congratulated 'their Roman Catholic countrymen on their being restored to the privileges of the Constitution', and expressed the 'prayer that the time may never more return when religious distinctions shall be used as a pretext for disturbing society, or arming man against his neighbour, and that intolerance of every kind may be trodden under foot'.[63] While Dickson, as Moderator, could not enter into the synodical debate, it is quite possible that the declaration owed its passage through the Synod to his influence with the members.

V

Dickson gives very little information in his *Narrative* about his actions in the years 1794, 1795 and 1796, except to report that in his neighbourhood it was not uncommon to see some Presbyterians and Catholics running from house to house under the impression that a massacre was to take place at any moment and that their neighbours with whom they had lived in peace and friendship were to be the perpetrators. These alarms he claims he exposed with success only to find that charges of sedition and threats of vengeance were directed against him for his pains.[64] His enemies contended that he occupied these years preaching inflammable and seditious sermons.[65]

On the death of the Rev James Bryson at Belfast in October 1796, there was a move to get Dickson to accept the vacant pulpit of Donegall Street congregation, with the additional inducement that he should set up an Academy in Belfast in opposition to the Rev William Bruce, Principal of the Belfast Academy (1790-1822).[66] A call from the congregation was presented to Dickson at a meeting of the Bangor presbytery on 7 February 1797, and supplies were appointed 'till Dr Dickson shall declare his determination with respect to the "call"'.[67] Dickson, however, eventually declined the call.

The government, with the aid of informers, became aware that the United Irishmen were reorganising on military lines; fearing collusion between them and the French Directory, it decided to act and rounded up the majority of the northern leaders in the winter of 1796 and the spring of 1797. Two of Dickson's ministerial brethren from the Volunteer days, the Revs T. Ledlie Birch and Sinclare Kelburn, were among those arrested but Dickson himself was left at large. However, efforts were made to procure evidence against him. Five or six members of his congregation were arrested in October 1796 and lodged in Downpatrick gaol. One member, by the name of Carr, was transported to Kilmainham gaol in Dublin where it was hoped that he would be able to provide material evidence to implicate Dickson. At the end of December Dickson took himself off to Dublin. His departure from Portaferry was noticed immediately by Col Savage of Portaferry House, who had been responsible for the arrest of Dickson's hearers.[68] Col Savage communicated the information to Lord Londonderry, Dickson's erstwhile political ally, and Lord Downshire, who in turn got in touch with Dublin Castle. Lord Londonderry, who surmised that Dickson had been appraised of the arrival of the French fleet off the coast of Cork – hence his departure south – described Dickson as 'one of the more violent and seditious characters in the country' and advocated that he 'should be hunted out in Dublin, and if possible taken up and detained as a suspicious personage'.[69] Col Savage in his letter to Lord Downshire warned that Dickson should 'by no means be allowed to see or hold any communication with any of the close prisoners, particularly with Carr', and expressed the hope that the Devil (Dickson's 'true friend') might leave him in the lurch. 'I'm sure,' he added, 'he must trip some time or other.'[70] Savage's apprehension lest Dickson be permitted to see Carr was well founded, for on a visit to some of the northern United Irishmen in Kilmainham gaol, Dickson was enabled, by a stratagem of some of the detainees, to overhear a discussion between Carr and other prisoners in the course of which Carr admitted that he had been offered £1,000 to provide information leading to Dickson's conviction.[71]

Dickson returned to Co Down after a fortnight in Dublin and spent part of his time over the next four to five months visiting and seeking the release of those members of his congregation lodged in Downpatrick gaol; eventually they were released at the Summer Assizes in 1797. He had also been present at the Co Antrim Spring Assizes held at Carrickfergus having been summoned, as had Lord Londonderry, Lord Castlereagh and the Rev John Cleland, in the trial of Joseph Cuthbert, a putative member of the United Irish assassination squad, 'in order to impeach' the character of the chief prosecution witness Belle Martin.[72] Belle Martin, a native of Portaferry, had been a barmaid at Peggy Barclay's Tavern in Sugarhouse Entry, Belfast, a regular meeting place for members of the United Irishmen and from time to time she had passed on information to the government. When the prisoner was arraigned, Belle Martin, who had been brought from Dublin for the trial, could not be found and the case against Cuthbert was dismissed for lack of evidence. The reason for her sudden disappearance became a matter of some conjecture but, as she had a reputation of being of a bad moral character, the Crown officials probably concluded that her evidence would have been easily discredited. Or as the editor of the *Northern Star* phrased it 'we suppose from prudential motives [she was] not brought forward'.[73]

Despite the continuing arrest and harassment of suspected United Irishmen and a general 'dragooning' of the province by the Crown forces under the command of General Gerard Lake, the spirit of reform remained strong. A number of Co Down magistrates and gentlemen, following the lead of two other Ulster counties, requested the High Sheriff of the County to convene a meeting of the freeholders at Downpatrick on 22 May, in order to present a petition to the King, calling for the dismissal of the Irish government ministers and a reform of parliament, as the means of restoring peace and tranquillity to the nation. On the refusal of the sheriff to comply, and learning of the intention of Generals Lake and Nugent to have any such meeting dispersed by the military, they cancelled the meeting, at the same time assuring the freeholders that alternative means would be speedily adopted to petition the King. On the day originally appointed for the meeting in Downpatrick, twenty-five of the petitioners met at Lord Moira's mansion in Ballynahinch, and resolved 'not to relax in our exertions by any legal and constitutional means to obtain a full and adequate representation of the people of Ireland in parliament without regard to differences of religious opinions'. W. S. Dickson, eager as always to promote parliamentary reform, was one of those who assembled at Montalto, and later published their resolutions in the *Belfast News Letter* over a period of three to four weeks.[74] The reaction of the government was to reject the petition and proclaim the whole county even more strictly under martial law.

In the latter part of 1797 and during the spring of 1798 Dickson states that he was largely confined to his home by reason of bilious attacks and attendant fever.[75] In March and part of April 1798 he was in Scotland attending to family business, visiting his wife's uncle who was dangerously ill. On his return, his servant, who had brought his luggage from Donaghadee, was stopped in the street in Portaferry and the baggage removed to the guard-house for scrutiny. The authorities suspected that Dickson had been to Scotland to promote the objects of United societies there, but no incriminating documents were found in the baggage.[76] In fact, it was customary for him 'out of his six weeks' leisure every year to spend four in Scotland, renewing his intimacy and friendships'.[77]

In the month of May Dickson travelled over parts of Co Down engaging in sacramental duties on behalf of some of his ministerial brethren; during that time he paid a number of visits to Belfast and attended the fair at Killinchy on the first Wednesday in May. On Tuesday 29 May he left the Newtownards manse of the Rev William Sinclair (who was later transported for his implication in the rebellion) with the intention of spending most of the day at Crawfordsburn with John Crawford, a magistrate favourable to the United Irishmen, and of continuing to Belfast later the same day; but on learning that Crawford was not at home, he proceeded directly to Belfast. Next day, Wednesday, he rode out to Bally-gowan, and spent the night at the home of Robert Rollo Reid, one of his former pupils and a United Irishman. At Saintfield Fair the following day, Thursday 31 May, Dickson sought to purchase a horse but failed to find a satisfactory mount; consequently Nicholas Mageean, a United Irishman and government informer, was sent to arrange for a horse to be provided the next day at a Capt Sinclair's near Belfast. Unable to get a meal at the inn in Saintfield, Dickson made his way to the home of David Shaw, another United Irishman, and after dinner there decided to ride to Belfast the same evening.[78] When he reached Ballygowan, however, he changed his mind and decided again to spend the night at Robert Rollo Reid's house. In his *Narrative*, Dickson gives no reason for his change of plans but, according to a deposition of his, when he arrived at Ballygowan he encountered a considerable commotion and saw a genteel young man, very drunk and with his nose cut, come run-ning out of a public house. On learning that the young man was a son of Dr Birch, a local doctor and brother of the Rev Thomas

Ledlie Birch of Saintfield, Dickson stayed with him till after 7 o'clock in order to prevent him fighting and then conducted him home to Ballybeen near Dundonald.[79]

Riding to Belfast on Friday 1 June, Dickson states that he was not successful in obtaining a new horse from Captain Sinclair; however he did meet up with a John Coulter of Collin, another United Irishman, and spent the night at his house. Then, on the Saturday morning, with a horse supplied by his host, he set out for Ballee, four miles south of Downpatrick, to carry out sacramental duties as previously arranged by his presbytery. On Saturday evening he crossed the Lough to Portaferry, crossed again to Ballee on Sunday morning and returned to his manse in Portaferry the same evening. On Monday he again officiated at Ballee and, after baptising a child for Mr John McNeown, set off for Ballynahinch where he spent the night at an inn.

The following day, Tuesday 5 June, Dickson rode out to the Spa on three occasions to take the waters for his bilious complaint, intending to do so for the remainder of the week. On his return to Ballynahinch that evening – two days before the Battle of Antrim – he was, at the instigation of Col Lord Annesley, arrested without a warrant by Captain Magenis and Lieut Lindsay of the Castlewellan Yeomanry.[80] At noon the next day a Col Bainbridge arrived from Lisburn, and gave orders for Dickson to be transferred there. Refused permission to ride, Dickson walked the eight miles to Lisburn under a blazing sun. Later the same evening he was transferred under guard by chaise to Belfast and lodged in what he describes as the 'black hole', then a guard house or prison. The following afternoon he was removed with other United Irishmen to the Donegall Arms, which was then being used as the Provost prison.[81]

Early in July he was transferred to the Artillery Barracks, where he had the melancholy task of offering spiritual comfort to Henry Joy McCracken a few hours before his execution on 17 July 1798.[82] On 12 August, he was removed to a prison ship in Belfast Lough. In September he was brought back again to Belfast prison and transferred once again to the 'floating Bastille' on 25 December – his

54th birthday – where he remained until 25 March 1799. During this period, repeated attempts were made by the Crown Law Agent, John Pollock, to obtain sufficient evidence to enable the authorities to convict and hang him. John Hughes, a Belfast bookseller and United Irishman who had turned informer, was placed among the prisoners in the hope that confidential conversations might be overheard by him and reported to the authorities.[83] Later Nicholas Mageean was planted among them for the same purpose, but Dickson and his friends became suspicious and the move proved a failure.[84] Pollock and the Rev John Cleland, Lord Londonderry's general factotum, endeavoured to trap Dickson into an admission of his guilt, but he proved too wily for them, refusing to sign any documents.[85] Pollock's efforts to secure grounds for a conviction were also somewhat thwarted when Nicholas Mageean refused to agree to testify in court about what he knew of Dickson's associations with the United Irishmen[86] or of his appointment as Adjutant General of the Co Down forces on 12 May 1798.[87] Pollock now concentrated on John Hughes who had been taken into protective custody and lodged in the Lower Castle Yard, Dublin. Pollock wrote to Viscount Castlereagh informing him that he had been in touch with Edward Cooke and Alexander Marsden at Dublin Castle in order to persuade them to prevail on Hughes to give evidence for 'so far as related to Dr Dickson, Simms, Tennent, etc. he can convict them'.[88] But as in the case of Mageean, Hughes refused to let the betrayal of his former comrades be made public in court. There is little doubt that, had these two informers been persuaded to testify, Dickson would have gone to the gallows in the summer of 1798.

The Rev John Cleland, for his part, persisted in the task of seeking further evidence against Dickson. On 4 November 1798, he prevailed upon Robert Rollo Reid of Ballygowan to swear an affidavit relating to a conversation which he had had with Dickson in his home on 30 May 1798, in which Dickson allegedly told him he had been appointed Adjutant-General of the Co Down forces.[89] Cleland also induced the United Irishman, Richard Frazer of Ravara, to swear an affidavit on 18 October 1798, which states that when Dr Dickson was asked on the day of Killinchy Fair in May if he would act 'in a public capacity', he had replied that he 'was willing to do anything he could to serve or be useful to his country'.[90] Even after Dickson's release from prison in 1802, Cleland sought to obtain from a former United Irishman, David Thomson of Saintfield, an admission that he had been one of a deputation from the County of Down Committee which gave the Doctor a high appointment at Killinchy Fair.[91]

During Dickson's incarceration in Belfast prison, his farm stock at Portaferry was seized and his family forced to flee for safety to Donaghadee.[92] To add to his misfortunes his eldest son, D. M. Dickson, a surgeon in the Royal Navy, died.

On 25 March 1799, Dickson, with several other northern prisoners, was put aboard the *Aston Smith*, which already contained a number of prisoners from Dublin.[93] The following morning the ship, with an armed escort, set sail for Scotland but, encountering a severe storm, did not reach destination till 30 March. The prisoners were landed at Gourock on the Clyde and conveyed overland to Fort George on the Moray Firth, ten miles north east of the town of Inverness, which they reached on 9 April.

In contrast to the cramped and vermin-ridden compartments, lack of warmth and poor food which had been their lot in the Belfast prison, conditions at Fort George were very favourable. Dickson states that the changes were such that he felt that he had been 'transported not only to a new heaven and a new earth, but to the society of the spirits made perfect'.[94] At Fort George the twenty prisoners each had a separate room with 'a neat four poster bed with good curtains'.[95] Dickson remarks on the fine cuisine they enjoyed.

> We have very fine salmon twice or thrice a week ... our beef, mutton, pork, veal, lamb, etc. are remarkably good. Latterly we have had plenty of garden stuffs or salading – and some young ducks and peas ... our wine and porter all have been uniformly good. And at supper we have occasionally had very fine crabs and lobsters.[96]

Those who wished could bathe every day of the week, as the season permitted, and clean bed linen was supplied once a fortnight.[97]

During his sojourn at Fort George Dickson refused to petition the government for his release, demanding instead that he should be brought to court and tried, but to no avail. In December 1801 came news of the impending release of some of the northern prisoners, and on 30 December, despite severe winter conditions, Dickson and his companions set out in three chaises for Greenock, where the sloop *Hazard* awaited them. They reached Greenock after minor mishaps on 9 January 1802, and on 12 January landed at Holywood, Co Down.[98] The following day, 13 January, Dickson and his friends entered into recognisances at Belfast and, to quote Dickson, 'were once more restored to the liberty of breathing the air, treading the soil, of our native land'[99] – three years, seven months and seven days after his arrest at Ballynahinch.

VI

Dickson was now practically penniless except for a small annuity of £25. The Portaferry congregation had continued to pay him his stipend until his pulpit was declared vacant by the Bangor presbytery on 28 November 1799. A new minister had been inducted on 5 June 1800, but not without opposition from some members of the congregation who were still supporters of Dr Dickson.[100] At the Synod meeting held at Lurgan on 28 August 1798 – two months after the rebellion – no mention was made either in the presbytery report or otherwise of Dickson's arrest and imprisonment in Belfast. The Synod, however, instructed presbyteries to institute a solemn enquiry into the conduct and conversation of their members and probationers with reference to their possible implication in the recent insurrection.[101] The following year, 1799, the Bangor presbytery reported to the Synod 'that the Revd Dr Wm Steel Dickson hath been from the beginning of June, 1798, a State prisoner, and is now such at Fort George in the Highlands of Scotland'.[102] Consequent to this Dr Robert Black, a minister in Londonderry and agent for the *Regium Donum*, sought the opinion of the Synod respecting payment of the *Regium Donum* to those members of the Synod then in confinement and it was agreed to suspend payment to them. Payment, however, was continued until Dickson's successor was appointed to Portaferry in June 1800.[103]

In the distressing circumstances in which he found himself on his return to Ireland, Dickson contemplated emigrating to America but, realising that his departure would be construed as an acknowledgement of his guilt, he courageously decided to remain. At this time the congregation of Donegore, near Templepatrick, was anxious to obtain a successor to its aged pastor, the Rev John Wright, and approaches were made to Dickson by some influential members of the congregation. Dickson contends that Dr Black and others prevented his settlement there, by insinuating that the *Regium Donum* would be withdrawn from the congregation and its aged pastor, should Dickson be appointed.[104] In 1802, although still without a congregation, Dickson was present at the Synod, which invited him to sit as an honorary member.[105] In the autumn of that year he received an invitation to become minister of a newly formed congregation in Keady, Co Armagh. Again, according to Dickson, Dr Black and his brother-in-law, the Clerk of the Synod, the Rev Thomas Cuming of Armagh, tried to block his appointment, but this time they were unsuccessful. Dickson was installed at Keady on 24 March 1802, the congregation promising him '£50 Stipend and whatever more the congregation could raise'.[106]

Dickson was not attached to any presbytery prior to the settlement at Keady. Nevertheless he wrote to the Clerk of his former presbytery of Bangor, informing him that the presbytery of Tyrone would probably require credentials from the presbytery concerning him. The Bangor presbytery promptly responded and issued the following statement showing the high esteem in which it still held its former presbyter:

We heartily congratulate our Fathers and Brethren of the Presbytery of Tyrone on the Drs. being added to their number. In learning as an accurate scholar, in manners as a gentleman, and dignity of moral conduct as becoming a Christian Divine, we hesitate not to say, he will do honour to any Presbytery. From what the publick have experienced of his literary abilities, and we of his improving fellowship, we conceive him justly entitled to the amplest credentials. We sincerely pray he may long live an useful member of your Presby, and an ornament to the Church of Christ.

Signed by order of Presby. John Watson, Modr.[107]

As Dickson's installation service did not include his signing the *Westminster Confession of Faith*, it was moved at the next meeting of presbytery, on 3 May 1802, that he should not be admitted as a member of presbytery unless he subscribed the Synod's formula of subscription to the *Confession*. This was found not to be the majority view of the members and Dickson was accordingly received as a member of the presbytery of Tyrone.[108]

During this time, the Dublin Castle authorities were still keeping a wary eye on Dickson and his movements. In June 1803, letters were received from officials in the Armagh district reporting on Dickson's settlement at Keady: while the writers did not take it upon themselves to claim that any positive charge of corrupting and influencing the minds of the people could be brought against him, they promised to keep the authorities informed.[109]

It would seem that Dickson paid a visit to Dublin early in July 1803, a few weeks before Robert Emmet's abortive insurrection in that city. He was seen by the Rev Mr Taylor, a Presbyterian minister of Harolds Cross, often in the company of Catholics and reportedly collecting money from them.[110] In August, according to a report sent to Lord Annesley, from his agent at Rostrevor, there was a rumour circulating in the Mourne country that Dickson was in the district awaiting the arrival of 30,000 stand of arms from France. Lord Annesley's informant was obviously no friend of the Doctor's for he stated that he longed 'to see Dickson's neck stretched'.[111] Lord Annesley, in a covering letter to the Castle authorities, writes that he has given orders for Dickson to be arrested.[112] However this time, unlike 5 June 1798, his Lordship's orders were either not carried out or else were countermanded by someone in higher authority, for Dickson remained at large.

VII

In 1804 the congregation of Second Keady, Dickson's congregation, presented a memorial to the Synod in which they asked why, in view of their formation as a congregation by the Synod in 1803, they had not received their share of the *Regium Donum*. The Synod, 'not considering itself competent at present to give the congregation any aid in this business', dismissed the application.[113]

The next year, 1805, the congregation presented a further memorial, but its commissioners, noting that a somewhat similar memorial presented by another congregation had been set aside by the Synod, then withdrew it. On the spur of the moment, Dr Dickson himself submitted a memorial requiring the Synod to declare explicitly 'whether or no he is alluded to in a part of the minute of 1799, which had been constructed into a reflection on his character as a man "implicated in treasonable or seditious practices" and if so to explain what they then meaned [*sic*] by being implicated in "practices treasonable or seditious",' but his memorial was unanimously dismissed.[114] At this, according to Dr Black, 'Dr Dickson rushed violently from his seat and having taken a few steps in the aisle, turned round and entreated the Moderator to hear him one word; a still silence ensued, when, laying his hand upon his breast he pronounced, with great emphasis, "farewell for ever" and left the house.'[115]

In the 1805 election in Co Down the contest was between Col John Meade and Viscount Castlereagh. Castlereagh was strongly supported by the Rev Dr Robert Black and the Rev Thomas Cuming. Dickson took the side of Meade and had the satisfaction of seeing Castlereagh, whom he had previously so vigorously supported, defeated. Dickson's impact on the voters must have been considerable for the Castlereagh camp produced a pamphlet containing an imaginary discussion between Dr Dickson and an erstwhile hearer of his from Portaferry. The pamphlet denounces Dickson as 'one who led some of your own brethren to the rope' and the 'parish to the brink of perdition' and speculates as to his fate had he not been taken up at Ballynahinch a few days before the battle. It also taunts him with his narrow escape in getting out of Dublin three days before Lord Kilwarden was killed at the time of the Robert Emmet insurrection, and with the still unpaid debts that he had left behind him at Portaferry in 1798.[116]

Dickson was absent from the Synod in 1806 because of illness. However, he attended in 1807, 1809 and 1810, and took part in the ordinary business of the court without alluding to his grievances against it.

In 1810 Dickson issued the prospectus of his *Narrative of the Confinement and Exile*, in which he declared that:

This Narrative will exhibit a detailed view of his sufferings, privations, and inflictions – the informations on which he was arrested, confined, dragged from prison to prison, on land to sea, sea to land, and country to country, as they appear in the reports of the secret committees of the Lords and Commons ... the respective treatment which he received in Irish and British prisons – the conduct of the Rev the General Synod of Ulster, towards him and his family, during and since that period, and the relation in which he stands to that body ... every circumstance of importance, relative to government, will be authenticated by official documents, and those, respecting the Rev the Synod of Ulster, by extracts from its own records.[117]

In the preparation of the work Dickson needed certain synodical records and decisions and these he sought from the Clerk, the Rev Thomas Cuming. Cuming refused to comply. Dickson presented a memorial to the Synod in 1811, complaining of the Clerk's conduct in refusing him copies of certain synodical papers, and petitioning the Synod itself to grant him his request. The Synod upheld the Clerk's reasons for refusing the papers, but then proceeded to grant Dickson his request.[118]

Dickson was politically active in the course of the year, taking part in the speeches at a Catholic Dinner in Dublin on 9 May 1811, probably becoming the first Irish Presbyterian minister ever to address a wholly Roman Catholic gathering. In his address he asserted that 'the great body of Presbyterians in Ulster are, at this moment, sincere and zealous friends to Catholic claims and that Catholics had no cause, either of fear or disgust, from the malicious rumours, industriously circulated that Presbyterians had become enemies of their interests, or, at least, lukewarm in their cause'.[119] He also spoke at a Catholic meeting in Armagh on 9 September but on his way home to Keady he was waylaid and beaten up. It was stated in some newspaper reports that Orangemen were responsible.[120] A sort of unofficial enquiry was held but no clear finding emerged.

The publication of his *Narrative* in May 1812 raised a major storm at the meeting of the Synod in June. The contents of his book were assailed by Dr Black and in the course of the altercation between Black and Dickson, Black challenged Dickson 'to stand up in his place, and declare that he was not concerned in originating, fomenting or fostering the rebellion of 1798, and that he would move his disavowal shall be recorded in the minutes of Synod'.[121] Dickson replied, 'I am astonished at such a proposal. What end could such a declaration serve? Or to what purpose would it be recorded in your minutes? Even Dr Black has not said that he would believe it. I will make no such declaration. If any man has a doubt of my innocence, let him prove me guilty.'[122] The Synod, very much under the power of Dr Black, declared its opinion that Dr Dickson's *Narrative* contained 'a number of gross mis-statements and mis-representations ... and that Dr Dickson should publicly retract' them.[123] The Doctor expressed his willingness to have the Synod prepare such a statement, but when it was set before him for his signature at a later meeting of the court he refused to comply, rejecting it with disdain. The Synod's first reaction was to suspend him *ab officio,* but an amendment, that the matter be postponed to the next Synod to allow Dr Dickson an opportunity of publicly retracting his statements, was agreed.[124]

Dickson availed himself of the interval to prepare and publish a pamphlet facetiously entitled *Retractations.* This was in effect a reply to a pamphlet issued by Dr Black under the title *Substance of Two speeches ... with an abstract of the Proceedings of Synod relative to the Rev Dr Dickson.* In his *Retractations* Dickson successfully answers most of the criticisms levelled at him by Dr Black and this, coupled with the publication of a series of letters in the *Belfast Commercial Chronicle* between July 1812 and February 1813, in which an anonymous correspondent carried out a sustained attack on Dr Black's pamphlet,[125] led to a reappraisal of his situation by the Synod in 1813. The Rev William Porter, assisted by the Rev Henry Montgomery, espoused his cause, and queried the accuracy of the wording of the Synod's statement of 1799 in relation to Dickson. It was agreed that the words 'implicated in treasonable and seditious practices', as applied to Dr Dickson, had been inaccurately used, but at the same time the Synod passed a resolution noting that certain statements made by Dickson in his *Narrative*, respecting the conduct of the Synod towards him while he was in confinement, were 'unfounded' and demanding an apology from him. At a later session Dickson handed to the Clerk a paper which purported to be an apology. This statement the Synod refused to accept as adequate, but in the circumstances decided to dismiss the whole subject and the paper was returned to Dickson,[126] a decision which a prominent member, writing in the August edition of the monthly *Belfast Magazine*, interpreted as the Synod saying in effect, 'It is true we have condemned Dr Dickson, but as we have found him such a stiff, unyielding, troublesome sort of a man, we will not have anything further to say to him.'

While neither the government nor the Synod was able to prove the charge that Dickson had been implicated in treasonable and seditious activities or that he had held the post of Adjutant-General in the United Irish forces in Co Down, most of the available evidence suggests that he certainly played a prominent part in the events leading up to the rebellion.

Nicholas Mageean, the United Irishman and government informer intimate with all the plans of the Co Down colonels, claimed that Dickson 'was the most active and persevering of the rebel traitors in promoting the system of the United Irishmen and the Rebellion'.[127] Another informer, John Hughes, the Belfast bookseller, informed the Committees of Secrecy of the House of Lords and the Commons that on Friday, 1 June [1798], Dickson told him that he was one of the Adjutant-Generals of the United Irishmen's forces in Co Down, and that he, Dickson, would go to Ballynahinch and remain there till Wednesday, as it was the central place from which he could issue orders to his officers. Dickson told him the reason why he would remain at Ballynahinch till Wednesday was that the Antrim colonels had adjourned till the Tuesday, and that he could receive their determination in Ballynahinch the day following [6 June]'.[128]

In addition, the Rev John Cleland was able to induce a number of former United Irishmen, in the aftermath of the rebellion, to swear affidavits that Dickson had accepted and held a high command in the movement.[129] Finally, two of Dickson's contemporaries in the ranks of the United Irishmen, C. H. Teeling and James Hope, stated (admittedly some years after Dickson's death, when he was well beyond the reach of the authorities) that he had indeed been Adjutant-General.[130]

However, there is a curious little incident that casts some doubt on his holding such a position. David Bailie Warden, a colonel in the United Irish army and a probationer of the Bangor presbytery, writing from America following his exile, recounted how, on the evening of 5 June (the night of Dickson's arrest) he and a companion, at the instigation of Nicholas Mageean, had travelled from Saintfield to Ballynahinch for the purpose of obtaining the latest news regarding the proposed rising. At the inn in Ballynahinch 'he happened *accidentally* to see Dr Dickson and conversed about ten minutes with him upon private business having a little before that entered the presbytery of Bangor' of which they were both members. Next morning Warden and his friend, apparently unaware of Dickson's arrest and still in the dark as to news of the rising, returned to Saintfield. There they again met with Mageean who told them that John Hughes of Belfast had sent a special messenger to him that day to invite the Co Down colonels to rise, adding that by twelve o'clock the next day Co Antrim would be in arms to attack the town of Antrim.[131]

Three possible deductions follow from this account by D. B. Warden: (1) Warden was not aware of Dickson's role as Adjutant-General and consequently did not seek from him any news concerning the rising; or (2) Dickson was not able to provide Warden with any news, as he was himself awaiting a report from the Antrim colonels; or, (3) Dickson was not an Adjutant-General, but simply a lawful citizen having a private conversation with a young ministerial colleague. This adds weight to Dickson's explanation for his presence in Ballynahinch at this time, namely to take the waters at Spa for his bilious complaint.[132] As to which one of these three hypotheses is correct, it is impossible to say, but the possibility that Dickson was not an Adjutant-General cannot be ruled out.

However, had he not been arrested later the same evening, following his conversation with Warden, it would soon have been evident to all whether he was an Adjutant-General or not. In the event, the precipitate arrest of Dickson on the orders of Lord Annesley[133] – an episode that was to cause John Pollock, Crown Law Agent, to cry out in frustration when interrogating Dickson in prison, 'You were taken at your post, but rather too soon. Had you been left to yourself, but a few days longer, the government would have been sure of you'[134] – and the refusal of the two informers to testify against him in open court, meant that Dickson was never formally charged.[135]

His response, when he came to write his *Narrative* in 1812, was first to state enigmatically, 'I may have been a general, for aught appears to be contrary, and I may not have been a general, though people said I was';[136] next to discredit the informers' reports regarding his actions and movements leading up to his apprehension by the military at Ballynahinch on 5 June;[137] and finally to assert defiantly, 'I have neither acknowledged nor denied the charge and I am convinced that there is not a man on earth capable of proving either its truth or falsehood, by any evidence entitled to credit in any court on earth.'[138]

In view of the deliberately ambivalent nature of his remarks, and of the open challenge to anyone to prove him either guilty or not guilty, and since one possible interpretation of his meeting with D. B. Warden suggests that he may not have been an Adjutant-General, a reasonable doubt still remains as to his position, if any, in the United Irish army. Was Dickson Adjutant-General of the Co Down insurgents or not? Only Dickson could supply the definitive answer to that question and he always studiously avoided committing himself.

VIII

Dickson was now approaching the age of seventy, but his interest in Catholic emancipation remained unabated. On 19 October 1813 he addressed a meeting of Co Down Catholics at Newry and referred to the recent declaration of the Synod in favour of emancipation, to which, he said, he could give only a limited approval because it did not go far enough.[139]

Still not satisfied with the Synod's ruling on his dispute with Dr Black, he sought leave to introduce a motion at the Synod of 1815 but was refused permission.[140]

The weight of years was now beginning to tell on him and on 27 June he resigned the pastorate of Second Keady, 'through infirmity and inconvenience of situation, to attend to the duties of the Pastoral office'.[141] Dickson did not receive the *Regium Donum* during or after his ministry of 13 years at Keady, presumably because the government never forgave him for the part he had allegedly played in events leading up to the rebellion of 1798. Consequently his means of support were never quite sufficient.

He retired to Belfast where he lived in a cottage provided by a Mr Joseph Wright, aided by a subscription raised by some of his friends and by a weekly allowance contributed by Dr Stephenson, William Tennent, Francis McCracken, John Barnett, Dr Tennent, Dr Drennan, Adam McClean and a few others.[142]

In 1817 he transferred from the presbytery of Tyrone to his former presbytery of Bangor[143] and in the same year published his last work, a volume of fifteen sermons.[144] His wife died on 15 July 1819 and it seems that the small annuity ceased with her death. He died two days after his eightieth birthday and was buried in a pauper's grave in Clifton Street Cemetery, Dr Henry Montgomery and eight or nine other persons forming the entire funeral procession. At the graveside 'an impressive and eloquent address' was delivered by the Rev W. D. H. McEwen.[145] Thus ended the earthly life of one who had endeavoured to neutralise the poison of prejudice and bigotry, fostered the seeds of religious liberty and sought to promote union and harmony among his fellow countrymen of all religious persuasions. The site of his grave was left unmarked for 85 years, till in 1909 F. J. Bigger erected a simple stone with the following inscription:

William Steel Dickson
patriot, preacher, historian.
Born at Carnmoney 1744
Died at Belfast, 27 December 1824
Do chum onóra na hÉireann
(*For the honour of Ireland*)

Notes

1   The Marriage and Baptismal registers of Carnmoney congregation are in the
     Presbyterian Historical Society's collection, Church House, Belfast. The
     Marriage record is as follows: 'Dec 6th 1743 John Dickson and Jane Steall
     married.' The Baptismal record states: 'Dec 30th [1744] William son to
     John Dickson was baptised.' Early Baptismal records do not give the date of
     birth. Dickson's date of birth is given as 25 December 1744 in his obituary
     notice in the *Belfast News Letter,* 31 December 1824.
2   Classon Porter, *Irish Presbyterian Biographical Sketches* (Belfast 1883), p. 10.
3   Dickson, W. S., *A Narrative of the Confinement and Exile of William Steel
     Dickson, D.D.* (Dublin 1812), pp. 3, 4. (Hereafter referred to as *Narrative.*)
4   Innes Addison, W., *The Matriculation Albums of the University of Glasgow,
     1728-1858* (Glasgow 1913), p. 69.
5   *Narrative,* pp. 3, 4.
6   ibid., p. 4. Principal William Leechman died on 3 December, 1785.
7   ibid., p. 6.
8   Ms. Minutes of Templepatrick Presbytery 1745-1770. p. 376.
9   ibid.
10   ibid., pp. 378, 379, 380, 381, 383.
11   ibid., p. 386
12   ibid., p. 368.
13   ibid., pp. 395, 418, 441.
14   Latimer, W. T., *Ulster Biographies* (Belfast 1897), p. 76.
15   *Narrative,* p. 6.
16   ibid., p. 7. Dickson nowhere refers in his *Narrative* to his wife's maiden
     name. W. T. Latimer and A. Gordon state that she was called Gamble, but
     the Ballyhalbert (Glastry) List of Marriages records 'August 21st, 1771 Rev.
     W. S. Dickson married Isabella McMinn.' The name McMinn reappears in
     the Christian names of their eldest son.
17   ibid., p. 185. There were six children of the marriage.
     The Baptismal Register of Ballyhalbert congregation records:
          Jane, baptised 5 December, 1775.
          David McMinn, baptised 14 June, 1776.
          Mary Charlotte, baptised 4 September, 1777.
     The Baptismal Register of Portaferry congregation records:
          John Echlin, baptised 14 September, 1780.
          Henry William, baptised 29 December, 1782.
          William Galaway, baptised 12 October, 1785.
18   *The Bible Christian,* 1830, p. 175.
19   *Narrative,* p. 7.
20   ibid., p. 8.
21   This sermon was preached to the 'Protestant Dissenting Congregation' of
     Ballyhalbert, 13 December 1776.
22   This sermon was delivered at Glastry (Ballyhalbert) on 27 February 1778.
     Dickson published two more sermons at the same time, entitled *On the
     Coming of the Son of Man.* Preached before the Particular Synod of Belfast at
     their Annual Meeting, November, 1777, and *On the Hope of Meeting,
     Knowing and Rejoicing with virtuous Friends in a future World* (Belfast
     [1780]). No indication of time and place of preaching is given.

23 *Narrative*, p. 8.
24 *On the Advantages of National Repentance*, pp. 21, 22.
25 ibid, pp. 21, 22.
26 *On the Ruinous Effects of Civil War*, p. 55.
27 ibid., p. 56.
28 ibid., pp. 57, 58.
29 *Narrative*, pp. 9, 10.
30 *On the Propriety and Advantages of Acquiring the Knowledge and Use of Arms in Times of public Danger*. Preached before the Echlinville Volunteers, on Sunday, 28 March, 1779 (Belfast 1780).
31 *Narrative*, p. 10.
32 ibid., p. 11.
33 ibid. The reaction of informed Catholic opinion to the sermon was summed up by Father O'Leary, ' … the discourse to the Echlinville Volunteers by Mr Dickson has done more good in one day, either by procuring relief for the distressed, or by provoking benevolence, peace and harmony amongst fellow-subjects of all denominations than the folios written on Pope Joan have done in the space of two hundred years'. *Miscellaneous Tracts*, (Dublin 1781), p. 153.
34 *Belfast News Letter*, 6-10 September 1776. (Hereafter referred to as *B.N.L.*)
35 ibid.
36 ibid.
37 ibid., 10-14 September 1776.
38 ibid., 7-10 October 1777.
39 ibid., 6-10 August 1779.
40 *Dictionary of National Biography*, v (London 1967), p. 951, s.v. 'W. S. Dickson'.
41 *Records of the General Synod of Ulster* (Belfast 1898), ii, p. 588.
42 ibid., iii, p. 26.
43 *Sermon Occasioned by the Death of the Revd. James Armstrong. Late Protestant Dissenting Minister of Portaferry: Preached by the Desire of the Congregation of that Place, November 14, 1779. And published by their request* (Belfast 1780).
44 *Narrative*, p. 311; Ms. Minutes of Committee of Portaferry Congregation, 24 October 1793.
45 Ms. History of Portaferry Congregation; in possession of the Presbyterian Historical Society, Belfast.
46 *Psalmody* (Belfast 1793), p. 27.
47 Robert Stewart Senior represented County Down as MP from 1771 till 1783.
48 *B.N.L.* 4-7 January, 18-21 January 1785.
49 Innes Addison, W., *Roll of Graduates of the University of Glasgow 1727-1897* (Glasgow 1898), p. 155.
50 *Narrative*, p. 42.
51 ibid., p. 24.
52 ibid., p. 23.
53 *Northern Star*, 18 July 1792; [H. Joy and W. Bruce], *Belfast Politics*, (Belfast 1794), p. 56.
54 ibid., 18 July 1792; *Belfast Politics*, p. 65.
55 *Belfast Politics*, pp. 104-107.
56 *Narrative*, p. 27.
57 ibid., pp. 28, 29.

58 *Northern Star,* 20 February 1793.
59 ibid.
60 ibid.
61 *Narrative,* p. 28.
62 Ms. Minutes of Committee of Portaferry Congregation, 24 October 1793.
63 *Records of the General Synod of Ulster,* iii, p. 157.
64 *Narrative,* p. 31.
65 Anonymous letter addressed to the Rt Hon Thomas Pellham, (*sic*) Dublin Castle, refers to 'William Steel Dickson DD, the Presbyterian Parson of Portaferry, who hath been long notorious for preaching sedition and who hath published inflammatory sermons ...'. National Archives, 620/26/135. Cf. Richard Musgrave, *Rebellions in Ireland* (Dublin 1802), i, p. 224.
66 Chart, D. A., (ed.) *The Drennan Letters,* no. 641, 12 November 1796.
67 Ms. Minutes of Bangor Presbytery, 1774-1790, pp. 178, 179. The Minister and congregation of Portaferry had been transferred from the presbytery of Killyleagh to Bangor presbytery in 1793.
68 *Narrative,* p. 31.
69 Lord Londonderry to Dublin Castle, 31 December 1796; National Archives, 620/28/5.
70 Col Savage to Lord Downshire, 26 December 1796; National Archives, 620/26/159.
71 *Narrative,* pp. 31, 33
72 ibid., pp. 193, 194; H. M. Hyde, *The Rise of Castlereagh* (London 1933), pp. 181-183.
73 *Northern Star,* 15 May 1797.
74 P.R.O.N.I., D 607/E/252 and 259; *B.N.L.* 15, 21 May, 2-29 June 1797.
75 *Narrative,* p. 41.
76 ibid.
77 *The Drennan Letters,* no. 621, July 1796.
78 ibid., p. 33, 34.
79 McClelland, A., 'Thomas Ledlie Birch, United Irishman', in *Proceedings and Reports of the Belfast Natural History and Philosophical Society,* Second series, vii (Belfast 1965), p. 30 footnote.
80 *Narrative,* pp. 46-50. The significance attached to Dickson's arrest is illustrated by the fact that Major-General G. Nugent, having informed Lord Castlereagh of the successful result of the Battle of Antrim, ended his dispatch of 8 June thus: 'The Rev Steele Dickson was taken up the night before last, and sent prisoner here, where he will be confined in a place of safety, as well as many others, whom it is now necessary to apprehend.' (*B.N.L.* 18 June 1798). Note that the General gives the arrest of Dickson as having occured on 6 June – the date on which he was transferred from Ballynahinch to Lisburn.
81 *Narrative,* pp. 54-57.
82 Madden, R. R., *The United Irishmen,* Second series, ii (1843), p. 492.
83 *Narrative,* pp. 62, 63.
84 ibid., pp. 64, 65.
85 ibid., pp. 68, 84.
86 J. Pollock to Viscount Castlereagh, 26 August 1798, National Archives 620/4/29/30.
87 *Black Book of the North of Ireland during the Rebellion,* P.R.O.N.I. D 272/1; Deposition of N. Mageean, P.R.O.N.I. D 714/2/21.

88 J. Pollock to Viscount Castlereagh, 26 August 1798, National Archives 620/4/29/30.
89 Black, R., *Substance of Two Speeches,* Appendix II, pp. 59, 60.
90 Deposition of Richard Frazer, P.R.O.N.I. D 714/3/37.
91 *Narrative,* p. 173.
92 ibid., pp. 77, 79.
93 *B.N.L.* 26 March 1799, referred to the prisoners, 'Yesterday Robert Hunter, Robert Simms, Wm. Tennent and the Rev Steele Dickson were sent down the Lough to be put aboard the vessel in which Arthur O'Connor and the other traitors were conveyed from Dublin.'
94 *Narrative,* p. 125.
95 ibid., p. 128.
96 ibid., p. 139.
97 ibid., p. 148.
98 ibid., pp. 178-181.
99 ibid., p. 182.
100 MS. History of Portaferry Congregation. The writer names a Mr Patr. Galway 'as the leader of a small but powerful opposition' to the induction of the Rev William Moreland as Dr Dickson's successor. Mr Galway at one stage in the dispute 'locked the meeting-house and carried off the key'.
101 *Records of the General Synod of Ulster,* iii, p. 212.
102 ibid., p. 216.
103 ibid., p. 223; W. S. Dickson, *Retractations* (Belfast 1813), p. 29.
104 *Narrative,* p. 280.
105 *Records of the General Synod of Ulster,* iii, p. 254.
106 Ms. Minutes of the Presbytery of Tyrone, 1781-1809, pp. 119, 120.
107 ibid. The credentials were drawn up at a meeting of the Bangor presbytery at Glastry on 21 March 1803.
108 Ms. Minutes of the Presbytery of Tyrone, 1781-1809, p. 120.
109 Ross, C., Armagh to A. Marsden, Dublin Castle, 16 June 1803, National Archives 620/66/24. Lieut J. Simpson, Linenhill to The Secretary of War, Dublin Castle, 24 June 1803, National Archives 620/67/55.
110 Lord Annesley to A. Marsden, Dublin Castle, 4 August 1803, National Archives 620/64/65. The Rev Mr Taylor was Philip Taylor, minister of Eustace Street congregation, 1770-1828.
111 William McGuire, Rostrevor to Lord Annesley, 2 August 1803, National Archives 620/64/65.
112 Lord Annesley to A. Marsden, 4 August 1803, National Archives 620/64/65.
113 Records of the General Synod of Ulster, iii, pp. 283, 284.
114 ibid., p. 302.
115 Black, R., *Substance of Two Speeches* (Dublin 1812), pp. 7, 8.
116 County of Down Election, 1805. [n.p. n.d.]. Dr Dickson's wife in a letter dated 6 April 1799, addressed to Mr Thomas McKibben, Portaferry, states that she knew that several people were anxious to have their accounts paid off and she was willing to give them any satisfaction she could by coming under Bond for the paying of them as soon as she had the power. *Report of the Presbyterian Historical Society,* 1912, p. 17.
117 *Rev Dr Dickson's speech at the Catholic Dinner, Dublin, May 9, 1811* [n.p. n.d.].
118 *Records of the General Synod of Ulster,* iii, p. 373.

119 *Rev Dr Dickson's Speech at the Catholic Dinner, Dublin,* p. 6.
120 *Narrative,* p. 318.
121 Black, R., *Substance of Two Speeches,* p. 39.
122 Dickson, W. S., *Retractations* (Belfast 1813), p. 62.
123 *Records of the General Synod of Ulster,* iii, p. 383.
124 ibid., p. 384.
125 The letters were issued in pamphlet form in 1813 under the title *Analytical Review of a pamphlet lately published by a person styling himself the Rev. Robert Black, D.D. In a Series of Letters: By an Elder.* (J. Haslett, according to F. J. Bigger Catalogue, Belfast 1930.)
126 *Records of the General Synod of Ulster,* iii, pp. 394-398.
127 P.R.O.N.I., D. 714/5.3
128 *Report from the Committee of Secrecy,* 1798, App. 15, p. 122; *B.N.L.* 14 Sept 1798.
129 *Vide supra,* p. 64–65, for details of those who made affidavits concerning Dickson's involvement in the United Irish leadership.
130 Teeling, C. H., *History of the Irish Rebellion of 1798* (Glasgow 1876), p. 121; James Hope, 'Autobiographical Memoir' in R. R. Madden, *Antrim and Down in '98* (Glasgow n.d.), p. 122.
131 P.R.O., H 0/10/86, *A narrative of the Principal Proceedings of the Republican Army of the County Down during the late Insurrection.* Italics mine. No writer's name is appended to this document, but internal evidence suggests that the author was David Bailie Warden.
132 *Vide supra,* p. 63.
133 ibid., for details of Dickson's arrest.
134 *Narrative,* p. 51.
135 *Vide supra,* p. 64, for details of the refusal of Mageean and Hughes to testify against Dickson.
136 *Narrative,* p. 51.
137 ibid., pp. 190-240.
138 ibid., p. 314.
139 *Belfast Monthly Magazine,* 1813, p. 403.
140 *Records of the General Synod of Ulster,* iii, p. 419.
141 Latimer, W. T., *Ulster Biographies,* p. 91.
142 *Irish Unitarian Magazine,* vol. 2, no. 10, p. 333. An illustration of his pecuniary circumstances is that a farm of his in the townland of Ringneal, Tullynakill, near Comber was sold by orders of the sheriff on a writ of Fiere Facias, the amount involved being £407.14.1. (*Belfast Commercial Chronicle,* 26 January 1814).
143 Records of the General Synod of Ulster, iii, p. 457.
144 *Sermons* (Belfast 1817).
145 *Irish Unitarian Magazine,* vol. 2, no. 10, p. 334. His death did not go unrecorded as both the *Northern Whig* and the *Belfast News Letter* a few days after his decease, carried an impressive and identical obituary notice which records, however, that 'his remains were accompanied to the grave by a considerable number of the most respectable inhabitants of Belfast'.

Presbyterian Ministers
and the Ulster Rising

William McMillan

It was in the 1780s and 90s when many Presbyterians 'came to regard the Roman Catholics as fellow-sufferers under the ascendancy
of the landed gentry and the Established Church, and to work for
an alliance with them by which that ascendancy might be over-
thrown'.[1] This attitude however was largely confined to the New
Light party*. At a meeting, held on 7 May 1792, the presbytery of
Killyleagh, regarded as the most heterodox in the Synod,[2] passed a
series of resolutions expressing delight at the downfall of the
Ministry which had involved His Majesty's dominions in civil war,
and their sympathy with the fettered state of their fellow Roman
Catholics, declaring that it was iniquitous 'To continue penalties
against obedient children for the disobedience of their ancestors,
and viewed it with detestation as a black branch grafted upon the
blasphemous doctrine of imputed Righteousness.'[3] On the other
hand, the Seceders and the Orthodox party within the Synod, although
professing Whig principles, were not ardent political reformers.
'When the people of County Down in 1784, petitioned in favour of
Parliamentary Reform, the Seceders petitioned against it.'[4] The New
Lights, not only in the presbytery of Antrim but also in the Synod,
were beginning to act compatibly with their religious liberalism.

The threat of a French invasion in 1776 led to the formation of
the Volunteer Movement with the object of supporting the defence
of the country; it incorporated into it many Presbyterian ministers
and soon the movement spread over Ulster. While it was exclusively

*The New Light, or Non-Subscribing, party were those who, in the eighteenth
and nineteenth centuries, refused to subscribe or sign *The Westminster Confession
of Faith* as a test of their orthodoxy. They were generally liberal and radical both in
theology and in politics.

Protestant, yet 'it reflected also the strong liberal sentiment characteristic of Ulster at the time,'[5] and because its services were not required its members began to take an active interest in politics. A
Convention of the Volunteers was held in the Dungannon
Presbyterian Meeting House in February 1782, and a far-reaching
political programme was approved although not all the Volunteers
were in favour of Catholic Emancipation and Parliamentary
Reform. The measures in favour of the Roman Catholics were supported mainly by the liberal Presbyterians, some of whom favoured
'a system of complete equality for men of all religious denominations, and looked upon the Roman Catholics as sufferers under the
ascendancy of the Established Church, living (as one Presbyterian
preacher put it) in "worse than Egyptian slavery"'.[6] The Rev William
Steel Dickson, a noted New Light theologian, in a Volunteer
Sermon of 1779, described as deficient in 'the sal evangelical'[7]
reprobated the injustice with which the Roman Catholics were
treated and pointed out the impolicy and danger of refusing them
entrance into the Volunteers. Naturally then, when the Society of
United Irishmen was formed in Belfast, on 14 October 1791, constituted for the purpose of forming a political union of Protestants and
Catholics, and thus maintain a liberal measure of reform, it was
strongly supported by New Light ministers and sympathisers. This
Society (decreed illegal in 1794) soon became identified with republicanism because of the interest and sympathy shown to the
French Revolution, which at first was warmly welcomed in Ulster.[8]
The anniversary of the Fall of the Bastille was celebrated in Belfast
and elsewhere, being regarded as a victory for liberty,[9] but when the
full extent of the terrors and excess of the French revolutionaries
become apparent, many timid reformers became frightened.
However, the most daring and enthusiastic of the Irish
Presbyterians were drawn into the Societies of the United Irishmen.
This inclination of Presbyterians and Roman Catholics, hitherto
fiercely opposed, perplexed and alarmed the British Ministry, but
about the same time a movement of a very different kind, directly
opposed to the United Irishmen was acquiring considerable
strength. From 1791-95 the Protestant 'Peep-o-Day-Boys', as they

were called, and 'Catholic Defenders', came into repeated conflict; this quickened the religious animosities of the past and thwarted the policy of the United Irish leaders. Those conflicts gave rise to the 'Orange Society' which was formed in 1795. The Orangemen were almost entirely composed of members of the Established Church and attached to the established government.

Lecky admits that the government wished to interfere as little as possible with the outrages committed by the Orangemen against the Roman Catholics.[10]

This revival of religious hatred was a fatal obstacle to that co-operation of Catholic and Protestant desired by the United Irishmen, but the Society did gain support by putting themselves forward as the champions of the oppressed, and many Catholic fugitives were sheltered in the Presbyterian homes of Co Antrim and Down.[11] Eventually, however, the aims of the United Irishmen resulted in rebellion and in 1798 their rising was put down with bitterness and cruelty. French help had been overrated and the poorly equipped rebels were soon routed. In Co Wexford and Co Wicklow the most formidable risings took place, and despite the fact that in Wexford no Quaker was maltreated or robbed by the rebels, the insurrection in these counties assumed a religious complexion and was afterwards viewed as a savage war of religion.[12]

In Ulster the rebellion was soon quashed, and after the Battles of Antrim and Ballynahinch the leaders were captured and executed. The Ulster rising has been referred to on many occasions as a Presbyterian rebellion, and Dr H. Montgomery, who was not 'ashamed to acknowledge that some of my own "kith and kin" fought in the ranks of their country', and who was 'proud to say that during the last forty years, I have found my best, my clearest-headed, and my warmest-hearted friends among the United Irishmen of 1798', also maintains that the rebellion was in 'its origin, and almost to its end … a Presbyterian rebellion'.[13] Indeed he said that the Ulster gaols were 'choked' with Presbyterian ministers. On the other hand, W. T. Latimer and Dr Killen, the church historians, are largely concerned in disassociating the Presbyterians from the rebels. They tend to suggest that the bulk of their church was solidly behind the government. Dr W. Killen, referring to Dr Montgomery's statement, said

that a very small portion of the Ulster gaols would have been sufficient for the accommodation of all the Presbyterian ministers who
were in confinement.[14]

When the Synod met in August 1798, it immediately forwarded
an address of Loyalty to the King, and the Lord Lieutenant; it
humbly besought the King 'not to impute to the whole the
transactions of a part', and contributed £500 to the defence of the
Kingdom. It further enjoined its presbyteries to 'institute a solemn
inquiry into the conduct and conversation of their respective members and probationers, to distinguish impartially between the innocent and the guilty, that the ministry may be blameless, and to
make a report at the next meeting under penalty of severe censure.'[15] The following year the presbyteries declared their satisfaction
that the conduct of their members 'had been conformable to order
and good Government, in the late afflicting circumstances of the
country. It appears of the comparatively small number who have
been implicated in Treasonable or seditious practices, two only, one
a minister and the other a probationer, have been executed. Two are
still in confinement; some have expressed their sincere contrition;
others are no longer connected with the Synod, and the remainder
have either voluntarily, or by permission of Government removed
from the Kingdom.'[16] The Synod therefore put on record that it
'reflected with sorrow upon the scandal brought upon its reputation, by the indiscretion and misconduct of a few misguided and
unworthy individuals, it feels confident in confirming that there is
no ground for suspecting its loyalty as a Body.'[17] This is interesting
when compared with a letter written two years before to Dublin
Castle in which it was said: 'The Presbyterian ministers are unquestionably the great encouragers and promoters of sedition.'[18] If this
resolution of the Synod stood alone, it might be contended that
only a few ministers became involved; yet there are indications
which tell in another direction and moderate the judgement of
both the Synod and the church historians. On 8 May 1800, Dr
Robert Black, the agent for the *Regium Donum*, wrote to Lord
Castlereagh and said: 'I will continue to impress upon my friends
the confidence in Government that I entirely feel myself, and I

doubt not with effect ... I know there is a fund of good sense, which will pre-ponderate when fairly appealed to.'[19]

This surely suggests that all was not quite as peaceful among the Synod members as the records would have us believe, and certainly it presupposes that there is at least a grain of truth in Dr Montgomery's remarks. No complete lists of ministers and probationers implicated in the insurrection has ever been drawn up, and historians differ as to numbers, but attached to this chapter is a list comprising of twenty-seven men, connected with the Synod and the presbytery of Antrim, all of whom were New Light in theology, and all of whom have been mentioned in different papers as being connected with the United Irishmen and the rebellion. As not one seceding minister seems to have been implicated, this tends to suggest that the radical theological outlook of the New Lights harmonised better with the United Irishmen's views concerning Roman Catholics then did the evangelical Calvinism of the Old Lights and their friends.

It must be pointed out, however, that at least three prominent ministers of the Old Light party were implicated in the rebellion.

The Rev Sinclair Kilburn, who was ordained minister of the Third Congregation, Belfast, on 8 February 1780, took an active part in the Volunteers, and in the rebellion. He is reported as having occupied the chair at a meeting in Belfast for petitioning Parliament in favour of Roman Catholic claims.[20]

A man of republican ideals, he was once asked to pray for George III, and after delaying as long as possible he said, 'O Lord, if it be possible, save the King.'[21] Imprisoned several times for seditious practices, he resigned his pastoral charge in 1799, 'on account of health'; this was announced at the Synod of 1800, at which Kilburn was present.

The Rev John Glendy was another fervent admirer of the United Irishmen. As minister of Maghera he baptised Henry Cooke. Accused of rebellion he made his escape to America where he became the chaplain to the House of Representatives, and to the Senate at Washington.[22]

The Rev Henry Henry, minister of Connor from 1788, also took a prominent part in the rebellion, and as a result suffered imprisonment; he continued to preach to his congregation until his death in 1840.[23]

At least one Reformed Presbyterian minister was implicated. This was the Rev William Stavely of Knockbracken, who on 25 June 1797 was arrested during Divine Service, later liberated only to be arrested the following year. His house was burned and furniture to the value of £200 was taken away. After an imprisonment of several months he was finally released.[24]

In fairness, it must also be pointed out that not all the New Light men viewed the rebellion with favour. Dr Robert Black, minister of the Dromore Non-Subscribing Church, opposed it bitterly. At first he had been friendly to the Volunteer Movement and to Catholic Emancipation, but later, horrified at the events of the French Revolution, he veered round, supported the government and the loyalists in their attacks upon the rebels.[25]

Dr Montgomery, too, while sympathising with the United Irishmen and their ideals on behalf of the Roman Catholics, believed that the society had erred in its judgements, and should have sought reform, as he was doing, by constitutional means; yet as a recent writer has put it, 'there can be little doubt that the boy of ten who watched his brothers march to the Battle of Antrim, would not have been a mere spectator had he been ten years older.'[26]

Further, the members of the First Non-Subscribing Church, Belfast, at a meeting of 'The Heads of Families' in June, 1798, forwarded an address of welcome to the new Lord Lieutenant in which they declared their 'Abhorrence of all foreign interference in the affairs of this Kingdom; of the Present Atrocious insurrection, and of all secret cabals... to subvert the constitution without the joint consent of the King, Lords and Commons in Parliament. As we have never been instructed in any doctrines favourable to such destructive measures so we totally disclaim, and from our hearts, adjure them.'[27] In spite of all this, however, it is true to say that, not only were the majority of the ministers concerned in the rebellion of the Non-Subscribing and Liberal principles, but also the majority of the leading laymen. Dr William Drennan, son of the minister

Rev Thomas Drennan, of First Church, Belfast, was an ardent reformer and a member of the select Committee of the Dublin Society of United Irishmen. So too was his brother-in-law, Samuel McTier, again a member of the Belfast Committee of the United Irishmen. Dr Drennan kept up a constant correspondence with Mrs McTier on the affairs of the day, and there is no doubt as to the politics of both brother and sister.[28] Archibald Hamilton Rowan of Killyleagh was one of the most notable rebels. Arrested early in the campaign he escaped to France, and although he had a government reward of £1000 on his head, two boatmen were determined to land him safely, saying: 'Our boat is small, but God watches over those, who like you, have the blessing of the poor.'[29] On his return from exile he supported Montgomery, being a staunch Arian, and he even attempted to bring over his old political friends to the aid of Montgomery in his fight against Cooke. In 1727 he wrote a letter to the Orthodox Leader, enclosing a notice requesting a meeting with him. In this he wrote, 'The contrariety of our political opinions would not alone have caused the proceedings which the enclosed notice announces ... but your conduct at the Synod proves to me the same spirit of intolerance prevails in your religious conduct.'[30]

The failure of, and the circumstances surrounding, the rebellion of '98, the rigour of its suppression, and the propaganda that it was a popish plot, gradually revived among all denominations the old fear of Roman Catholics. The insurrection was the beginning of the end for liberals in politics and theology, and the reaction told in favour of Toryism and Orangemen.

However, the power of the New Lights was far from dead after the rebellion, and when Daniel O'Connell, pleading in Dublin for Catholic Emancipation, and denouncing the religious dissensions 'which the enemies of Ireland have created', called for a union of Catholics and Protestants, his cry was heard by the Presbyterians of Ulster.[31] The Synod of 1813 made a 'strong and unanimous declaration in favour of Catholic Emancipation'[32] and declared 'that from the abolition of political distinctions on account of religious profession, so far as may be consistent with the principles of the constitution, we anticipate the happiest consequences. Hence, we conceive, would arise a union of interest ... while the baleful operation of party spirit would be restrained.[33]

MINISTERS, LICENTIATES AND PROBATIONERS
IMPLICATED IN THE '98 REBELLION

Arthur McMahon, Holywood

The Rev Arthur McMahon, of Holywood, deeply implicated in treason, and later to turn informer, was one of the most interesting personalities of the presbytery of Antrim. The second son of Alexander McMahon, a farmer of Dunanelly, he was educated in the University of Glasgow where he graduated MA in 1777. Licensed by the presbytery of Antrim he later joined the presbytery of Killyleagh.[34] This presbytery, says Dr Killen, was probably the most heterodox connected with the General Synod.[35] In 1789 he received a call to the church at Kilrea, where he was ordained on 12 October. On relinquishing his charge he returned to the presbytery of Antrim when he was installed at Holywood in 1794.

McMahon appears to have been a man of daring character, and of considerable scholarship. For a period he acted as tutor to the Londonderry family. Principal Alexander Gordon maintains that Lord Castlereagh received his classical education from Mr McMahon.[36] Lord Castlereagh was a co-religionist of Mr McMahon's, and at this time had not been lured by ambition to change his politics and his religion.

His settlement at Holywood lasted less than three years. He was compelled to seek refuge in Scotland in June 1797. It would seem that in 1797 'some Irish officers who had been in the service of Austria arrived in Dublin to assist the revolution'.[37] Some of these men toured the country, and at Randalstown a meeting was held of the provincial committee of the United Irishmen. This meeting was attended by the Rev Mr McMahon. In the report of the Secret Committee of the House of Lords, issued in 1798, it is seen from the sworn testimony of one John Hughes of Belfast, who had also attended the Randalstown meeting, that the Rev Mr McMahon reported to the assembly, that he had been sent 'by Colonels of the

County Down' to state to those of Antrim, that the 'Colonels of Down were ready to rise…'[38] From the testimony we learn that the Rev Mr McMahon was at this period a member of the National Executive, and 'One of the seven Colonels of the County of Down who had been selected and appointed leaders'. It was while McMahon was returning home from this meeting at Randalstown that he was informed of his impending arresting. As a result of this warning he took a boat at Bangor and crossed over to Scotland.

When he left Holywood it would seem that he hoped to return. Certainly he did not resign his pastoral charge, and the congregation was left in some perplexity. At the August meeting of the Antrim presbytery delegates from the congregation were present, seeking assistance and advice.[39] When the presbytery met in November, the Moderator, Dr Bruce, was asked to write to the clerk of the Bangor presbytery requesting probationers from that presbytery to supply the Holywood congregation. In May 1798, the presbytery received a letter submitted by Mrs McMahon, which announced her husband's resignation, and at this stage the pulpit was proclaimed vacant. At the same time Mrs McMahon wrote a letter to the members of the Holywood congregation, which betrays hostile feelings between the former minister and his congregation. She wrote: 'Were the emoluments double what they were, he (her husband) would spurn the idea of wishing to return to the congregation', and she concludes her letter with a prophecy that her husband would soon return 'and with honour acquit himself of the unjust insinuations thrown out to his prejudice'.[40]

Mrs McMahon's prophecy was to remain unfulfilled; her husband never returned to Ireland.

It is evident that the government knew all about McMahon's activities from the moment he arrived in Scotland. From there he made his way to London, where he met a Roman Catholic priest, named Coigly, or Quigley. He too had been obliged to leave Ireland, and was later hanged (7 June 1798). In London both these men were engaged in forming Societies after the plan of the United Irishmen, and their force was estimated at 40,000.[41] Apparently they were soon forced to seek refuge in France. Wolfe Tone in his diary notes, on 1 February 1798, that McMahon was among the Irish refugees in Paris.[42] On the same date we learn that a meeting of the Ulster Committee met in Shane's Castle, where it was stated that Mr McMahon 'had opened a communication with the "United Britons", a matter deemed of great importance.'[43]

From 1798 until 1804 little is known of Mr McMahon's activities, but it can be assumed that following the failure of the rebellion, he was forced by poverty to sell his information to England. The letters which have led to the impression that he became a spy for the English and the French, appeared in Bourrienne's *Memoirs of Bonaparte*,[44] and are reproduced in Fitzpatrick's *Secret Service under Pitt*.[45]

In 1804, Marshal Berthier, the French Minister of War, had recommended to Bernadette two Irishmen then in Hamburg, as spies. One of these was Mr McMahon. It was discovered however by the French Ambassador in Hamburg, that the Irishman rendered himself more serviceable to England than to France, a fact which the ambassador communicated to Bernadette, who in reply wrote: 'I never had great confidence in the fidelity or intelligence of McMahon. He was never trusted with any business of importance and if I furnished him with any means of subsistance, it was because he was recommended to me by the war minister, and, besides, his unfortunate condition could not but excite pity....'[46]

The Rev Mr McMahon's grandson, who became a Lieut General in the American Army, attempts to vindicate his grandfather of this charge,[47] but he fails to produce sufficient evidence to the contrary.

Whatever the true facts of the case may be, it is perfectly clear that he was befriended by Marshal Berthier, and later received a commission in the Irish Legion when it was formed by Napoleon in 1804. Five years later he was a prisoner of war in England, where he remained until the fall of Napoleon in 1814 when the prisoners were released. He then returned to France, and was ordered to join a French regiment. Dr Killen believed that he became distinguished as General Mack,[48] but this cannot be substantiated. His own family believe him to have fallen at Ligny, or Waterloo.[49]

William Sinclair, Newtownards

Rev William Sinclair belonged to a family which had old Presbyterian associations: Rev Robert Sinclair, minister of Larne Non-Subscribing Presbyterian Church, was his uncle.[50]

William had been educated at Glasgow University (1775), and for a period had acted as an 'usher' at a school near Dublin, under the principalship of a Mr Mercer. He was also assistant tutor for a time at a day school run by his uncle at Larne. In 1794 he received a call from the Newtownards Non-Subscribing Church, and was duly ordained on 10 March, his uncle officiating at the service. There is no mention of an ordination as such on the records of the Antrim presbytery, but the matter was communicated by the presbytery to the General Synod in June of that year.[51] Twice during his ministry he acted as Moderator of the presbytery, in 1785 and in 1789.

In his unpublished *History of the Newtownards Church*, written during his ministry (1827-1888), Rev Hugh Moore describes Sinclair as a popular preacher, 'one who was amicable and exemplary in his demeanour, thereby securing the esteem and affection of his townsmen of every denomination'.[52] While in Newtownards Sinclair opened a boarding school at his Manse. Here the sons of the most respectable inhabitants of the town as well as the adjoining district received the rudiments of a liberal education, a fact communicated to Rev Hugh Moore by one of the first pupils, Captain McCullough of Bangor.[53] It was during his ministry that John Wesley, in his eighty-sixth year, visited the north of Ireland, and on his arrival at Newtownards was refused admission to every pulpit in the town with the exception of that occupied by Sinclair. Rev Mr Sinclair's interests were not confined to teaching and preaching: he appeared to have found ample time to indulge in political activity. He was a member of the United Irishmen. As such he was present and spoke at a meeting in Belfast on 25 December 1792. This meeting was held in the Second Presbyterian Church (Non-Subscribing), and had been called for the purpose of expressing opinion 'on the present state of public affairs, and to enter into such measure as might be deemed expedient for the accomplishment of the great object – an equal representation of the people in Parliament'.[54]

I have been unable to ascertain the exact part played by Sinclair in the rising of '98. It is perfectly clear, however, that he was arrested, tried by a court martial and found guilty of treason and rebellion. He was sentenced to be transported for life.[55] Later he was permitted to leave for America.

At a meeting of the presbytery of Antrim on 10 October 1798, three months after the rebellion, two representatives of his congregation, Messrs Cooper and Moore, appeared, applying in the name of the congregation to 'be disannexed from Rev William Sinclair'. It was thereupon resolved by the presbytery, 'that it is not conducive to the interest of religion that the connection between the congregation and Mr Sinclair be continued, and that it be thereupon dissolved'.[56]

No reason has been recorded in these minutes why Mr Sinclair's connection with the congregation was not conducive to the interests of religion, but in view of his court martial, and the fact that the leading lay personality of the congregation was none other than Lord Londonderry, it can be well understood.

At the time of his arrest, Moore tells how the loyalists set fire to the Manse and everything it contained save such articles of furniture as could be carried away. Even the hay and grain in his stackyard, as well as his farming implements did not escape 'their vindictive rage'. Among the loyalists were members of his own congregation, and, continues Moore, 'I have lately been informed that one of them I well knew … carried off his clock, an article of furniture I most frequently have seen, though I had not the slightest idea of its history at the time, being called upon in discharge of my pastoral duties to visit the individual himself … during a long illness terminating in death.'[57]

In February 1799, a letter from Sinclair was received by the Antrim presbytery requesting that body to apply to Lord Londonderry and the congregation 'for a fulfilment of the engagements made him at his settlements'.[58] It was resolved that Sinclair furnish the Moderator with a statement of the accounts which it was his contention were still to be paid, and that the presbytery would endeavour to obtain a settlement. At the April meeting negotiations were still in progress. The stipend book which would have furnished the evidence of the debt due to the late minister was missing. It transpired that 'they had been taken out of the Session house by persons unknown and destroyed'.[59] In consequence of this the presbytery could proceed no further in settling the accounts between the congregation and its former minister.

It is an interesting fact that in the Session room library there is at present an old account book of this period, the centre of which has been cut out.

The presbytery did, however, furnish Sinclair with a certificate of his ordination signed by the Moderator. It is as follows: 'that Mr William Sinclair was ordained minister of Newton in March 1784, that it appeared he had discharged the duties of the pastoral office to the satisfaction of his congregation.'[60] Shortly after this he left for America, but little is known of his activities there. Moore says, 'I have learned, however, from undeniable authority that he died in comfortable circumstances, that he was in the habit of sending for several years annual presents to old servants, neighbours and members of his congregation to whom he felt under an obligation for their faithful services and unswerving fidelity.'[61]

Rev John McIlwaine

It would appear from further extracts in Moore's unpublished *History*, that political reasons were also responsible for the resignation of Sinclair's successor, the Rev John McIlwaine.

Mr McIlwaine had been licensed by the presbytery of Tyrone in 1792[62] and was ordained in Newtownards on 19 March 1799. At his ordination it was agreed to pay him an annual salary of £30. To this was added the sum of ten guineas from Lord Londonderry as a pew rent, plus three pounds fifteen shillings for that of his Lordship's servant, together with 'the yearly value in cash of the fields formerly occupied by Mr Sinclair'.[63] In August 1799, Mr McIlwaine applied to the presbytery of Antrim for its advice as to the propriety of his continuing minister of the congregation. The presbytery adopted the following resolution: 'that with a perfect approbation of Mr McIlwaine's principles and conduct ... we recommend him for a regard to the interests of the congregation, as well as his own comfort to resign the pastoral office ...'[64] There is no indication in the minutes of the events leading to this situation. Moore, however, details some interesting occurrences narrated to him by an uncle who took an active part in the proceedings. It would appear that Lord Londonderry learned from some source that the Rev McIlwaine had a brother who had been implicated in the rebellion, so much so that he was forced to flee to America. His Lordship thereupon concluded that the new minister was imbued with the same principles as his brother, and insisted on his ceasing to be minister. Mr Hugh Moore, a small farmer at Killearn, maintained in open meeting that it was contrary to the principles of Presbyterianism that any member, no matter what his standing in society might be, should take the liberty of acting in such an arbitrary manner. He himself had voted against the appointment of Mr McIlwaine as the minister, but, as he had been chosen by a large majority, he 'for one would not join in the movement set on foot by Lord Londonderry to dispense with the services of Mr McIlwaine as their pastor, more especially as it was founded on political motives alone'.[65] Lord Londonderry, reports the author of the narrative, 'took the matter very coolly and candidly admitted the force of the arguments placed before them and quietly said, "if you do not accede to my request to sever the connection now subsisting between Mr McIlwaine and the congregation, I will withdraw altogether from your membership, and not only that, but I will withhold every farthing of the sums I have hithertofore contributed for the support of your minister".' This was blackmail; yet such a step would have had disastrous effects upon the congregation. The matter was left to the presbytery, specially convened for the purpose. The result of their deliberation was to advise Mr McIlwaine's resignation. He was subsequently installed in the Presbyterian Church at Kilkeel on 23 December 1800,[66] and died in his charge on 16 March 1839.

The congregation at Newtownards having submitted to the decision of the presbytery of Antrim, Lord Londonderry became more conciliatory. He wrote to Dr Black of Londonderry who recommended Rev Joseph Osborne. He was a licentiate of the presbytery of Derry and had been ordained to the pastoral charge of Corboy and Tully, originally known by the name of Longford, on 16 March 1792. He resigned his charge in 1799. It was alleged that for his own personal safety he had been forced to leave. He was a 'loyalist', and had, in fact, attended Lord Longford, as private minister, on the field against the rebels. Wounded in battle he had received from his patron a gold watch and sword as a parting gift.[67] This was the man whom Lord Londonderry invited, offering him thirty pounds yearly stipend, plus a new manse, over and above what he would receive from his congregation.

It is generally believed that he was never officially installed, and that Lord Londonderry was instrumental in disposing with the formality.[68]

The records of the Antrim presbytery state that on 9 June 1800, Rev W. H. Drummond of Second Church, Belfast, reported that he had attended Newtownards when a call was made out to Mr Osborne, 'which call Mr Osborne accepted. He thereupon took his place as a member of the presbytery'.[69] There is no mention here of an installation. The Rev Hugh Moore, who succeeded him in 1827, says, 'there was a coolness on the part of the presbytery towards Mr Osborne, there was even a disposition on the part of some to regard him as not one of themselves, and not entitled to the privileges of membership ... (but) it soon passed off, for he was, so far as I can remember, up to the time of his resignation a respected member of the presbytery.[70]

Futt Marshall, Ballyclare

Mr Marshall was also a member of the presbytery of Antrim, and his name appears on lists of those implicated in the rebellion, though he does not appear to have suffered any imprisonment. There is some mystery concerning his arrival at Ballyclare. In the minute book of the presbytery his dates are given as 1785-1813, yet on 27 August, 1783 his name is given as among those who attended a presbytery meeting. There is no record of his ordination or installation on the minutes, but it can be assumed that he was ordained on 9 February 1795, as a sermon 'preached at the ordination of the

Rev Futt Marshall by the Rev William Bryson', was afterwards published in Belfast.[71] This is undoubtedly the Futt Marshall who became a rebel. The McSkimmon's Mss. state that he was present
with the rebels on Donegore Hill on 7 June 1798, and that following the defeat of the insurgents at the battle of Antrim he 'retired
home'.[72] He continued in his charge and died in 1813.

James Worrall, Larne

A native of Limerick, Mr Worrall was brought up a member of the
church as then established by law. He was educated at Trintiy
College for the ministry of that church, and there graduated BA.
His religious views changed, however, and he applied to the presbytery of Antrim to become a probationer under their care.
Pending his call to a church, he acted for a time as tutor in the family
of Mr Turnly of Rockport. Here he became acquainted with a
member of the Larne congregation, Mr Farrell, and on his recommendation, Mr Worral received a call and was ordained on 16
March 1796.[73]

As a minister he was active in catechising, and discharging his
other congregational duties, and has been referred to as an 'amiable
and accomplished gentleman'.[74]

In politics he was not only an advanced liberal, but also a member of the United Irishmen. As the recognised leader of the insurgents, he was locally known as 'the lieutenant', and in the judgement of one who followed him in the Larne pulpit 'he was con-
nisant of measures contemplated, if not perpetrated, against hearers
of his own, which should never have been connived at, or silently
observed, by a minister of the Gospel of Peace'.[75] As a United
Irishman he opened his pulpit to Rev James Porter of Greyabbey,
whilst he was making a tour through the province, nominally deliv-
ering lectures on natural philosophy, but really swearing in United
Irishmen.[76] As a result of his political activities he was arrested and
paid the penalty by a short confinement in Carrickfergus Castle,
and because of his strong sympathies with the revolutionary movement, many families of good social reputation were alienated from
his congregation.[77]

A consistent liberal he voluntarily relinquished a stipend which was secured for the Protestant Dissenting minister of Larne, from the tenants, of all religious persuasions, on the Kilwaughter estate.

For this he was accused of having lowered 'the social position of his congregation', by doing away with an arrangement which had existed for centuries.[78] Following his release from prison he read from the pulpit an explanation of his political opinions, but even this did little to reconcile many of those who had left the congregation.

He had always been a man of delicate constitution, and for health reasons he was advised to seek a warmer climate. Accordingly he resigned his charge in 1802 and removed to Clonmel in the south of Ireland, where he died two years later on 28 Novermber. In the south his political opinions took a completely opposite turn, so much so that the violent language and manner in which he was said to have expressed his new-born Protestant zeal shocked even the Orange Squires of Tipperary.[79]

James Porter, Greyabbey

The only ordained minister of the Presbyterian Church to be executed for alleged treason was the Rev James Porter of Greyabbey. In the estimation of the Roman Catholic historian, Dr Richard Madden, the Rev Mr Porter was one whose qualities 'were calculated to gain the friendship of men who had some knowledge of their fellows and had ample opportunity of discriminating between the pretenders of worth and the possessors of it'.[80]

A native of Ballindreat, in Co Donegal, Mr Porter was born in 1753. On the death of his father he became a school teacher in Dromore, Co Down, where he was married by Dr Black in the Non-Subscribing Presbyterian Church. Later he moved to Drogheda and then entered the University of Glasgow at the age of thirty. Licensed by the presbytery of Bangor he received a call to the congregation at Greyabbey where he was ordained on 31 July 1787.[81] The Rev James Bryson of Belfast, a well-known Arian, preached at the ordination on the text 'Search the Scriptures'.[82] He was an accomplished scholar, and was said to have possessed one of the best private libraries and collections of apparatus for experimentation in natural science in that part of the country.

A determined New Light theologian, he was soon drawn into the vortex of revolutionary politics and took an active interest in continental affairs. There is no record of his having been a sworn member of the United Irishmen, but by his tongue and pen he openly espoused the cause which the organisation was established to promote. Dr Montgomery, writing in 1847, tells how fifty years before he saw Mr Porter 'when under cover of lecturing upon some popular branches of Natural Philosophy, he made a tour for the real purpose of exciting discontent ... whilst assembling crowds to see the ascent of his little Montgolfier balloons, and to feel the shock of his tiny electric battery, he was exceedingly successful in spreading the principles of the United Irishmen, and was everywhere followed as a popular idol.'[83] He also served the rebel cause most assiduously as a contributor to the pages of the *Northern Star* newspaper. Between the years 1794-1795 he published in this paper a series of poems afterwards reprinted under the title 'Paddy's Resource'. The following year he submitted a series of letters which soon became famous as the 'Billy Bluff' letters. In these the author, by a skillful use of the dialect and habits of speech common to the district, held up to public opprobrium the exactions of the Squirearchy from the peasants, and satirised the conditions then prevalent of spying, espionage and feudal tyranny. The characters in these letters were Squire Firebrand (representing the local Squire Mr Montgomery) who had in his employment Billy Bluff (representing Billy Lowry, the bailiff on Montgomery's estate) whose office it was to carry all the news to the Squire and to report on all suspected persons. The Squire's agent was Lord Mountmumble (representing Lord Londonderry, father of Lord Castlereagh). So popular were these letters that the peasantry committed large portions of them to memory. They were later issued in a pamphlet which was reprinted in 1816, 1840 and 1868.* A further series of letters

---

* A sample of his wit can be seen from the following extract. Billy Bluff is informing Squire Firebrand of a conversation he had with R (a suspected United Irishman) who made 'a pretty talk about titles ... says he, but these are fine times, blessed times, lordly times, all our Squires are turned Lords, all our Lords Earls, all our Earls Marquises, all our Marquises Dukes. And why but they should, said I. Very right, said he; a Lord is a new creature, he can see through a stone wall as easily as through a pane of glass; he can see in the dark better than a cat; he can hear a

from Mr Porter's pen appeared in 1797 under the signature of 'Sydney'. These were addressed to the Marquis of Downshire and contained a violent attack upon William Pitt, who was charged with bringing the country and the constitution to the verge of destruction. In that same year the government appointed a Fast Day in thanksgiving for the dispersion of the French fleet by a storm off Bantry Bay. Mr Porter preached on this occasion, 16 February 1797, and his sermon was afterwards published under the title 'Wind and Weather'. The deliverance he attributed to Divine Providence, not to the English, and for the future he suggested that care should be taken lest Providence be found wanting. Even Dr Madden has remarked on the inappropriateness of this political sortie from the pulpit. It is not surprising, therefore, that when the rebellion broke out he was arrested. He had not taken up arms, nor had he joined the insurgents, but an informer swore that Mr Porter was present when the mail from Belfast to Saintfield was captured by the insurgents. The postboy in charge of the mailbag failed to identify him, yet on the unsupported evidence of a perjured renegade the minister of Greyabbey was condemned to death by hanging. His wife with her seven children went to Lord Londonderry to beg for his life. She was refused an interview. Even one of his Lordship's daughters who had studied under Mr Porter attempted to intercede, but 'Lord Mountmumble' could not be appeased. Thus the execution took place in sight of his own home and Meeting House. His tombstone bears the following inscription: 'Sacred to the memory of Rev James Porter, Dissenting Minister of Greyabbey, who departed this life July 2nd, 1798.' Dr Montgomery correctly re-

whisper five miles distance; a musket would not pierce his skin; he is wiser than Solomon and he never dies. Then you know I knew he was making fun. Why Billy it is true enough, a Lord never dies, the man may die but the title lives on for ever...

Then R went on, says he, what a fine thing to see in one day Mr changed into Lord, Mrs into My Lady; Jack-a-dandy into My Lord likewise and all the little Misses turned into My Lady A., My Lady B., My Lady C., My Lady D...

Did you ever see mushrooms growing on a dunghill, said he? Many a time, said I. Then, said he, you have seen what our new race of Lords and Earls resembles; they have rotten roots, flimsy stems, spungy heads and start up when nobody suspects it, in 24 hours. *The Billy Bluff* marks that it should have read, 'Murdered by Martial law for the crime of writing Billy Bluff.'

Following his death the Synod tried to deprive Mrs Porter of the Widows' Fund, but this attempt failed.

One of his sons, Alexander, who fought as a boy with the insurgents at Ballynahinch, had to seek asylum in America where he became a Senator; and another son, James, became the Attorney General of Louisiana.[84]

Dr Madden prefixed to his memoir of Mr Porter the Shakespearian motto, 'Man might pardon him and neither heaven nor man grieve at the mercy.'

Samuel Barber, Rathfriland

Mr Barber, who had been educated at Glasgow and licensed by the presbytery of Templepatrick, was a 'fearless advocate of the Right of Private judgement in matters of faith and a steady friend of civil and religious liberty'.[85] He was ordained at Rathfriland on the 3 May 1763 and took an active part in the Volunteer Movement; he became Colonel of the First Newry regiment but not, as Witherow says, of Rathfriland.[86] In 1790 Mr Barber was elected Moderator of the Synod and his retiring sermon was afterwards published. It is said that when he heard of a young man of Newry having been hanged in his own garden without either judge or jury, he thereupon remarked: 'The Country had best look to itself when such things could be done.' For this he was arrested and tried for rebellious principles and was sentenced to seven year's banishment or two years in jail.[87] He went to jail and the officer in charge took the prisoner through his own parish and town of Rathfriland, in order it was thought to excite an attempt at rescue, but Mr Barber's calmness and firmness prevented that. When his friends would have crowded round him, he declared, 'not to come near nor speak to him and no harm would come to him but any interference would be fatal'.

Mr Barber was lodged in Downpatrick jail.[88] Dr Montgomery described Mr Barber as 'possessing a singularly vigorous mind, a cultivated taste, a ready wit, a fluent elocution, a firm purpose, an unsullied character, and a most courteous demeanour,'[89] and Professor Witherow says he was Unitarian in theology.[90] He died in his charge in 1811, after a long association with 'Gratton and other illustrious patriots of the time'.[91]

William Steel Dickson, Portaferry

The Rev Dr Dickson, one of the 'ablest and most unfortunate of the Presbyterian Ministers of Ireland', was educated in Glasgow under John Millar, professor of Civil Law, and Principal Leechman; 'from the former he derived his political principles and from the latter his New Light Theology'.[92] He was licensed in March 1767, by the presbytery of Templepatrick, and in 1771 he was ordained at Ballyhalbert, from where he moved in 1780 to Portaferry.[93] Early active in politics he was an admirer of the Volunteer Movement and took a leading part in its proceedings. He was also responsible in 1783 for securing the election of Colonel Stewart for Co Down. Colonel Stewart was later Earl of Londonderry, and father of Lord Castlereagh; the latter was overjoyed by Dr Dickson's exertions on behalf of his father. Dr Dickson spoke of Lord Castlereagh at this time, as a 'dear boy', but later the relationship between him and the 'dear boy' was sadly changed.[94] A true friend of Catholic Emancipation and Parliamentary Reform, the minister of Portaferry joined the Society of United Irishmen in 1791, and was undoubtedly a leading figure in the movement. In May of 1798 he attended the fair at Saintfield to buy a horse 'intended as his charger as Adjutant-General of the forces of the United Irishmen'.[95]

Consequently, on the eve of the Battle of Ballynahinch he was arrested and taken to Belfast. He was, however, never brought to trial and after a confinement in the Prison Ship in Belfast Lough, he was transported as a 'State Prisoner' to Fort George in Scotland. In 1812 he sought to mitigate the charges brought against him in 1799, but there can be little doubt that they were true, as in contemporary United Irishmen's papers he is referred to as 'Commander' and 'Deputy Adjutant General'.[96]

He remained at Fort George until 1802 and on his release received a call to the congregation of Keady which had just been formed. The congregation, however, was unable to pay more than fifty pounds, and so as a new congregation they applied to the Lord Lieutenant to be put on the list of congregations who were to receive the *Regium Donum*. In 1804 the congregation presented a memorial to the Synod, in which they asked the reason for the withholding of the grant, but the Synod 'considering itself incompetent at present to give the congregation any aid in the business, resolved to dismiss the application'. The following year the same procedure was adopted. For these hardships Dr Dickson cast the entire blame on Dr Robert Black, the government agent, and friend of Lord Castlereagh. He also blamed Dr Black for having the minute entered on the Synod's record of 1799, in which reference to Dr Dickson is given as having been implicated in treason. This feeling led in 1812 to the publication of his *Narrative of confinement and Exile*, published by subscription. The *Narrative* was severely criticised in the Synod of 1812 by Dr Black who called it a 'Disorderly and ill arranged mess, where everything which is not mistated, is discoloured and preverted.'[97] The Synod unanimously resolved that 'it contained a number of gross misstatements and misrepresentations which were highly injurious to the reputations of the ministers of that Body', and called upon Dr Dickson to retract them, but he refused. In 1813 the Synod did, however, resolve that the words of its resolution of 1799, 'implicated in treasonable and seditious practices', as applied to Dr Dickson, had been inaccurately used'.[98] In this debate Dr Black was strongly opposed by the Rev William Porter, of Newtownlimavady, an Arian and afterwards Clerk of the Synod; by Dr Montgomery, and by Dr Patrick, a lifelong Arian reformer and supporter of liberal political principles. The efforts of these three men lead to Dr Black's first defeat in the Synod of Ulster.[99]

In 1815, Dr Dickson was forced to resign his charge and he died in 1824 in his 80th year. Dr Montgomery said of him that in his early years he had been the honoured guest in the mansions of Belfast 'where alternately his patriotic wisdom commanded acquiescence, and his sparkling wit "set the table in a roar". Yet without one stain upon his character, I saw the earthly remains of that great man, ... deposited in a pauper's grave, where not even a stone marks "the narrow house of his repose". Some eight or ten individuals formed the entire funeral possession, the late warm hearted W. D. H. McEwen, pronounced a pathetic oration, and we left the melancholy spot moralising on the value of public gratitude, the permanency of political friendship, and the advantage of popular applause.'[100]

Thomas Alexander, Cairncastle

The second son of Robert Alexander, Knockcair, Crumlin, he was born on 1 January 1770, and received his university education at Glasgow, where he graduated in 1791. The following year he was licensed by the presbytery of Templepatrick, and on 17 December 1793, he was ordained as assistant and successor to Rev John Lewson, at Cairncastle. Mr Lewson died in 1802, and his assistant remained in charge of his congregation until his retirement in 1833, after a minsitry of almost forty years.

He married the daughter of the senior minister and widow of Mr Shaw of Ballygally, all of whom sympathised with the rebel cause.

During the early years of his ministry, Mr Alexander conducted a school in the town. One of his pupils later became minister of Antrim, and he tells[101] how as a young boy he was dismissed early from his class at the Manse on 7 June 1798, and on the following Saturday 'saw his schoolmaster commanding a company of rebels and marching at their head'.[102] This must have been one of Mr Alexander's assistants as he himself was later to tell the Rev Classon Porter that on the date in question he was at the home of his sister in Crumlin who had died. He returned by an unfrequented road arriving in Cairncastle on the Saturday. The following day he preached in the church. He was, however, an active member of the United Irishmen and was one of those who attended a meeting of the Society in Larne a few days before the rebellion. At this meeting it was proposed that the town of Larne should send a deputation to the French Convention, a proposal which was adopted.[103] It was shortly after this that he was arrested under the following circumstances. A man called Bob Major of Belfast had taken refuge in Cairncastle, and for several weeks escaped detection in the houses of the two ministers of the town, Rev Mr Lewson and Rev Mr Alexander, and in the home of Mr Shaw of Ballygally. It was arranged to have a boat in Ballygally Bay to take him off, and Alexander and Shaw were among those who went out a little from the shore to reconnoitre at the time appointed. The boat, however, had been taken by a revenue cruiser, and they too were caught, and made prisoners. Alexander and Shaw were confined in a military guardhouse in Carrickfergus. There does not seem to have been sufficient evidence to convict them and after a short imprisonment they were released.[104]

Later in his life Rev Mr Alexander joined in the Arian Controversy and took the side of the Non-Subscribers, withdrawing with his congregation from the General Synod and joining the Remonstrant Synod in 1830. A son, Henry Alexander, became minister of the Unitarian Church in Lancaster, and later the Non-Subscribing congregation of Newry.

Robert Campbell, Templepatrick

Mr Campbell, a licentiate of the Templepatrick presbytery, was the minister of Templepatrick from 1796 when he was ordained on 20 December.[105] Later he too withdrew with his congregation from Synod and joined the Remonstrants.

While there is no mention of his name in any record of implicated men, he appears to have had sympathy with the cause of the United Irishmen, and while there is no evidence that he was a member of the Society, many of his congregation were.

The minister of Templepatrick was, however, responsible for saving the life of Dr Agnew, an ardent member of the Society, and a member of his congregation.[106] On the disarmament of the Belfast Volunteers, two six-pounder guns were kept back and were given into the charge of a Templepatrick man. Shortly before the outbreak of the rebellion these guns were taken from Belfast in the carts of 'Mr James Blow', a printer,[107] and taken to the house of Dr Agnew, whence they were taken by night and hidden in the Rev Mr

Campbell's Meeting House. One of these guns was used at the Battle of Antrim.[108]

John Smith, Kilrea

A licentiate of the Tyrone presbytery, he was born in 1766, and educated at Glasgow University, where he graduated in 1785.[109]

He succeeded the Rev Arthur McMahon, and was ordained on 17 March 1794. A man of talents and celebrity, he has been described as being 'of independent mind, great imprudence, great misfortunes, and somewhat secular in his pursuits' and in his day was regarded as 'a dangerous character'.[110] Charged with 'seditious practices', Mr Smyth suffered severe imprisonment in Londonderry, Carrickfergus, Belfast and Fort George.[111] He was released unconditionally, but meanwhile his farm had been taken from him, and he was left homeless and beggared on his return to his congregation. Later he was again arrested as a 'rioter', and again sentenced to several months imprisonment.

Throughout his troubled life the congregation still adhered to him and he died in his charge in 1821.

Dr Robert Acheson, Glenarm

Dr Acheson was the nephew of the Rev Thomas Reid of Glenarm, and, following his education in Edinburgh, he was licensed by the presbytery of Templepatrick in 1784. He was ordained assistant to the Rev Thomas Reid on 17 July 1792. 'In June 1799 he was removed to Donegall Street', then the Synod's Second Congregation Belfast and later Unitarian.[112] Before his ordination in 1792 he had conducted a school at Glenarm and was among the first to join the Society of United Irishmen. He has been described as a 'Commander of the insurgents on Ballaire Hill, 8 June 1798'.[113] As a result he was charged with 'treason and rebellion', but he was later acquitted. He died in 1824.

Adam Hill, Ballynure

Mr Hill was licensed by the presbytery of Route in 1782, and ordained for America, but in 1783 he was installed in Ballynure.[114] It would seem that from an early date he too had sympathy with the rebel cause, and on 14 October 1797 he accompanied 'The Martyr of the Insurrection', Willaim Orr, to the gallows at Carrickfergus. Mr Orr was a member of the Non-Subscribing Presbyterian Church at Antrim, and his death was looked upon as a national calamity. 'Remember Orr' was the watchword of the rebellion and medals were struck with his name. The Irish historian says that the minister of Antrim, the Rev William Bryson, was not popular and so, at the request of Mr Orr, the Rev Mr Hill accompanied him as chaplain.[115] Mr Hill was himself a member of the United Irishmen, and he was tried by court-martial for being a leader on Donegore Hill on 7 June.[116] He was found 'partly guilty' and sentenced to a year's imprisonment. Mr Classon Porter reports that he was told that because of the evidence of a soldier, himself a Presbyterian, and who therefore refused to identify Mr Hill, the minister of Ballynure escaped the gallows.[117] He continued in his charge after release from prison and died in 1827.[118]

Robert Scott, Duneane

Educated in Glasgow, Mr Scott was licensed by the presbytery of Route and ordained at Grange and Duneane on 28 June 1762. What part he played in the rebellion I have been unable to ascertain, but he was court-martialled on the charge of high treason, though later acquitted. He died in 1813.[119]

James Simpson, Newtownards

Following an education at Glasgow University, Mr Simpson was licensed by the presbytery of Letterkenny in 1783 and was ordained in the First Presbyterian Church, Newtownards, in August 1790. He was not a member of the presbytery of Antrim as the McSkimmin's Mss. had said,[120] though he was New Light in theology. What part it was he played in the rebellion is unknown but he was arrested and tried by court-martial. His sentence was 'transportation for life', but he was later permitted to emigrate to America.[121]

William Dunlop, Strabane

Mr Dunlop, 'a man of cultured taste and varied accomplishments', was also educated at Glasgow. He was licensed by the presbytery of Strabane in 1789 and ordained at Badoney in the remote district of Co Tyrone.[122] It was in the last year of his ministry there that the rebellion broke out, and while there is no evidence of his ever having been a member of the United Irishmen he certainly had their cause at heart. Classon Porter tells how on the night before the rising Mr Dunlop undertook to deliver certain important papers of the United Irishmen, and attiring himself in a blue, half-military coat, and putting the papers in his grouse bag, he rode through a troop of the Tipperary militia assuming 'an air of official importance'. The sergeant in charge of the troop attempted to stop him, 'but the officer in command, deceived apparently by Mr Dunlop's half military dress and confident bearing, ordered him to desist, saying, 'Sir, would you attempt to stop a Government express?' In that capacity Mr Dunlop was allowed to proceed, with a bundle of treasonable documents in his wallet, the detection of which would have cost him his life.[123] The military blue coat was preserved in his family 'as a member of his courage and self possession'. Mr Dunlop also served the cause of the United Irishmen by the use of his pen, writing several patriotic songs of which the following is a sample:

'Long had Hibernia's warlike sons in strife inglorious bled,
and long from her discordant isle had injured freedom fled;
at length her genius from above, descending stood confused,
and thus in bold persuasive voice the listening realm addressed:
Unite my warlike sons, and yet be free,
Unite, and from oppression's chains you'll gain your liberty.'[124]

He was never arrested and in 1798 moved to the congregation of Strabane where he ministered for twenty-three years. In 1810 he was chosen Moderator of the General Synod, and in the course of his synodical business called the government agent Dr Black to order; such independence was recorded in a poem proclaiming his fame and 'look majestic' when he denounced the great Doctor: 'And all your glorious acts at once to crown, you turn yourself averse, and sternly cry: I will not hear you Dr Black, Sit down.'[125] Mr Dunlop died in 1821, and his funeral sermon was preached by the Rev John Porter of Limavady, an Arian by repute, and a close friend.

David Bailie Warden, Killinchy

This highly gifted man was born at Ballycastle in the year 1772. He entered the University of Glasgow, and was licensed by the presbytery of Bangor as a probationer in 1797. This meant that he could preach, but could not dispense the sacraments. He was a man, who, in his own words, 'felt too sensibly for my countrymen', and because of this was tempted to join the ranks of the United Irishmen. In this Society he became a Colonel, and was referred to as Rev Mr Warden who acted as aide-de-camp to General Munroe and who was formerly a tutor at the School of Rev Mr Porter.[126] Following the rebellion he took refuge in Killinchy, where the people, fearing that their village would be burnt, decided to hand him over to the yeomen.

Instead he surrendered, and was sent to a prison ship in Belfast Lough. Here he remained several months without being brought to trial.

His trial had on four occasions been postponed for lack of sufficient evidence. Among his fellow prisoners was Dr Dickson, who tells how his own suffering would have been worse 'had it not been for the lively, rational and entertaining conversation of Mr David Bailie Warden ... a poor probationer.'[127] Finally Warden agreed that if he was released he would emigrate to America, and remain an exile for life. This was granted, and he immediately applied to the Bangor presbytery for a certificate of his official position as a probationer so that he could be received as such by a church in America.

The presbytery however, 'from motives of prudence unanimously refused to grant it'. As a result of this he published a pamphlet entitled *A farewell address to the Junto of the Presbytery of Bangor which met in Belfast on 6 November, 1798.* It was printed in Glasgow, and is extremely interesting as it indicates that this presbytery was then generally composed of men who, theologically, had accepted New Light opinions.

He reminded the brethren how they had all preached that 'reli-

gion was a personal thing, that Christ was the Head of the Church';
and that everyone of them had both 'publicly and privately' circulated
republican morality. Despite the fact that he had never been convicted, the presbytery by its refusal to grant him credentials had
taken upon itself to condemn him, for motives of fear lest their
share of the *Regium Donum* be withdrawn. If this is true, there can
be little doubt that Lord Castlereagh was responsible for instigating
the proceedings taken by the presbytery against him.

His trenchant accusation is in the following words:

> 'I may venture to say that such a proceeding was never equalled
> either in ancient or modern times. A presbytery who were the
> most strenuous advocates of reform and Catholic emancipation
> ... to refuse a certificate of what they themselves thought me
> worthy appears inconsistent and I must say absurd in the ex-
> treme ... I call it the perfection of cruelty ... Everyone of you
> has both publicly and privately circulated republican morality;
> that religion is a private thing, that Christ is the Head of the
> Chuch... that the will of the people should be the supreme law,
> and now from terror, to show your fatuous glow-worm loyalty,
> you have met as a military inquisition, incorporated the mild re-
> ligion of Jesus with your selfish, serpentine cunning, and the
> present political fermentation superceded the court of enquiry,
> and court marshal, and deviated from justice and honesty ... If
> I have committed errors, they are errors of a young mind, not
> able to distinguish what was practicable from what was vision-
> ary, but, can you lay your hands upon your hearts and say, you
> were not zealous in cherishing the principles of Reform.'

He concludes:

> 'From terror and from a false mistaken ideal of gratitude on ac-
> count of your *Regium Donum* you would sacrifice your honesty,
> your friends, your name. Your proceedings have been desultery,
> unmanly and unjust'.[128]

That this letter had little effect upon the presbytery can be understood from the fact that they reported to the Synod in June of the
following year that David Warden had sailed for America and was
no longer considered a probationer under their care.[129]

In America he resumed his study of medicine which he began at Glasgow, and obtained the degree of Doctor of Medicine, and later in his life became the American Consul General in Paris; as such he attended the Congress of Vienna and met Lord Castlereagh. No doubt he opposed the latter's aims and desires. In 1813 he published a work on the *Origin, nature and influence of Consular establishments,* which was translated into different languages. This work procured his election as a member of the Institute of France, the only Irishman thought to have acquired the distinction. He died in Paris in 1845.

Warden was not the only probationer of the presbytery of Bangor to be so dealt with. He had at least three companions who were dealt with by the presbytery.

James Hull, Ballyvoran, near Bangor

He was licensed in 1795, and was the third son of the Rev James Hull, a man of avowed New Light principles, who became Moderator of the General Synod in 1770. His synodical sermon was later attacked for advocating such principles.[130] His son was also non-evangelical, and a United Irishman. The exact part played by him in the rebellion I have been unable to ascertain. He was reported to have been executed, but this is an error.[131] The Bangor presbytery notified the General Synod of 1799 that he had been charged with being concerned in the rebellion, and had sailed for America.[132]

John Miles, Monereagh

Licensed with John Warden by the presbytery of Bangor, reported to Synod on 5 September 1797, he was never ordained, though his name was given in an official list of those implicated as the Rev John Miles.[133] His name does not appear in the McSkimmon's Mss. but he too was forced to seek refuge in America.[134]

William Fox, (address unknown)

That Mr William Fox was a probationer of the Bangor presbytery is clear from a narrative which he wrote in 1798. This tract is fairly long and a copy of it was in the possession of the late Dr Charles Dickson, of Killiney, Co Dublin. It is entitled *A Narrative of the Principal Proceedings of the Republican Army of the County Down, during the late Insurrection: To the Men of Down.* Having described various proceedings of the United Irishmen from the month of May till the night previous to 5 June, he tells how he went to Ballynahinch and there 'happened to meet Dr Dickson. I conversed with him about ten minutes upon private business having a little while before that entered the presbytery of Bangor...'.

There is no record of Mr Fox having suffered imprisonment, but he was forced to go to America and from there he wrote his *Narrative.*[135]

At least two students suffered for their disaffection on the gallows:

Archibald Warwick, Kircubbin
He was licensed by the Belfast presbytery in 1797, was found guilty of treason by a military tribunal and executed at Kircubbin in October, 1798.[136] Latimer maintains that he was the only licentiate who suffered capital punishment;[137] but in this he was in error, as Robert Goudy (Gowdy), Dunover, suffered a similar fate. In contemporary papers he is referred to as the Rev Mr Goudy, who was court-martialled on 27 June, and charged with having been in touch with General Monroe, and bringing back a message to Alexander Orr. For this he was executed at Newtownards on 2 July.[138]

The Rev T. L. Birch states that he was the grandson of 'the late Rev and pious Mr Goudy of Ballywalter', and that on the gallows he observed to the 'Earl of Londonderry and others that he would shortly argue the matter with them before a tribunal where there would be an impartial hearing'.[139]

In addition the following students were also implicated:

Benjamin Mitchell, Ballymoney
Born near Maghera, and educated at Strabane, he was a licentiate of the presbytery of Route. He was imprisoned in Londonderry for alleged treason, but was later released, and on 12 November 1800 he

was ordained as minister of Ballymoney where he remained until his resignation on 9 May 1815. He died the following August.[140]

Charles Wallace

A licentiate of the presbytery of Tyrone, he was long imprisoned in Belfast, and in the prison-ship stationed in Garmoyle Pool in Belfast Lough. He was transported to America.[141]

William Adair, Ballygraffin, near Comber

A commander of the Battle of Saintfield, he effected his escape to America.

James Townsend, Knockbracken, and Greyabbey

A leader at the Battle of Saintfield, and second in command at the Battle of Ballynahinch, he was referred to as a tutor at Rev Mr Porter's at Greyabbey, and as a probationer. He escaped to America.[142]

Thomas Leslie Birch, Saintfield

Born on 24 April 1755, Mr Birch was later educated in Glasgow and was licensed by the presbytery of Dromore in 1775; he was ordained in Saintfield on 21 May 1776 and here he remained until 1798. I have been unable to find any evidence that he was a member of the United Irishmen, but his sympathies were with them, despite the fact that he was a 'No Popery' man. In 1794 he published a sermon in which he fixed a date for the fall of the papacy.[143] A decided non-evangelical he also attacked the Seceders in another published sermon. He was responsible for the formation of the first Society of the United Irishmen at Saintfield on 16 January 1792, but left the town on the eve of the battle. However, he was arrested and imprisoned for sedition. Apparently he had preached to the insurgents at Creevy Rock, on Sunday 10 June, taking as his text: 'Let every man come forth with his slaying weapon in his hand.'[144] At a court martial in Lisburn he was found not guilty of being at Creevy, but of being present and encouraging the rebels at Price's Castle, and Ballynahinch.[145] Due to the influence of a brother who was a medical doctor at Newtownards, and a loyalist, he was permitted to transport himself to America.

Boyle Moody, Newry

Mr Moody, who had been licensed by the presbytery of Armagh, and who later retained connection with that presbytery when it was split, was installed at Newry in 1740 without any formal induction as he refused to subscribe the *Westminster Confession of Faith*. What part he played in the rebellion is not recorded in any of the United Irishmen's papers, nor indeed is his name.

However, Dr Campbell quotes a letter, dated 1800, which referred to 'the late minister of Newry, his crime was his profession, his liberal principles, his avowed friendship to Catholics, nothing else was alleged'.[146] Dr Campbell notes that 'the late minister referred to was Mr Moody, who was imprisoned and, as a result of his persecutions, he died in May 1799'.

In addition to these, the name of John McNish, Clough, Co Antrim, appears in the McCanse papers as having been implicated and transported. He is referred to as the Rev Mr McNish, but no doubt he was only a probationer. I have been unable to acquire any further information about him.

James Connell of Garvagh, another probationer, escaped to America, as did Robert Steel, John Pinkerton and Ruben Rogers, licentiates of the presbytery of Derry. What their theological position was cannot be ascertained.

Notes:

1   *Ulster since 1800,* pp. 23-24.
2   Reid, James S, *History of the Irish Presbyterians,* (Belfast 1902), vol. 3, p. 479.
3   *Belfast Newsletter,* 17 May, 1782.
4   Latimer, W. T., *History of the Presbyterian Church in Ireland,* ed. W. D. Killen (Belfast 1867), p. 375.
5   *Ulster since 1800,* p. 13.
6   ibid., pp. 14-15.
7   Witherow, T., *Historical and Literary Memorials of Presbyterianism in Ireland,* (Belfast 1879-80), vol. 2, p. 228.
8   McDowell, R. B., *Irish Public Opinion, 1750-1800.*
9   ibid., pp. 146-148.
10 Lecky, W. E. H., *A History of Ireland,* vol. 3, p. 438.
11 McNeven, *Pieces of Irish History,* p. 117.
12 Dickson, Charles, *The Wexford Rising in 1798,* p. 19.
13 *The United Unitarian Magazine,* vol. 2, pp. 333, 335.
14 Reid, op. cit., vol. 3, p. 398, note 48.
15. R. G. S. U., vol. 3, pp. 209, 212.
16 ibid., vol. 3, p. 221.
17 ibid.
18 Lecky, op. cit., vol. 3, p. 479.
19. *Memoirs and Correspondence of Viscount Castlereagh,* vol. 3, pp. 304-305.
20 *Annals of Ulster,* pp. 7ff.
21 *Ulster in '98,* p. 67.
22 Witheroe, op. cit., vol. 2, pp. 313-315.
23 *Fasti of the Irish Presbyterian Church,* p. 206; *Annals of Ulster,* p. 12. A nephew of the Rev John Glendy, the Rev Wm Glendy, took the side of the Arians in the early nineteenth-century struggles. He was minister of Ballycarry. Mention of him shall appear later.
24 *Annals of Ulster,* p. 102, also pp. 11 and 55.
25 Witherow, op. cit., vol. 2, p. 268.
26 *The Non-Subscribing Presbyterian,* June 1958.
27 The Committee Book, vol. 3, 1791-1819, pp. 54-55. Dr Wm Drennan was born on 3 May 1754. For his opinions regarding the execution of Wm Orr, the first martyr of the Rebellion see *Drennan Letters,* pp. 261-3. His sister, Mrs McTier, organised voluntary schools and was secretary to a Maternity Society, the 'germ of the Present Belfast Maternity Hospital'.
28 *Record of Unitarian Worthies,* p. 374, also *Irish Public Opinion, 1750-1800,* pp. 198-9.
29 Lecky, op. cit., vol. 3, pp. 234-5.
30 Porter, J. L., *The Life of Henry Cooke,* p. 126ff.
31 Gallagher, Frank, *The Indivisible Ireland,* pp. 46-47.
32 Crozier, John A., *The Life of the Rev H. Montgomery,* p. 95.
33 R. G. S. U., vol. 3, p. 397.
34 *The Northern Whig,* 21 April, 1825 and 28 April, 1825.
35 R. G. S. U., vol. 3, p. 117.
36 Reid, op. cit., vol. 3, p. 479.
37 Gordon's unprinted Mss., p. 172.
38 *Annals of Ulster,* p. 57.
39 Fitzpatrick, W. J., *Secret Service Under Pitt,* p. 292.

40 Minutes of the Presbytery of Antrim, vol. 2, p. 44.
41 ibid. p. 49.
42 Fitzpatrick, *Secret Service under Pitt*, p. 293.
43 *Life of Wolfe Tone*, vol. 2, p. 460.
44 *Annals of Ulster*, p. 62ff.
45 op. cit., vol. 2, pp. 295-6.
46 op. cit., pp. 290-291.
47 ibid., p. 290.
48 Letter of Lieut. General McMahon, *Ulster Journal of Archaeology*, vol. 15, pp. 134, 137.
49 Reid, op. cit., vol. 3, p. 392, note 34.
50 *Ulster Journal of Archaeology*, vol. 15, p. 137; *The Christian Freeman*, July 1871.
51 *The Fasti of the Presbyterian Church*, says that William was a brother of the Rev Rober Sinclair of Larne, and of the Rev James Sinclair of Ballyhalbert, but Alex Gordon (unprinted Mss) refers to him as a nephew of the Larne minister, a fact supported by Rev H. Moore in his unpublished work.
52 R. G. S. U., vol 3, p. 62.
53 *Historical Sketches of the First Church Newtownards*, p. 58.
54 *Historical Sketches*, p. 59.
55 *Annals of Ulster*, p. 17.
56 *Ulster in '98*, p. 67.
57 Minutes of the Presbytery of Antrim, vol. 2, p. 51.
58 *Historical Sketches*, p. 61.
59 Minutes of the Presbytery of Antrim, vol. 2, p. 55.
60 Minutes of the Presbytery of Antrim, vol. 2, p. 55.
61 ibid., vol. 2, p. 57.
62 *Historical Sketches*, p. 62.
63 *Fasti of the Irish Presbyterian Church*, p. 281.
64 Minutes of the Presbytery of Antrim, vol. 2.
65 Minutes of the Presbytery of Antrim, vol. 2.
66 *Moore's Historical Sketches*, p. 67.
67 A. Gordon's unpublished Mss., p. 204.
68 *Moore's Historical Sketches*. Editor's notes, information received from Joseph Osborne, a grandson.
69 ibid., p. 72, also *Fasti of Presbyterian Church*, p. 226.
70 Minutes of the Presbytery of Antrim, vol. 2.
71 *Moore's Historical Sketches*, p. 72.
72 The Sermon was published in 1786, and was based on the text, John 5:39. A copy of this is at present in the possession of Mr A. McClelland, Belfast.
73 *Ulster in '98*, p. 67.
74 Minutes of the Presbytery of Antrim, vol. 2.
75 Congregational Memoirs of Larne and Kilwaughter, p. 73.
76 ibid., p. 75.
77 ibid., note, p. 75.
78 *The Christian Unitarian*, vol. 3, p. 299.
79 ibid., vol. 3, pp. 298ff.
80 ibid., vol. 3, p. 300.
81 *The Lives of Henry Joy McCracken, Henry Moore, James Hope, Wm Pitman McCabe and Rev James Porter*
82 Minutes of the Bangor Presbytery, p. 138.

83 Millin, S. S., *History of Second Congregation Belfast*, p. 35.
84 *The Irish Unitarian Magazine*, vol. 2, p. 331.
85 *The Irish Unitarian Magazine*, vol. 2, p. 332. Other references: *The Christian Life*, vol. 32, p. 19. G. Porter, *Irish Presbyterian Biographical Sketches. Dictionary of Natural Biography, XIVI*, p. 180, and Witherow, *Literary and Historical Memorials*, vol. 2, p. 293.
86 *The Belfast News Letter*, September 1811.
87 *Ulster Journal of Archaeology*, vol. 15, p. 30. Witherow, op. cit., vol. 2, p. 168.
88 *Ulster in '98*, p. 66.
89 ibid., p. 92.
90 *Irish Unitarian Magazine*, vol. 2, p. 291, also *The Christian Unitarian*, 1886, p. 359.
91 op. cit., vol. 2, p. 169.
92 *Ulster Journal of Archaeology*, vol. 15, p. 156.
93 Witherow, op. cit., vol. 2, p. 227.
94 *Fasti of the Irish Presbyterian Church*, p. 138.
95 Porter, Classon, *Biographical Sketches*, p. 11.
96 ibid., p. 12.
97 op. cit., D.O.D., 714.
98 *Substance of Two Speeches, delivered at the General Synod of Ulster at its annual meeting in 1812, by the Rev Robert Black, D. D.; with an abstract of the proceedings of the Synod relative to the Rev Dr Dickson*, p. 16.
99 R. G. S. U., vol. 3, pp. 394-396.
100 Crozier, op. cit., p. 43.
101 *The Irish Unitarian Magazine*, vol. 2, p. 333-334.
102 Rev Robert Magill, 'Recollections of '98 in Broughshane'; partly reproduced in *Ulster in '98*.
103 ibid., p. 15.
104 Porter, Classon, 'Stories about '98, and United Irishmen', partly reproduced in *Ulster in '98*.
105 ibid., p. 19.
106 *Fasti of the Irish Presbyterian Church*, p. 193.
107 *Ulster in '98*, p. 20.
108 James Blow's father was the printer usually employed by the Non-Subscribers as he sympathised with their principles. His business originated about 1694. See Latimer, op. cit. p. 299; also noted, in *Ulster in '98*, p. 20.
109 *Ulster in 98*, pp. 21, 41; also *Annals of Ulster*, p. 30.
110 *Fasti of the Irish Presbyterian Church*, p. 231.
111 *Ulster Journal of Archaeology*, vol. 15, p. 37.
112 ibid, p. 38; also *Ulster in '98*, p. 67.
113 *Belfast News Letter*, February 1824.
114 *Ulster in 98*, p. 67.
115 *Fasti of the Irish Presbyterian Church*, p. 206.
116 Francis Joseph Bigger, *William Orr*, p. 16.
117 *Ulster in 98*, p. 66.
118 ibid. Note, p. 67.
119 *Northern Whig*, 26 July 1827.
120 *Fasti of the Irish Presbyterian Church*, p. 172; *Belfast News Letter*, April 1813.
121 *Ulster in '98*, p. 67.

122 *Fasti of the Irish Presbyterian Church*, p. 230.
123 ibid., p. 200.
124 *Biograpical Sketches*, p. 20.
125 *Ulster in 98*, p. 51.
126 *Biographical Sketches*, pp. 22/23.
127 Unedited Papers of the United Irishmen, D.O.D. 714.
128 Dickson's *Narrative*.
129 'A farewell address, etc.,' *Ulster Journal of Archaeology.* vol. 13.
130 R.G.S.U., vol. 3, p. 216.
.131 Witherow, op. cit., vol. 2, p. 110.
132 *Ulster in 98*, p. 66.
133 R.G.S.U., vol. 3, p. 216.
134 Unedited papers of the United Irishmen, D.O.D., 714.
135 R.G.S.U., vol. 3, p. 216.
136 Communicated by Dr Charles Dickson.
137 R.S.G.U., vol. 3, p. 217.
138 op. cit.
139 *Ulster in 98*, p. 67; and unedited papers, D.O.D., 714.
140 Birch, T.L., *A letter from an Irish emigrant to a friend in the U.S.*,
      Philadelphia, 1799, p. 29. Typewritten copy in possession of A. McClelland,
      Belfast.
140 Gordon's Unprinted Mss., p. 45; *Fasti of the Presbyterian Church*, p.223.
141 R.G.S.U., vol. 3, p. 217.
142 Unedited Papers, D.O.D., 714.
143 ibid., and D.O.D., 162 (100), p. 9.
144 Witherow, op. cit., vol. 2, p. 285.
145 *Ulster in '98*, p. 66.
146 Unedited Papers of the United Irishmen, D.O.D., 714.
147 op. cit., p. 125.
148 Unedited papers, D.O.D., 272.
149 *Ulster in '98*, p. 67.
150 Communicated by Mr A. McClelland, Belfast.

Father James Coigly

Réamonn Ó Muirí

On a sultry summer day, 7 June 1798, Fr James Coigly (Quigley), aged 36 years, priest of the archdiocese of Armagh, was hanged at Penenden Heath, a mile to the north-east of Maidstone, Kent, England. He was a United Irishman and had been convicted on a charge of high treason. At the end of his oration to the crowd present he said, 'I have now finished. But, gentlemen, I recommend to you – I do recommend to you, men of Kent, in time to come, beware how you permit any persons to take advantage of you, and to guard against the snares of the crown-lawyers. It has been the fate of your country to shed the blood of a poor helpless innocent stranger. May Almighty God forgive all mine enemies, and I desire of you all to pray to God to grant me grace to support me in this moment, and to enable me to die in a manner worthy of my integrity. I have many sins to answer for, but they are the sins of my private life; and I am innocent of the charge for which I die.'[1]

Was he innocent of the charge for which he died?

While he was in prison Fr Coigly penned a number of letters outlining his life to his friend and distant relative, Valentine Derry, a fellow United Irishman who visited him at the prison and was present to comfort him at his execution. The 'Life'[2] is a stylised *apologia pro vita sua* but from it, from state papers and other literature, it is possible to give a sketch of his life and ponder the circumstances that led to his death.

Family Background

Fr Coigly was born in the year 1761 in the townland of Castleraw in the parish of Kilmore, Co Armagh. Kilmore was called *Ceil Mor Enir* in the Irish annals, *Magh Enir* being the name of the plain

lying between Loughgall and Portadown. At the Plantation of
Ulster all Catholics in the parish were dispossessed but some were
allowed to remain as tenants. A pattern of a mixed population, with
a Protestant majority and pockets where Catholics remained numerous, emerged in the next two centuries. The Parliamentary
Returns of 1766 indicated that there were 791 Protestant and 491
Catholic families in the parish and one Catholic priest. Fr Coigly
was baptised by Fr Owen Laverty on 8 August 1761. His Christian
name is given as James on his baptismal certificate[3] though in some
places he is referred to as James John and John James. His parents
were James Coigly and Louisa Donnelly. He respected them and
honoured them. It caused him great suffering to think that they
would have to bear the sorrow of his horrific death as aged people
in their late seventies: 'Never did I knowingly injure any one – was
ever an obedient child, dearly beloved and cherished by my parents.
Alas! my untimely fate will bring down their hoary hair with sorrow
to the grave' … 'I have not courage enough to write to my father.
May the God of our forefathers give him and my distressed mother
consolation!'[4] His baptism sponsors were James Marlay and Jane
O'Donnelly. He was confirmed by Bishop Troy of Ossory, who on
9 March 1777 had been appointed Apostolic Commissary to the
troubled diocese of Armagh under Archbishop Anthony Blake. Fr
Coigly had three brothers: Hugh, the eldest, a linen merchant, who
lived near the family home in Castleraw; Robert who is known for
the seven articles he wrote on 'Orangeism' for *The Morning Chronicle*
in 1821, 1835 and 1837; and Michael, a soldier who became an informer in the days of Robert Emmet. There is a tradition that the
Coiglys or Quigleys originally migrated to Co Armagh from Co
Derry in the 18th century. The family is now represented by two
branches, one Catholic and one Protestant.

Fr Coigly pays tribute to his father, 'a plain honest farmer' who
he said gave him 'an education superior to his situation'. He was educated at a Dundalk grammar school, probably the Free School
where he learned mathematics, Latin, Greek and modern languages. His 'Life', written within the confines of prison, has quota-
tions from Latin authors, obviously from memory, an indication of

his pride in his proficiency in Latin. Dundalk was to be much associated with the Coigly family. Our first reference to a 'Quigley' in Castleraw is to Hugh, father I would say of James and grandfather of Fr James – '1745 - Road from Kilmore to (?) to be repaired by inhabitants of Castleraw and Kincon, Hugh Quigly, overseer'.[5] There is a tradition[6] that three brothers migrated from Derry in the 18th century; one settled in Castleraw, one went to the Castletown-Roche district near Dundalk and another to the vicinity of Killylea village, Co Armagh. In the light of a Hugh in Castleraw in 1745, the tradition can either be interpreted as referring to this Hugh and two brothers or to three sons of Hugh, James and two others. 'Captain' Robert Quigley, the County Master of the Defenders at the Battle of the Diamond was a Killylea Quigley. The Dundalk relatives could have influenced James's choice of school. Fr James's parents and elder brother Hugh took refuge in Dundalk, probably with their relatives, when they were forced out of their homes at the Battle of the Diamond, 1795. James and his son Hugh later returned to Castleraw. James was still alive in 1807. There is a reference to his will, dated 3 October 1807, in an Index of Armagh Diocesan Wills. Only two Quigleys are listed in the Tithe Applotment Books (1833), Kilmore Parish, Castleraw townland: James with an acreage of 20a 2r 20p and Jane with an acreage of 23a 1r 10p.[7] As Hugh was the only other member of the family to have a household, I presume that by 1833 he was dead. No Quigleys are listed for Kilmore in Griffith's valuation, 1864.

Fr Coigly served as a priest in Dundalk, as curate and chaplain to the prison. His name appears as witness to marriages in a Dundalk parish register on 8 November 1793 and 16 March 1796. Occasionally priests acted as second witness when only one witness was present. His ministry there lasted three years, 1793-96. One of his great friends in Dundalk was Valentine Derry who wrote in the preface to the 'Life', 'I lived in the same Town with Mr Coigly nearly three years, spent most of my vacant days and evenings in his company, and found his conversation always chaste, edifying and cheerful. I was delighted with his vivacity, pleased with his virtue and talents as a clergyman, and amazed at the solidity of his understanding and heroic principles. In argument he displayed much erudition, particularly historical knowledge, of which he had a wonderful store. His disposition was mild, liberal and charitable – feelingly indignant of injustice and cruelty. All my acquaintance loved and admired him: he was on the most intimate footing with them, and was as the child of the family in every house.'

Dundalk

Dundalk proved a good central station for Fr Coigly in his political activities in Louth and the North. Prominent among the United Irishmen there were Valentine Derry, Anthony 'Croppy' McCann of Corderry, Joseph Moritz, and the brothers John and Patrick Byrne. The mother of Bartholomew Teeling, Lisburn, was one of the Taffee family of Smarmore, Ardee. Teeling lived with John Byrne at the well-named 'Union Lodge', Dundalk, in 1796. John Hoey and Anthony Marmion were convicted and executed in 1798 on the evidence of Dundalk apothecary and government spy, Dr John Conlon (Connellan). Connellan mentions Fr Coigly and other Dundalk United Irishmen in his reports and notes. The local magistrates, Thomas Gataker of Dundalk, Colonel John Ogle of Carrickedmond and Forkhill, Neale McNeale of Faughart and Norman Steele of Inniskeen were very active against the United Irishmen. Fr Coigly grew to love Dundalk. In a letter to Derry three weeks before his death he instructed him, 'You will please to give my last adieu to my friends at Dundalk, in particular to Woods, Joe, Isabella, etc. etc. etc. I cannot name them all.' The Woods mentioned here, I think, is Dr James Woods,[8] apothecary in Dundalk, born at Lough Ros, near Crossmaglen, about 1758, a learned man who had studied for the priesthood on the Continent but had changed to medicine after his health broke down. He was a Gaelic poet and was an important figure in the strong literary Gaelic society in Dundalk in the first half of the nineteenth century. He is mentioned in the evidence against James Matthews of the Royal Dublin Militia who was sentenced to death at Blaris Camp for his membership of the United Irishmen, 5 July 1797.[9] Matthews and other soldiers attended United Irish meetings in Dundalk.

Matthew Browne of the Dublin regiment militia testified, 'The prisoner Matthews had such intercourse with one Woods, an apothecary at Dundalk, and the prisoner often told the deponent that he understood from the intelligence that was conveyed to him by Wood(s), that there were a number of people at Belfast ready to assist the French when they landed, and that disturbances would begin sooner than we imagined.'

Fr Coigly's name still survives in Dundalk. An area to the west of the former Magnet Cinema is called 'Fr O'Coigley place' on the Ordinance Survey map of Dundalk 1937.

Collège des Lombards, Paris

Following the custom of many young men who aspired to the priesthood at that time, probably after an educative apprenticeship to the local parish priest, James was ordained priest in Ireland before setting out to receive the more formal theological training in a seminary on the European mainland. His bishop sent him to the Collège des Lombards in Paris, then an Irish seminary. On 31 December 1784 and on 1 and 2 January 1785 Dr Richard Reilly, Coadjutor Bishop and Administrator of Armagh diocese conferred on him Tonsure and Minor and Major Orders in the parish church of St Anne in Dungannon. When Fr Coigly was arrested in 1798 in England, his treasured church certificates were found in a pocketbook. They are printed in Howell's *State Trials*. There is a certificate of his baptism and confirmation in Latin written by Fr Dudley Devlin, parish priest of Kilmore, and dated 12 December 1784 (obviously necessary documentation for his bishop before ordination), a certifcate of ordination, and a letter of recommendation to assist him on his journey to France and assure his admittance to the Collège des Lombards. These latter were drawn up by Fr Matthew White, secretary to Bishop O'Reilly, at Drogheda, 30 March 1785. Fr Coigly must have collected them in Drogheda on his way to France. He arrived in Paris on 8 June 1785. Fr Dudley Devlin referred to him as a youth of excellent character, born of pious Catholic parents. He gives his surname as 'O'Coigly' which is also the form used in French documentation in the Irish College, Paris. Fr Coigly objected to this version at his trial and seems to have preferred 'Coigly'. He used occasionally the name 'Fivey' as a by-name, implying that it derived from the Irish *cúig* ('five'), but this is incorrect.

Fr Coigly was a popular person and endeared himself to others by his mild temperament and his good manners. However, he was a 'fighter' by nature and this he admits himself. 'I was from my entrance in life as a man, continually involved in disputes, always in favour of the poor trodden-down subjects against the gigantic strides of overbearing tyranny'.[10] His crusade for justice began in the Irish College, Paris. One can imagine how mature ordained priests chaffed under the discipline of a college, especially if they never had the experience of boarding. In Coigly's view the régime was too harsh. He took the first opportunity of opposing the *status quo* when he claimed the Maginn burse in the college. In 1677 Abbé Patrick Maginn and Fr Malachy Kelly gained permission to use the Collège des Lombards as a college for educating priests for the Irish mission. Abbé Maginn founded burses for the education of priests from his own diocese of Down and Connor and from Dromore. Priority was to be given to ecclesiastical students of the families descended from his relatives, Maginn, Magenisse and O Neill; failing that, they were to be selected from ancient families of Down and Dromore, and after that a burse was open to other families in Ulster. Coigly claimed a share, contesting the rights of Fr John Mac Allistair of Dromore and Fr Edward Mac Mullan of Down who enjoyed free places. Fr J. O'Laverty in his *Historical Account of the Diocese of Down & Connor* outlines Coigly's case from a document which is now classified as 1CP. 2FA.23 in the archives of the Irish College. According to O'Laverty, Coigly argued that he was 'the nearest descendant from Arthur Magenisse, and that he had obtained from the nearest male heir of the family of Magenisse a nomination and presentation directed to the Prior of St Victor. He produced a certificate that he was born in the parish of Kilmore, that he was baptised ... ; he produced certificates signed by Messrs Royer (Rogan), Ross, and Constanine Magenisse, Arthur O'Neill, and Simon Donnelly, that he descended from the family of Magenisse mentioned in the will. These certificates attested that the Rev James O'Coigly was the legitimate son of James O'Coigly and Louisa O'Donnelly, the daughter of Christopher O'Donnelly, son of Chevalier Neill O'Donnelly and Louisa, daughter of Arthur Magenisse, son of Chevalier Hugh O'Donnelly, and Margaret, daughter of Eugene O'Neill, son of John O'Donnelly, of Donaghmore, and Mary, daughter of Con Magenisse.' Coigly maintains in his 'Life' that he was opposed in his claim by Fr John Baptist Walsh, rector of the College, and by two Irish bishops, that even the King without his knowledge was made a party against him, that he was repeatedly threatened by a *lettre de cachet* either from the King or Archbishop. We are left to his word that the matter ended in a compromise. The petition of Fr Mac Allastair and Fr Mac Mullan, from which this information is drawn, was dated 8 March 1788. Coigly describes the affair as a 'tedious suit'.

Fr Coigly's pride in his noble ancestry was typical of many familes in Ireland in the 18th century; the grievance of their dispossesion in the 17th century was still fresh. Many of them had lost relatives in the 1641 Rising and the war of James and William. The genealogy outlined in the lawsuit is probably correct; genealogy played an important part in Irish society and consequently in Irish literature. Coigly returned to this theme in his 'Life' – 'I am the descendant of ancient Irish tribes.' He was also proud of his forefathers' prowess in fighting for the restoration of their lands – 'My great-grand-father O'Donnelly, together with seven of his brothers, were slain at the head of the tribe, bravely defending the bridge at the battle of the Boyne ... it was my great-grandfather Coigley who invented and constructed the famous boom at Fort Culmore for the block-ade of Derry. He with three of his brothers were afterwards killed at Kilcommoden, commonly called the Battle of Aughrim, gallantly fighting at the head of his regiment, after the infamous Lutterell had betrayed his country and cause.' The relation of these stories at the beginning of his 'Life' infers that he, like his forefathers, will die bravely for his country. Contemporary documents do not support the tradition that his great-grandfather Coigley constructed the 'boom'; it is clear, however, that a certain John Donnelly of

Portadown assisted in that work and he may indeed have been the great-grandfather of the story, for Fr Coigly's mother was a Donnelly from Ballyhagan in Kilmore parish.

Having obtained a copy of the charter of the college for the pursuance of his lawsuit, he succeeded in gaining student control of the administration of food and drink; he accused Fr Walsh of profiting from the provision funds; next he pushed for the election of superiors as laid down in the charter. He says, 'John Baptist Walsh left no means untried to persecute me, and ruin my character: he even wrote to my bishop in Ireland, praying to have me removed to some other Irish college; and this fact he denied upon oath, until I produced my bishop's letter against him.'[11] We do not possess Doctor Walsh's arguments in this dispute but, since he goes down in history on the testimony of others as an honourable man who showed courage in the French Revolution period, was imprisoned, and weathered the storm to ultimately restore the two Irish colleges in Paris into Irish hands, one can assume at least that he also had right on his side.[12] The revolution interrupted Coigly's new campaign. He fled Paris on 12 October 1789, narrowly escaping a lynching from the mob, as he relates. He reached Dieppe, was arrested the next morning and 'with great difficulty obtained permission to embark in the Brighton packet-boat'.

The Armagh Outrages

Although much has been written in recent years[13] pointing to a contemporary political cause for the disastrous sectarian strife that broke out in his native place, the Loughgall-Kilmore region of Co Armagh, in the 1790s, the basic reason always lay under the surface even in peaceful times, namely the resentment of Catholics who had lost their lands in the previous century and the fear of Protestants that fair play to Catholics would end in their own dispossession and loss of power. The beginnings of the granting of some measures of relief and some political reform concessions, combined with the growing campaign for Catholic emancipation, and even the short period of the benign Lord Fitzwilliam as Lord Lieutenant, were enough to alert some of the Protestants of

Loughgall and Kilmore to the dangers of Catholic power. The Church of Ireland members, ever strong among magistrates and the landed class, began to retreat from ideas of reform and ultimately threw in their lot with 'ascendancy' and sectarianism. The lure of profits and patronage in the establishment was too much to sacrifice. Catholic freeholders had gained a vote in 1793. There were Catholics who could earn money in the linen cottage industry and indeed some had become prosperous and were employers in the linen trade, like Fr Coigly's brother Hugh. A flush of money among this class meant they would be prepared to pay higher rents and some landowners, assured of their votes, welcomed the attraction of higher rents. Catholics began to migrate to areas where they could exercise their new bargaining power. Jealousy and resentment naturally awoke the religious differences and prejudices on both sides that dated back to the Reformation and the Counter-Reformation. The interplay of tension among the more prosperous roused the poorer classes to seek change. Poor Catholics, when the wind of change began to blow, sought relief from high rents, tithes, cesses and litigation fees. They organised the Defender movement formally into lodges as a secret oath-bound society. Protestants organised under the secret Peep-o-Day-Boys. The parties fought their disputes at local level. Guns entered the faction fights; there were mutual plunderings of arms, intimidating assemblies increased, there were riots and murders.

Presbyterians and poor Protestants too had their grievances; rents, tithes, cess and legal fees upset them too, but their political exclusion as second class citizens galled them most. The Presbyterians resented the Church of Ireland's monopoly of the privileges of power. Some Protestants in Co Armagh became members of the United Irishmen, especially the Presbyterians, but deep down they could not countenance a joint campaign with Catholics, especially the Defenders. In the end most of them threw in their lot with the Protestant loyalists who had formed the Peep-o-Day-Boys, and these merged into the Orange Order in 1795; former United Irishmen sometimes became more loyalist than the loyalists themselves. By 1798 both government and military unashamedly used sectarianism and the Orange Order as another weapon in their arsenal to combat the United Irishmen.

This local scene, ironically, is staged against a greater background of political excitement caused by the American and French revolutions, copious examples of good will between denominations, and a revived volunteer force with pretensions to a 'National Guard'. There were lulls of peace and occasions of distrust and conflict in the years 1792-93. One of the big challenges to Protestant trust was the question of Catholics possessing arms. Many Irish Catholics entered the British army and the newly formed militia; they were badly needed since Britain went to war with France in 1793. In some areas the revived volunteers welcomed Catholic recruits not only in theory but in practice. The Loughgall volunteers had passed a resolution as early as 1784 rejoicing in the relaxation of the penal laws against Catholics and inviting them to join their ranks and receive instruction in the use of arms.[14] That never happened. In fact the raiding of Catholic houses for arms by Protestants symbolised their reaction against growing Catholic influence and was a major feature of the misdeeds of the Peep-o-Day-Boys (who were themselves well-armed with the weapons of the old Irish Volunteer force). The magistrates took little action against sectarianism.

When Fr Coigly arrived home from Paris in 1789 he was faced with the growing tensions, 'On my arrival in my own country, to my grief, I found the inhabitants of that devoted county, Armagh, engaged in a civil war, and *religion made the pretext!* Although my health was very low, I immediately attempted to reconcile the parties, but was much discouraged by several leading gentlemen of that county [*Atkinson of Crow Hill, Verner of Churchill, and Richardson of Richhill*], who often told me at their tables, "*That it was of great utility to the Irish government that such religious disputes should exist between the Dissenters and Catholics,* and that at any rate it would be more easy to mix oil and water together than to make those two parties agree between themselves." Notwithstanding, I continued my endeavours and succeeded with many: the country became nearly tranquil, but my endeavours on that great object, an union of the Catholics and Dissenters, continued the same. Witness my efforts in 1791, 1792, and 1793 at Randalstown, Maghera, Dungiven, Newtown and Magilligan; in a word wheresoever I happened to be. It is true, I had to combat many deep-rooted prejudices on both sides; and my success would have been comparatively trifling, had it not been for the spirited exertions of that truly respectable, virtuous, and enlightened body, the Dissenters of the county of Antrim, but chiefly and in particular those of Belfast.'[15]

On his return from France, Fr Coigly lived in his parental home in Castleraw until he went to Dundalk in 1793. This was probably due to his poor state of health. Sickness seems to have affected him all his life. His work of reconciliation in the local district from 1792-93 was recognised by one of the landlords of the area, Colonel Robert Camden Cope of Loughgall Manor, who wrote in 1792, 'This district has been in a state of disturbance for some time past. Scenes worse than those in France are witnessed nightly between the Peep-o-Day-Boys and the Defenders. A Roman priest, O'Quigley, residing in my estate in the townland of Ballyrath [*the old name of Castleraw*], a French student, has exerted himself to placate the Roman Catholics, and I have been doing the same with the Protestants.'[16]

Defenders and United Irishmen

After two years living in Dundalk, mixing no doubt with Defenders and United Irishmen, Fr Coigly caught the new thinking on civil liberties and political change. The grievances he already understood and he already had the gut feeling for the underdog. The new ideas of liberty emanating from the French Revolution were now more to his taste. Valentine Derry, who lived in Dundalk at this time, relates, 'I saw him shortly after he first came from France. He gave me the most satisfactory account of the causes and commencement of the Revolution that I have obtained from any quarter. His memory was so remarkably tenacious, that he seldom omitted the minutest circumstances in his longest narratives, let the subject be ever so complicated. He certainly was not then a friend to the French revolution: and if he had latterly changed his princi-

ples, I am confident it was brought about, as it is with the majority
of the Irish Nation, by calumny, false suspicion, prejudice, and unjust persecution.'[17] Fr Coigly now set out on his travels once more
but it was reconciliation plus a political doctrine of civil liberties
that he preached. He found a willing ear with the Covenanters, a
Presbyterian sect who were numerous in counties Down and
Antrim. Dr William James Mac Neven, United Irishman, who re-
viewed the 1798 period in his book *Pieces of Irish History*, mentions
him in relation to the Covenanters, probably May 1795: 'The
United Irishmen were at this time beginning to spread very rapidly
in the counties of Down and Antrim; and the effects of their system
might easily be traced by the brotherhood of affection, which, pur-
suant to the words of their test, it produced among Irishmen of
every religious persuasion. Men who had previously been separated
by sectarian abhorrence, were now joined together in cordial, and
almost incredible amity. Of this perhaps, no instance more remarkable can be conceived, than the conduct of the covenanters, a sect
still numerous in those two counties. By all the prejudices of birth
and education, they appeared removed to the utmost possible extreme, from any kind of co-operation or intercourse with Catholics
… They were, however lovers of liberty, and republicans by religion
and descent: their concurrence in the general system was, therefore,
not unimportant. … Covenanters in numbers became United
Irishmen, and the most active promoters of the system. After this
had gone on for some time among them, Quigley, a Catholic priest,
went to a part of the country where they were settled, and was introduced as a fellow labourer in the common cause. The affection
those poor men shewed to one whom, shortly before, they would
perhaps have regarded as a daemon, was truly astonishing.
Intelligence was dispatched to every part, of his arrival, and from
every part they crowded to receive and caress him. But when they
learned this Romish priest was so sincere a lover of liberty, as to
have been actually fighting at the capture of the Bastile, their joy
was almost extravagant.' Fr Coigly was hardly present at the capture
of the Bastille but I am sure he used his Paris experience to good
dramatic effect. Samuel McSkimin in *Annals of Ulster* alludes to a

'friar' who 'heedless of the extirpation of his order in France, per-
ambulated the counties of Down and Antrim, preaching in fields
... and the subject of his discourses were invariably brotherly love,
with allusions to the great work going forward for the renovation of
mankind'.

The assault on the homes of his parents and brother on 20
September 1795, the day before the Battle of the Diamond, pushed
him further into politics. He had worked hard for peace but the
conflict between Defenders and Peep-o-Day-Boys came to a head
in 1795, the year of the loss of Lord Fitzwilliam and the triumphal
return of the ascendancy. The Defenders had grown in strength in
counties Armagh, Down, Antrim, Derry, Louth and Monaghan. Fr
Coigly was not present when the homes of his parents and brother
Hugh were wrecked. The story is related by him in the 'Life' and by
his brother Robert (in 1821 and 1837) in the *Morning Chronicle*.
Fr Coigly tells it in the context of planned provocation by the establishment to separate the union of Catholics and Dissenters; an
organised mob began the infamous 'wrecking' which led to the
Diamond fight and the expulsion of thousands of Catholics from
Kilmore and Loughgall. He says, 'My unfortunate county, Armagh,
was chosen as the proper place for action; as, comparatively speaking, the established Churchmen were stronger, and the Catholics
weaker than in any other county of Ireland. A Church and King
mob was raised; and it has been proved upon oath, by some of the
most respectable gentlemen and landholders in that county, that
the said mob, unprovoked, attacked with fire-arms the unoffending
Catholics. Then they proceeded to what they called racking houses,
that is to destroy every species of furniture, windows, window
frames etc. ... This Church and King mob, calling themselves
Orangemen, commenced their bloody system by attacking my
father's house about two years ago. My helpless hoary parents, the
younger of whom is seventy-seven years, carefully avoided even the
semblance of resistance, by throwing open the doors and windows
at their approach; yet they wantonly fired over one hundred shots
into the house, one of which slightly grazed my father's head – My
mother fell seemingly lifeless on the spot; and though she still lives,

yet she is rather an object of general compassion, dragging on a
wretched and miserable existence.' His father's life was threatened,
the house wrecked, the goods taken away, the remainder destroyed
including valuable books and papers. 'The above-mentioned mob
proceeded afterwards to my elder brother's house, where they committed similar outrages. He being extensively engaged in the linen
manufacture, kept some hundred hands at work. Those worthy
supporters of government, to do him the greater injury, destroyed
his account-book entirely, containing an account of debts to a considerable amount.' Robert Coigly's narrative adds, 'they had the
proprietor on his knees, every moment expecting death; and at the
same time the soldiers, under the command of the magistrates,
were within shot of them'.

It is clear that the Coiglys were marked out as targets because of
their prosperous situation and influence. Fr Coigly's reconciliation
crusades and his forays into Antrim and Down would not have endeared him to the Peep-o-Day-Boys. Robert Coigly's actions in
procuring the intervention of magistrates and military left him a
marked man. Years later he wrote in the *Morning Chronicle*, 'With
the Orangemen, Roman Catholics and Defenders were synony-
mous terms, and those amongst them who had realised a little
property by hard industry, were called Captains or Chiefs.' Another
factor brought odium on the Coiglys. Two of the leaders on the
Defender side, 'Captain' Robert Quigley, Killylea, and Arthur
'Switcher' Donnelly, were relatives.

One of the results of the Battle of the Diamond was the founding of the Orange Order, a second was the persecution of Catholics.
Many thousands in North Armagh were driven from their homes.
Fr Coigly in his 'Life' mentions that he personally engaged Leonard
McNally for the Lent Assizes in Armagh in 1796 (many years later
McNally was revealed as an informer; he reported Fr Coigly's activities in a letter to government, 5 February 1797). He says, however,
that the Attorney General 'would not permit Mr Mac Nally, nor
any of our lawyers, to interfere'. The truth was that the Attorney
General, Arthur Wolfe, acted fairly. The local magistrates were at
fault. They failed to investigate the atrocities in a proper fashion.

The juries were extremely partial, even ignoring directions from the judge. The subsequent reprieves of Peep-o-Day-Boys disgusted the victims. Fr Coigly mentions the notorious case of William Trimble (alias Trumball alias Captain Wrackall)[18] who was capitally convicted for the murder of Fr Coigly's neighbour and intimate friend, Daniel Corrigan; his execution was respited and his sentence was committed to transportation. Robert Coigly explains Trimble's execution reprieve, 'he declared they durst not execute him; for if they attempted to do so, he would produce the written instructions that he received from the higher powers'. Corrigan lived in Lurgancott (Roughan) and Trimble in Dromard, the next townland. Another friend of the Coigly family, Bernard Coyle, a wealthy linen merchant in Lurgan who worked for peace and sought justice in the courts, found himself ensnared in a trumped-up counter charge of treason. The Orangemen wrecked his business. When he finally cleared himself, he had to take up residence in Dublin. The persecution of Catholics and the corruption of law in the wake of the Battle of the Diamond threw some of the leaders of the United Irishmen in Antrim and Down behind the Defenders. One constant factor regarding the Armagh 'troubles', recognised by Lord Gosford and government officials, was the 'supineness' of the local magistrates who either took no action or showed favour to the Peepo-Day-Boys. The partisan writer, Sir Richard Musgrave, in his *Memoirs of the Different Rebellions in Ireland,* argues for the magistrates that the art and integrity of the organisation of the Defenders, a 'low people', betrayed a higher intelligence behind them. He writes, 'We cannot be surprised at this, when it is very well known, that the famous father Quigley was very active among the defenders. As he interested himself very much in their concern, it is not improbable that their organisation was on the French plan, as it has been discovered that he made a practice of going often to France.'

We have no proof that Fr Coigly was a member of the Defenders. Musgrave's reference to trips to France is irrelevant; they were subsequent to the Armagh 'troubles'. If he was not a member, however, it is true that he was closely associated with them.

Members, like himself, belonged to the old dispossessed noble families who had been pushed into the bogs and the mountains. They had long memories and strong traditions. The rapid growth of the Defenders inevitably caught the attention of the urban United Irishmen who were then faced with the task of investigating them with a view to an alliance or a union. Napper Tandy, a leading United Irishman, met a group of them at Castlebellingham in 1793. Richard Madden says that he was introduced to them by Fr Coigly.[19] The oath of secrecy was administered, an informer gave information, and Tandy to avoid prosecution had to flee the country. In 1797, as we shall see, Coigly and Tandy joined forces in a special mission in Paris.

There is quite a strong defence of the Defenders in the pamphlet *A View of the Present State of Ireland, with an account of the origin and progress of the disturbances in that country and a narrative of facts addressed to the people of England,* written by 'An Observer' and published in London in 1797. I have long argued the possibility that it was written by Fr Coigly because it was published in England and directed towards a British audience. The style is similar to his 'Life', he was acquainted with radicals in England and he himself was part of the 'British dimension' in republican politics. It gathers together many of his themes – the disastrous war with France, the distinguished energy of the reasonable reforming London Corresponding Society, the disinterest of corrupt government in Ireland, the valid *raison d'être* of the Defenders, their persecution by military and corrupt law, the praiseworthy efforts of the United Irishmen to bring union and their just campaign for radical political reform, the catastrophe of the recall of Lord Fitzwilliam. Noteworthy in the pamphlet is a strong reference to Daniel Corrigan and Arthur McCann of Kilmore and their murder by their neighbour William Trimble; also underlined is the tragedy of the 'seven hundred' Catholic families driven from their homes, their property burned and destroyed by Orangemen. Significantly the writer states, 'Months would be insufficient to enumerate all the acts of wanton cruelty which were inflicted on the inhabitants of Ireland from the first of April to the 24th of July. Since the latter

date, I am not personally acquainted with the state of that country.'
The last sentence gives a key to the authorship – Fr Coigly had just
left England at that time – he went to France in July 1797.

One of the remarks that 'Observer' makes in defence of the
Defenders is contrary to Musgrave's thought: 'The Defenders were
suffered to proceed until they became very numerous, and had
committed such excesses as must ever result from the assemblage of
large bodies of men, groaning under the lash of persecution and oppression, without the guidance of either prudence or talent to conduct them. The great object of administration was now complete,
for the Protestant was irritated and enraged against the unhappy
Catholic, beyond the example of former times; and *division*, the
bane of Irish prosperity, and *sole cause* of Irish misfortune, had
spread its deleterious effects in every village and hamlet, while
private confidence and social intercourse withered by its noxious
influence.'

It is difficult to know when exactly Fr Coigly became a member
of the United Irishmen. I think he was already a member in 1796.
John Binns, United Irishman, one of the men charged with treason
along with Coigly, said in a memoir written in later years for
Madden's *United Irishmen* that Valentine Lawless (later Lord
Cloncurry) made Coigly a United Irishman in his father's house in
Merrion Street, Dublin. Lord Cloncurry on the other hand (less
credible) asserts that he met Coigly for the first time on his way to
France in 1798.[20] A letter[21] of Coigly written from Dundalk dated
27 July 1796 to John Shaw of Rosemary Lane, Belfast, talks amiably
of 'united' affairs and indicates that his political activity is not to
the liking of the clergy: 'We have judged it prudent not to think of
going to Belfast according to appointment, yet it is more than
probable that I will be with you myself in three weeks or there-
abouts. Affairs continue to wear a favourable aspect in this quarter. I
have written once more about *The Star*. Some nights all the papers
are charged, but generally about the one half of them. The subscribers are exasperated against the ... more especially as the news is
become so interesting. We can't expect I believe to receive *The Star*
more regularly unless by a carrier. Be convinced that the negligence

of the proprietors as to that point has done a vast deal of harm to the cause. All friends here are well. And now for myself. I think it more than probable that my stay in Dundalk will not be of long continuance. The clergy are leagued together in order to make me unhappy.' On 9 August 1796 Edward Boyle, 55 Mannor Street, Dublin, reported Fr Coigly's movements to government, 'Their (sic) is now in town three Gentlemen from the North, a Mr William Small from Dungannon, a Mr Quigley from near Armagh and a Mr Coyle from Lurgan that was in Armagh Gaol, all in the line. Should you wish to know any particulars from them, your giving me directions shall be respectfully attended to'.[22] John Foster wrote from Collon, 16 August 1796, to under-secretary Cooke at Dublin Castle, 'Quigley is curate to Martin the Priest of Dundalk a busy medling man but the most warm and indiscreet priest we have is McArdle who is a friar and spends his time between Dundalk and Drogheda. If Quigley shews or Campbell comes here, let me know here and I will get them well watched at least'.[23] On 5 February 1797 Leonard McNally the informer reported to government that Coigly, whose political mission was at Dundalk and Armagh, had met Richard McCormick and made daily visits to the state prisoners at Kilmainham. McNally reported 'the tenour of his conversation'.[24]

The year 1797[25] was to date the most eventful year in the history of the United Irishmen. The arrival of the French at Bantry Bay on 21 December 1796 heartened the ardent members in Ulster and Leinster and awakened Munster and Connacht. The gathering of arms accelerated, recruits flocked to the society. The idea of a French invasion, however, opened differences between the prudent, who would wait for a new arrival of French troops before action at home, and the anxious, who saw that time was not on their hands and that immediate insurrection to entice the French to invade was necessary. Edward Lewins was sent to negotiate with the French authorities. He was well briefed and he naturally allied with Wolfe Tone. Both of them, however, were soon to lose touch with the more militant at home who under oppression could not wait. In the race for time the government won the day. The Bantry Bay

scare initiated the sending to Ireland of proper reinforcements and
a reorganisation of the army in Ireland. The loyalists panicked.
Lord Camden, who had succeeded Lord Fitzwilliam as Lord
Lieutenant, advised new and extraordinary measures of legislation
and allowed the military a free hand to make arrests. From 3 March
1797 General Lake began to disarm Ulster. Repression aroused bit-
ter resentment among all classes but in the end it was successful.
United Irish leaders in Ulster and Leinster were arrested. The rump
that remained in Ulster were young and militant. Among others,
Coigly now came to the fore. Finally these had to flee before immi-
nent arrest. Among them were Samuel Turner of Newry, Joseph
Orr of Derry, Alexander Lowry of Linenhill, Katesbridge, Co
Down, Bartholomew Teeling of Lisburn (who had been living in
Dundalk), Fr James Coigly and Rev Arthur Mac Mahon, a
Presbyterian minister from Holywood, Co Down.

The resentment of Ulster people to the government's campaign
of oppression is indicated by a formal protest in Armagh city.[26] On
17 April 1797 a meeting of the nobility, clergy and freeholders of the
county of Armagh was held there under the chairmanship of Sheriff
Sparrow. Three Addresses of various shades deploring the state of
the country were put before the assembly, a loyal Address, a call for
moderate reform and an 'inflammatory' Address condemning the
war with France, the lack of proper parliamentary power in Ireland,
and the oppression of the coercive acts. Sensationally it was the 'republican' Address that was passed at the meeting.

Fr Coigly maintains in his 'Life' that he worked for the acceptance of this Address and that it was the persecution that followed
that forced him to seek refuge in France. He writes, 'In April 1797,
it was agitated to address the Throne for Peace, but above all for the
removal of our task-masters, commonly called His Majesty's
Ministers. – This was during the Assizes at Armagh; and, indeed, I
was as active on that occasion as possible. The meeting was to con-
sist of the gentlemen, clergy, and freeholders only, in order that the
call might be strictly regular, and palatable to the High Sheriff. The
time was so short, that I was obliged to ride over a considerable part
of the county, to distribute the printed notices, and exhort the free-

holders to attend and do their duty. The meeting was well attended; a strong address to his Majesty for the above purposes was carried, with only two dissentient voices. From Armagh I was subpoen'd to attend as a witness on the part of a prisoner at the assizes of Carrickfergus; and from thence I returned by Downpatrick, where I overheard the late Marcus Beresford, Lord Castlereagh, Earl Annesley, and Nicholas Price, mark me out as a victim of their vengeance. When I came home, I was informed by a gentleman connected with that party, but more honest than his associates, that it was not safe for me to remain in the country; the active part I had taken in the business of the address, etc. had decided the ministerial faction to get rid of me at any rate; and the usual means of false witnesses would be resorted against me.' This man he said held a position under government. He continues, 'In a few days after, some of my particular friends were arrested, without cause, as appeared aferwards, and thrown into prison at Dundalk, where I lived; and, what may appear surprising, they did not attempt to arrest me, but placed my warrant in the – hands. This honest man gave me notice thereof; and yet, conscious of my own innocence, I would not go out of the way, until forced to it by my friends the day following.' It was Denis Fitzpatrick, the gaoler, who warned him that he had a warrant for him. He obviously knew Coigly from his visits to the gaol. Joseph Nugent, an informer, wrote, 7 August, to Edward Cooke, '(*Quigly*) is connected with Mr Dardis now confined at Mullingar, Mr Burn of Dundalk and Mr Barnwell of Bloomsbury near Kells, Co Meath.'[27]

Fr Coigly had drawn the government's attention to himself by his strong activity at the Armagh and Carrickfergus Spring Assizes in May 1797.[28] Marcus Beresford's report to Thomas Pelham, chief secretary at Dublin Castle, is contained in the latter's notes for Saturday 6 May 1797. Beresford appeared at council for the crown in Armagh. The notes read: 'No case, as it was brought forward on the table, so strong as to be able to say that the jury found a wrong verdict. A publication to intimidate the jurors circulated. A committee went round to all the circuit assisting the prisoners. Samuel Turner, of Newry, Patrick Byrne, and Quigly, a Catholick clergyman of Dundalk, and Alexander Lowrie were the principal. They interfered only in the defence of prosecutions on the part of the crown. Constantly in court under the counsel employed by the prisoners, assisted them in challenges, and seemed to give general directions about the trial.' The way was open for Fr Coigly's arrest. He sensed with foreboding the whispering campaign against him from a formidable combination of Beresford, who as we see reported him to government, Nicholas Price, Lord Castlereagh, once a mild liberal type, now a harsh opponent of the United Irishmen, and Earl Annesley. Annesley, the leading landlord in the Castlewellan and Downpatrick area, was related to the Beresfords and was violently anti-Catholic. He combined with Lord Downshire to split the United Irishmen with a view to destroying them in a weakened state. Nicholas Price, landlord of Saintfield, Co Down, scourge of United Irishmen, moved the next month to arrest Coigly's friend, Rev Arthur Mac Mahon.

When Fr Coigly was subpoenaed to appear in court for a prisoner at the assizes in Carrickfergus, he visited in the prison Joseph Cuthbert, a dedicated United Irishman, who had been tried the day before for a conspiracy to murder. Rev Edward Hudson wrote of the incident to Lord Charlemont, 9 May 1797, from Portglenone, 'You have heard of the famous tailor, Mr Cuthbert. After his trial at Carrickfergus, a gentleman whom I know went to see him in the gaol. The tailor was reclining on a bed. At the fire sat a clergyman of our church belonging to this county, a Presbyterian preacher from Down [*Arthur Mac Mahon*], and a Papist priest from Louth [*Fr Coigly*]. The tailor cried out to his visitor, 'By G–, sir, you might travel an hundred miles before you would meet such a trio!'

People like Joseph Cuthbert, James Coigly, Jemmy Hope, Samuel Neilson, Henry Joy McCracken, Thomas Russell and later Robert Emmet, were closer in their sympathy for the labouring people than the more intellectual types in the United Irishmen like Wolfe Tone and Arthur O'Connor. Sectarian strife and sectarian discrimination disturbed them. Coigly owed Cuthbert a visit. Cuthbert and Henry Joy McCracken had visited Co Armagh at the time of the outrages and showed solidarity with those who had suffered. Fr Coigly probably became aquainted with McCracken at this time. In 1798 he joined him in the more militant faction who saw the urgency of revolt if the help of France was to be a reality.

The man who made the arrests in Dundalk and who had issued a warrant for Fr Coigly was Colonel John Ogle of Forkhill. This information is given in a letter of Joseph Nugent, to the Marquis of Hartford, London, 12 August 1797: 'With great humility I beg leave to inform your lordship, that there is now in London four persons that fled from the County of Down and Armagh for treason and sedition, whom I find warrants of apprehension were issued against them by a Mr Price of Saintfield, and Col Ogle of Dundalk: their names are, Revd Mr Magaulay – Revd Mr Quigly – Priest, Councillor Turner of Newry, and Mr Magawley who served his time to a Doctor Musgarve, now in confinement at Dublin, for Treason.'[29]

In England, 1797

Coigly managed to leave Ireland in the general exodus of Ulster leaders in June 1797. Their differences with the the Dublin section of the Executive Committee of the United Irishmen on the urgency of revolt were exposed at a meeting in Dublin in the first week of June. There followed a less than unanimous meeting of the leaders with Ulster delegates at Randalstown. Then the government moved against them. Warrants were issued for their arrest and they fled.

Fr Coigly's destination was France. He was a French speaker and was obviously delegated to investigate the imminence or otherwise of French help. During his stay in England he played a significant part in reviving the campaign for radical reform among the labouring class. Although Irish people in Britain naturally gravitated to their own living places and their own taverns, there was quite a friendship among Irish and English, and that despite an ulterior motive in the United Irish propaganda there, namely, to harness all the opposition possible in Scotland and England to the benefit of Ireland should the French invade Ireland or Britain.

One of the key figures in creating a voice for the artisans was Thomas Hardy, a shoemaker, who founded the London

Corresponding Society (LCS) in 1792.[30] Its main political goal was 'Universal Suffrage and Annual Parliaments'. It had a ready ally in the Society of Constitutional Information, a movement of groups of educated and articulate reformers. In the opinion of the LCS France provided a model for political reform and from the beginning the Society looked to the French with friendly envy. In the next six years the government, through a series of laws, arrests and trials, greatly reduced its strength and impact. Then at a period of low ebb in 1797 a new society made its appearance, the United Englishmen (later referred to as United Britons in London), modelled on the United Irishmen, oath bound, intent on infiltrating the armed forces and arming for revolution. Some members left the LCS to join the more extreme active society; others like John Binns and his brother Benjamin, immigrants from Dublin and Presbyterians, retained dual membership. Not unexpectedly others withdrew from the LCS.

On his arrival in England in June 1797, Fr Coigly lost no time in making contacts with the radical reformers in Manchester. In the usual convention of communication between reforming groups, he presented them with an official Address from the Ulster United leaders. His discussions with the radicals, comprising Irishmen, members of the United Irishmen and United Englishmen, were held at Isaac Perrins's public house, the Fire Engine, Ancoats Lane.[31] Perrins was employed by Messrs Bolton and Watt to repair and regulate their steam engines in and near Manchester. He was thus in a position to be acquainted with radical artisans and they frequented his inn. He diplomatically steered the most dedicated to private meetings with Coigly. The priest's strongest Ulster contact was James Dixon, a native of Belfast, weaver and cotton spinner. Dixon had provided members of the Manchester Corresponding Society with copies of the United Irish constitution and their secret oath and test. On this initiative the United Englishmen in Manchester were founded. The branch secretaries were invited to meet Coigly. Thirty-five out of thirty-seven met at the lower Ship Inn on Strude Hill, Manchester, where they voted to finance his journey to Paris. He spoke openly of the imminent insurrection in

Ireland, the need for a simultaneous rising in England and the hope of a French invasion of both countries. The ties with Ulster were strengthened at these conspiratorial encounters and plans were forged to set up more permanent contacts. Joseph Cheetham, County Committee member of the United Englishmen in Manchester, a master spinner and manufacturer, raised funds of 100 pounds to help buy arms for the United-Irishmen and donated 10 pounds to Coigly to help him on his way to France.

Mary, the wife of Isaac Perrins, in an examination,[32] 14 April 1798, said that Priest Quigley stayed at the Inn in Whitsun week last and remained three days and three nights. In his company were two men, O'Hara and Cassidy, who stayed with him the whole of the time. 'Quigly,' she said, 'is a stout lusty man and O'Hara is lame of one leg and has a high heel shoe ... Cassidy is a tall thin man of a black complexion ... Quigley's hair was cut short'. Coigly referred to these as Irishmen from Dundalk and pronounced O'Hara a 'shopkeeper' come to buy goods. O'Hara is mentioned in another statement as an attorney from Dundalk. Coigly also met at the inn an old acquaintance from Loughgall, James Hughes who, at his request, brought him on a visit to the 'Romish chapel'.[33] Thomas Towall from Banbridge also met him and accompanied him to Stockport to see two of his relatives called Cassidy.[34]

Robert Gray, an auctioneer's clerk, a United Englishman and an active radical, summoned the meeting at Strude Hill. He described Coigly at this time as 'about 5 feet 9 inches, a good looking man; he had a rough greatcoat and had a florid face'.[35]

In London Fr Coigly naturally entered the circle of the more extreme members of the London Corresponding Society, including some of its leaders, who had come under the influence of Irishmen like the brothers John and Benjamin Binns and Dr Thomas Crossfield. Benjamin Binns, in a memoir for Madden's *Lives of the United Irishmen*, claimed that he first met Coigly in 1796, 'passing through London on his way to France'. On that occasion Coigly was supposed to have brought with him an Address from the Secret Committee of England to the French Directory. There is no evidence for a journey to France in 1796. He obviously refers to his journey to France in 1797.

In London Coigly also met with the United Englishmen, among them Colonel Despard,[36] a native of Co Laois, and Thomas Evans,[37] former secretary of the LCS. His motivation was surmised in two letters of Thomas Nugent.[38] Writing to Edward Cooke from London on 7 August, he reported, 'I beg leave to inform you that the Revd Mr Quigly Roman Priest, late of Dundalk, whom I find has fled for sedition is now here with Mr Macmahon of the County Down, a Dessenting Clergyman, his coleague, on their way to Paris as Delegates from United Irishmen as the(y) term it to propose easy and efectual plans for the French to invade the land. They are secreted. I have found them out and informed Government of them. ... A subscription is now caryed on to forward them to Hambourg on their way to Paris by the London Corresponding Society. The(y) have for some time been active in their information the(y) made of efecting a Revolution in Ireland and here and have plans where the French may land a party to efect that Plan.' In his letter of 12 August to Lord Hartford, Nugent mentions Councillor Turner and Mr Magawley also as members of the party sojourning in London on their way to Paris via Hamburg. By this time, however, Turner was already in Hamburg, arriving on 10 June. He and Bartholomew Teeling had been commissioned by the Lord Edward Fitzgerald and Arthur O'Connor militant faction to voice support for a prompt French invasion. It was Fitzgerald and O'Connor who in 1796 had opened up the first diplomatic channels with the then French ambassador to Switzerland, François Barthélemy. Parallel with the Teeling and O'Connor action, in the frustrating absence of news from Lewins and Tone, William James McNeven was sent by the Dublin leaders to further the official negotiations.

Samuel Turner,[40] who had fled Ulster in June 1797, became an informer on 8 October 1797, when he visited Lord Downshire in London. He faced a personal crisis in his life. Being a staunch Presbyterian, he came to believe that the United movement had taken too much of a Catholic turn, notable in the cautious attitude of Lewins in Paris and the over prudent timidity of the Catholic leaders at home. After the June 1797 meeting in Dublin, when Ulster delegates attended, the 'prudence or cowardice' of the Papist

leaders disgusted him. Some of his frustration is shown in the particular aversion he developed towards priests and his contempt for
the much maligned Lewins, a rival negotiator. Turner and Coigly
had belonged to the same district organisation of the United
Irishmen and they would have met frequently in Dundalk. Turner's
report to government at the end of 1797 gives us the best retrospect-
ive picture of Mac Mahon and Coigly in London in the summer of
1797. He places Mac Mahon in the rôle of the stronger partner.

Turner reported: 'They stayed together in London, imitating
the Patriots in the mode of forming Societies after the plan of the
United Irish. They had heard of the expedition at the Texel being
intended for Ireland, and it was agreed on that an insurrection
should be attempted in London, as soon as the landing was effected
in Ireland. Colonel Despard was to be the leading person, and the
King and Council were to be put to death, etc. Their forces were estimated at 40,000, ready to turn out. McMahon, hearing he was
traced to London, resolved on going for France, and took Quigley
as his interpreter: he got a subscription made to pay Quigley's expenses, and collected twenty-five guineas, fifteen of which were
given by a Mr Bell, of the City, (summoned on the trial of O'Connor),
and ten guineas by Chambers, of Abbey Street, Dublin, who had been
this long time in London, keeping up a correspondence (as I believe) between Lewins, etc.

'McMahon and Quigley went over to Cuxhaven, thence directly
for Holland, were on board the fleet [*the Dutch invasion fleet assembled in the Texel*], and, when the expedition went off proceeded to
Paris. They there found Lewins, but could get no satisfactory answers from him relative to his communications with the French
government. A quarrel was the consequence; and Quigley was dispatched privately by McMahon to London, to get some one sent
over to represent the Patriots of both nations, and to replace
Lewins. A paper drawn up by Benjamin Binns, and which they had
brought over to sketch out something from, was made no use of;
but Tom Paine told Quigley he might assure the English that
France only made war against their government. Quigley returned
with Mumphort.'

In France, 1797

Coigly in his 'Life' says that in his poverty he was assisted in Paris by an 'old college companion, now an officer of distinction in the regular forces'. This was probably James Bartholomew Blackwell,[41] from Ennis, Co Clare, who had been with Coigly in the Collège des Lombards. Another ex-student of the college was William Duckett, a native of Kerry. Nicholas Madgett, an important bureaucrat in the Ministry of Foreign Affairs, born in Kinsale, employed Duckett as an agent. Duckett did his work admirably, his inscrutable nature lending to his natural talent for intrigue. He made missions to Ireland and Britain and concentrated on promoting disturbance in Britain. Fr Coigly turned down a temporary post as priest, offered by his 'college friend' Blackwell, which would have solved his financial difficulties.

The Civil Constitution of the Clergy of 1790 had made law the popular election of bishops and priests and the severing of the church in France with Rome. Fr Coigly could not in conscience take an oath against the church.

In France James Coigly and Arthur Mac Mahon fulfilled their duty. Contrary to Turner's comment in his information, they did make use of Benjamin Binns's Address (it was in his handwriting), editing it slightly and attaching their own names to it. They presented it as a memorandum to the French Directory on 4 October 1797.[42] It was styled as a message from the 'members of the chief revolutionary committee of England' to the Directory of France. The committee enumerated popular grievances. They promised 'to secure the leading members of the Privy Council (the King only excepted) and thus paralyse the government at least for a time'. They asked for a guarantee of separate republics in Ireland and Britain if there was a French invasion. Early in October 1797 Coigly set out for Paris.

The death of General Hoche on 19 September 1797 was a severe blow to the diplomatic drive of Tone and Lewins. He was sympathetic to the Irish cause. The fact that Napoleon regarded him as a rival did not augur well for their future overtures. Following the persecution at home, many United Irish leaders had congregated in

Paris, Napper Tandy among them. They understood better than Tone and Lewins the shifting situation on the ground in Ireland. Their impatience relayed the frustration of O'Connor and Fitzgerald at home. In the coming months Tandy took the lead in a campaign against Tone and Lewins. Coigly joined the Tandy camp. It was his natural inclination. Tandy and Coigly called a meeting of Irish in Paris to force Tone and Lewins to reveal the state of negotiations with the French. Lewins did not attend. Tone wrote in his diary on 1 February 1798, '(*Tandy*) began some months ago by caballing against me with a priest of the name of Quigley, who is since gone off, no one knows whither; the circumstances of this petty intrigue are not worth my recording. It is sufficient to say that Tandy took on him to summon a meeting of the Irish refugees, at which Lewins and I were to be arraigned, on I know not what charges by himself and Quigley. Lewins refused to attend, but I went, and when I appeared, there was no one found to bring forward a charge against me, though I called three times to know, "whether any person had any thing to offer". In consequence of this manoeuvre, I have had no communication with Tandy.' At this stage it was probably clear to Coigly that he could do no more. He would have concluded that Lewins must be replaced; the French might listen to the intelligent aristocratic Arthur O'Connor who had initiated the Irish-French diplomatic talks; this new leader, partner of Lord Edward Fitzgerald, would be the only one who could appeal for immediate help from France in the present crisis.

Back in England, 1797

Samuel Turner, in his report at the end of 1797, mentions Fr Coigly returning with Mumphort.[43] He would have met Coigly in Hamburg on his way home. Coigly arrived in Yarmouth just after Christmas. In London he renewed his mission to the militant elements in the London Corresponding Society and the United English (now United Britons). He carried the prestige of having visited France; possibly in the veiled rôle of agent he could overstate the readiness of France to act if there was a rising in Britain and Ireland. He met the United Britons' committee on 3 January 1798 at Furnival's Inn Cellar. Turner already had sensed the plotting in

London when he wrote at the end of 1797, 'Colonel Despard, a Mr
Bonham, young Lawless, and Robert Simms, are the only persons
in whom the Irish at Paris said I ought to place my confidence, in
case I either wrote or came to England or Ireland.' During his three
weeks in London Coigly consulted Valentine Lawless, resident representative of the United Irishmen. This must have been known to
government. The three United Irishmen, Lawless, James Agar, and
John Bonham, all of the legal profession and frequenters of
Furnival's Inn Cellar, were under surveillance from October 1797.
A visit to Lawless would be enough to alert government to Coigly's
return and have him watched. He discussed affairs with the Binns
brothers who were prominent members of the United Britons in
London. Other important Irish members were Colonel Edward
Marcus Despard and Dr Thomas Crossfield, who became secretary.
William Hamilton from Enniskillen and Edmund O'Finn from
Cork, United Irishmen, and William Bailey from Co Down, were
also part of this British-Irish alliance. O'Finn was sent to Hamburg
and Paris to meet William Duckett and Léonard Bourdon on be-
half of the new grouping. Coigly at first had tried to persuade John
Powell Murphy,[44] a teacher of languages, and a native of Tandragee,
Co Armagh, to undertake this task. Murphy later went to Hamburg
but subsequently became an informer for the government. Thomas
Evans and Thomas Stuckey were the leading Englishmen in the
United Britons in London.

The Binns brothers, awaiting the return of Fr Coigly from France,
had been busy preparing Addresses to be brought to the executive of
the United Irishmen in Dublin as part of the build-up of solidarity between the revolutionary associations of Ireland and Britain. Addresses
both from the LCS and the United Britons were prepared to support
the O'Connor/Fitzgerald faction. It was decided to send Benjamin
Binns and William Bailey with Coigly to Dublin. Coigley met the
United Britons Committee on 3 January at the favourite haunt of reformers, Furnival's Inn Cellar. O'Connor did not risk going there.

On 5 January a detailed description of Coigly was sent to government.[45] It was unsigned but was obviously sent by James Powell,
the spy within the LCS-United Britons circle. It reads:

'Jan. 5. 98

'I have this moment left Quigley, Crossfield & Despard. Quigley cannot dine with me on Sunday. He sets off for Ireland tomorrow at two o'clock. He will be at Crossfield's between 10 & 11 c'clock.

'Below is an accurate description of his person & dress this evening.

'Height about 5 feet 9 inches. Stout & well made. Very handsome for his age, apparently about 50. Very bright dark eyes. Fresh coloured, particularly on the cheekbones. Dark beard, & sharp nose, rather long faced. Hair dark, but grey, particularly about the forehead, & on the top of the whiskers, no powder. Good white teeth, which he shews. Very small mouth.

Dress this evening

'Dark olive striped Coat, single breasted, with large buttons of the same colour, rather shabby. Waistcoat, double breasted, like the one I generally wear. I have enclosed a pattern. Under Waistcoat buff Marseilles dimity, both dirty. Under Waistcoat round coloured upper lapelled. Dark grey overalls with white buttons inside of the thighs, lined with black leather sew. New dark grey great coat, black velvet collar, round hat. Looks like a Priest. B. Binns I believe goes with him.

'I thought it necessary to give this information immediately.

'The conversation that passed I will give you on Sunday morning when I shall wait on you. He has papers of consequence with him.'

In Ireland, 1798

Coigly, Binns and Bailey left London on 6 January 1798 with the two Addresses and arrived in Dublin on 9 January. According to intelligence they also carried 'a Certificate & Instruction signed & sealed by Crossfield and a seal of the United Irishmen which ... is a passport to the French Directory. There are few of them cast, & they are only in the Hands of the most sacred & confidential Officers.'[46]

Contact was made with Lord Edward Fitzgerald and Binns and

Bailey presented the Address of the United Britons to Henry Jackson, one of his associates. The Address was put before the national committee of the United Irishmen. The object was to establish the principle of coordination, 'England, Scotland and Ireland as all one People acting for one common Cause.' The provincial leaders were issued with copies for their committees. The matter was reported at a meeting of the Ulster provincial committee on 1 February, at Antrim and at the Armagh County committee on 27 January. Meanwhile Binns met Catholic leaders in Dublin and then proceeded to Cork to meet associates of O'Connor. When he gave information before the Secret Committee of the House of Lords, 1798, John Hughes, Belfast bookseller, said that in February priest Quigly had introduced him to 'citizen Baily, who was an officer in the East-India Company's service' and to Benjamin Binns.

On 14 January Coigly wrote a letter[47] to Lord Edward Fitzgerald to arrange a meeting for the following day. Obviously he would have detailed to Lord Edward his meetings in Manchester and in London and would have brought him up to date on the situation in Paris. The logical conclusion would have been a new mission to France led by O'Connor to finally oust Lewins and impress on the French government to act quickly. In the 'Life' Fr Coigly maintains that Frederick Dutton, an infamous informer whom he once saved from the gallows, having heard of his presence in Dublin, hastened there to arrest him. Two other informers were interested in his presence in Dublin. Francis Higgins deputised Francis Magan to watch him. Two letters of Higgins[48] to under-secretary Cooke, 12 and 16 January, relate how Magan gave Higgins a description of Coigly. Magan had met Coigly in 1797 at James Dickson's house at Kilmainham where he had sheltered before going abroad. It seems Magan did not find Coigly although he watched Dickson's house, Dr Mac Nevin's and Bond's. Dickson's house was a favourite haunt of 'liberals'. Leonard McNally reported the presence of the the emissaries to government on 6 February, 'Father Quigley of Dundalk, after whom you enquire, has lately returned from France, in dress *à la militaire*, and passes as Captain Jones. He sent a long message from N. Tandy to his son; but the latter cautiously avoided giving him an interview'.[49] Binns too was under observation. A Bow Street Runner had followed him from London and with help from the Castle observed his movements in Dublin.

Manchester and London, 1798

Valentine Derry, in his Preface to the 'Life' says, 'I went with him, on the night of the 31st, from Dublin to Rush, and parted with him the next day, within a mile's distance of that place.' Fr Coigly continued his journey to Belfast. The provincial meeting at Shane's Castle, Co Antrim, on 1 February, was told that 'the reverend priest Quigley now returned to Belfast, and formerly of the county of Louth from which he had fled some time ago, was one of the Delegates lately returned from France, and that he and the Reverend Arthur McMahon of Hollywood, who fled from thence on the general apprehension in the county of Down last summer were the principal persons who opened the communications with the United Britons.'[50] Fr Coigly left Ireland in the first week of February 1798.

Coigly spent three days in Manchester. He met with twenty-seven secretaries of the Manchester United English divisions and was quite open about the purpose of his new journey to France. He said he would meet Arthur O'Connor in London, 'and the main part of that business was left to him … their purpose was to give the French assistance in their plan of invading' Ireland, Scotland, and finally, England.[51] As previously, a subscription was organised to defray his expenses to London. Robert Gray, a United English secretary, describes meeting Coigly on 8 February by accident on the street in Manchester. He was wearing a military dress, a blue coat and cape and blue pantaloons; without it he said he would not have been able to come from Ireland.[52] Coigly arrived in London on 11 February. He says in the 'Life' that 'an attempt was made to arrest me, as I suppose, between nine and ten o'clock, in Piccadilly, by two Bow-street runners'.[53]

Meanwhile a quarrel developed in Manchester between Robert Gray and William Cheetham.[54] Gray took fright at the momentous idea of an imminent revolt and was hurt by Cheetham's taunts that he was not a true republican. On 8 February, just after he saw

Coigly for the last time, he approached Nathaniel Milne, the clerk
to the Manchester Bench and made detailed revelations of the plotting. Milne, perhaps not giving Gray's information full credence,
did not act until he heard of O'Connor's arrest and then he brought
the information to senior justice Thomas Butterworth Bayley. The
Home Office had already been alerted to the existence of the
United Englishmen in Manchester by an Irish Catholic priest, Fr
John Waring, who relayed the information of a man called Kerr, a
native of Armagh.[55] Gray's long statements, studied discerningly by
Whitehall, filled in another segment in the government's picture of
the Manchester embryonic revolutionary movement and the
Coigly/O'Connor conspiracy.

In London Fr Coigly and John Binns stayed in a room in Fetter
Lane that Thomas Evans had rented to Benjamin Binns. Both attended the meetings of the United Britons' committee. Fr Coigly
was given an Address by them for the French Directory. Although it
was dangerous play, especially since Britain was at war with France,
Addresses were constantly exchanged among reforming groups. It
was the normal mode of rhetorical greeting and fraternity between
the radical societies, between those in Ireland and Britain, and between Ireland and France. Benjamin Binns had written a more serious, more practical and more dangerous Address for Coigly on the
previous mission to France. This new Address[56] had been drawn up
by Thomas Crossfield on 25 January and was in his handwriting.
Two paragraphs will illustrate its inflated propagandist nature:

> 'Already have the English fraternized with the Irish and Scots
> and a delegate from each now sits with us. The sacred flame of
> liberty is rekindled, the holy obligation of brotherhood is re-
> ceived with enthusiasm; even in the fleets and the armies it
> makes some progress – disaffection prevails in both, and united
> Britain burns to break her chains. ...

> 'United as we are, we now only wait with patience to see the Hero
> of Italy [*Napoleon*], and the brave veterans of the great nation.
> Myriads will hail their arrival with shouts of joy; they will soon
> finish the glorious campaign! Tyranny will vanish from the face
> of the earth, and, crowned with laurel, the invincible army of

France will return to its native country, there long to (*sic*) well earn't praise of a grateful world, whose freedom they have purchased with their blood.'

Fr Coigly attended a meeting of United Britons at Furnival's Inn Cellar, Holburn, in mid-February, where, no doubt, the United Irish reaction to the United Britons Address was discussed. Colonel Despard at one stage consulted secretly with Coigly, John Binns observing that 'they are gone to work'. Despard then met O'Connor at Osterly in Middlesex. While in London, Coigly contacted Valentine Lawless once more and also met Alexander J. Stewart. It was probably at Lawless's lodgings that he handed over to O'Connor the document from the United Irishmen, a parchment adorned with green, black and red seals, that formally assigned charge of the new Irish mission to France to O'Connor. Alexander J. Stewart from Acton in Co Armagh, a former member of the grand jury in Armagh, had been a compassionate defender of Catholics at the time of the Armagh outrages. He was a high-ranking United Irishman whose political activity was well-known to the government authorities. He was later accredited as being Adjutant General of the United Irishmen in Co Armagh. One of the English radicals who met Fr Coigly in London at this time was Francis Place.[57] He 'saw him three or four times, and liked him much, he was a good looking man of remarkably mild manners, kind and benevolent.'

Arrangements for the journey to France were delayed by Arthur O'Connor's elaborate preparations. The travelling party consisted of O'Connor, Jeremiah O'Leary, who from boyhood had been in O'Connor's service, Fr O'Coigly, and John Allen,[58] a young acquaintance of Lord Edward FitzGerald, now a friend of the priest. Arthur O'Connor posed as a 'Colonel Morris', Fr Coigly as a 'Captain Jones'; the other two men filled the rôles of servants. John Binns, through London Corresponding connections, worked hard to find a means of getting the party to France. He visited Whitstable and Deal, towns on the Kent coast, without success. After great difficulty he was confident that he had succeeded in engaging a vessel at Margate. The party of four men on their journey

to the coast, loaded with baggage, naturally aroused the suspicion
of people in Whitstable. The four and John Binns finally got together in the King's Head Inn at Margate. After spending the night
there, they were arrested in the morning, 28 February, by two Bow
Street runners, John Revett and Edward Fugion, and four light-
horsemen. The Chief Magistrate of the Bow Street Office, Richard
Ford, had organised a watch on Coigly and his acquaintances and
had built up a lot of information on their activities from informers.
Naturally, too, customs officials had been alerted to O'Connor's
impending departure to France. The prisoners and their baggage
were brought to Canterbury and on the next day, 1 March, to the
police office in the Strand in London. According to John Binns,
writing on the subject years later,[59] and this was also collaborated by
O'Connor,[60] it was there that Fr Coigly told them that there was a
treasonable Address to the executive of the French Directory in the
pocket of his greatcoat. This gives the impression that they did not
know until 1 March of the existence of this Address. That is incredible. O'Connor's servant, O'Leary, had the opportunity to dispose
of his master's incriminating documents down the privy of the
King's Head Inn.[61] Coigly, the first to be arrested, had been careless
in leaving his greatcoat over a chair in the breakfast room where it
was confiscated by the police. The prisoners were examined by the
magistrates on the afternoon of 1 March and their statements,
which pleaded innocence, were written down. They were then
brought before the Privy Council. Coigly, who appeared on 5 March,
admitted that he had seen Colonel Despard and Dr Crossfield, denied that he had any connections with O'Connor and refused to
say whether he was in orders or not. He admitted possession of a
dagger on his person when arrested.

On 7 March all the prisoners were committed to the Tower of
London. Fr Coigly was put in the cell above the Traitor's Gate. On
7 April they were moved to the prison in Maidstone to await trial.
Efforts were made through the appointed Catholic chaplain, Fr
Griffiths, to get Fr Coigly to turn approver, something that hurt
him very much. The government's priority was the conviction of
O'Connor.[62] He was an important member of the national execu-

tive of the United Irishmen. He had already served a six months
sentence in Dublin and the authorites there, thinking they had
been cheated by his release, sought an opportunity to convict him
of treason. The Whitehall authorities were faced with a dilemma.
They were in possession of ample knowledge regarding the treasonable designs of Arthur O'Connor and Fr Coigly, but informers
such as Samuel Turner, Robert Gray and James Powell would not
come to court or were too valuable to be exposed as witnesses. The
documents that made up the case against Coigly and O'Connor
were the Address to the executive of the French Directory, Coigly's
French passport (found at John Binns's lodgings) and his letter to
Lord Edward Fitzgerald of 10 January 1798 (found in a search of
Leinster House), and a letter from O'Connor to Fitzgerald complete with its cypher.

The court opened at Maidstone on 21 May 1798 at 8 am. The
trial[63] began with a sensation when the defence exposed the Rev
Arthur Young, a magistrate at Dover, for influencing jurors on the
panel to bring in a verdict of guilty. Whitehall was embarrassed that
he was discovered. Their officials were playing the same game behind the scene. The lists of possible jurymen in Coigly's trial, now
preserved in the Treasury Solicitor's papers, the Public Records
Office, London, are carefully marked by the law officers of the
Crown seeking to eliminate radical sympathisers. They are classified G (good), B (bad) and D (doubtful).[64]

O'Connor was ably defended by his counsel, Mr J. Plumer.
O'Connor himself browbeat the judges with a number of interventions and even shamefully pushed the guilt on to Coigly, earning a
reprimand from the judge and the future contempt of other United
Irishmen. He lined up a formidable array of Whigs to testify on his
behalf, including Charles James Fox, thus inferring that reference
to inviting the French to invade Britain in his letter to Fitzgerald
could only be regarded as ridiculous, coming as it did from a friend
of English Whigs whose constitutional politics he shared. It was
impossible to prove that any of the other prisoners knew of Coigly's
Address document and therefore impossible to make the charge of
treason stick in their case. Seeking to go to France while Britain was

at war with that country was an offence that warranted a charge
and imprisonment, but it was not treasonable.

The charge of treason against Fr Coigly was that he was present
when the Address was drawn up, that he wrote it, and that he was
the bearer of it to France. The court did not convincingly prove
that the greatcoat was his. It did not accept the possibilty, since it
was unguarded, that the Address could have been placed there by
another person. There was a credibility gap in the police officers'
evidence as to the time and place of their marking of papers confiscated, thus allowing a possibilty of documents being planted. One
of the Bow Street Runners who had arrested Coigly, Edward
Fugion, testified that the Address was in the pocket-book which he
found in Coigly's coat but, in an earlier affidavit, he had sworn that
he found it loose in Coigly's pocket along with the pocket-book.

The trial had been delayed from 11 to 30 April while government officials sought a witness who could identify Fr Coigly's writing. One asks the question, at what stage did they realise that
Coigly did not write the Address? They knew he was in Dublin on
25 January, the date the Address was written. Colonel John Ogle of
Forkhill, who had issued the warrant for Fr Coigly's arrest in June
1797, wrote from Armagh on 25 March,[65] 'Inform me if one person's evidence respecting Quigley's signature will be sufficient, as I
had a correspondence with him some time ago. I can perhaps prove
it myself, and say when the evidence will be wanting and if at
Maidstone. I am sorry to find a pardon has arrived for *eleven*
United Irishmen. Depend upon it, lenity will not have the wished
for effect, for the dispositions of a great majority of the people are if
possible, *worse* than usual. Direct to Dundalk or Forkil.' Probably
before this letter arrived, Cooke wrote to Wickham, 29 March,
'Thomas McFillin, farmer, near Magherafelt in the County of
Derry, will also be sent over. He is a man of excellent character, was
an United Irishman and left their Societies when he found their
desperate object. He will swear to Coigley's person and will prove
his having sat with Quigley in three Provincial Meetings of United
Irishmen, that Coigly was a Delegate from the County of Louth,
and that he acted in a Deputation from a Provincial Committee to

the Executive Committee of Ulster, and that he was a Priest. I have
not got a person who can swear to Coigly's handwriting, but I have
sent to Dundalk. Woods, Guager [*Gauger*] of Dundalk will, I expect, prove it.'[66] As it was, Ogle's offer was not taken up and Woods
did not travel. In the end the government brought forward the notorious informer and thief, Frederick Dutton, an Englishman, who
had lived at Newry and Dundalk. He claimed to have seen Coigly's
handwriting on the ticket of a lottery which the priest had organised to help a prisoner in Dundalk gaol. He swore to Coigly's handwriting on the Fitzgerald letter and the passport; significantly he
was not asked to swear to the handwriting on the Address.
Valentine Lawless, at Coigly's request, had succeeded in procuring
funds for his defence. Mr Plumer had been engaged to act as counsel for O'Connor and Coigly. He devoted hours in the court defending O'Connor but, mysteriously, hardly spoke a word in
Coigly's defence. John Foulkes had been engaged as his solicitor.
He was an experienced defender of radicals. How could he allow
counsel to ignore his client? After the trial Foulkes battled bravely
to bring up serious matters of discrepancy with the Duke of
Portland and visited under-secretary William Wickham at
Whitehall but to no avail. Fr Coigly had written to Dublin, probably
to Valentine Derry, to get him, Bernard Coile and others to testify
on his behalf, but they were connected with the United Irishmen
and, on second thoughts, it may have been judged that their evid-
ence would have proved counter-productive. He listed witnesses
summoned against him: Wood, said to be a revenue-officer at
Dundalk; Denis Fitzpatrick, the gaoler at Dundalk; Frederick
Dutton; Charles McFillin of Ballymulligan (near Magherafelt);
Marian, a king's messenger; and Oliver Carlton, high constable of
Dublin. Of these only Dutton testifed against him. Alexander J.
Stewart, a friend, gave a cautious testimony in court in his favour.
His careful choice of words was not surprising, since Whitehall had
at its command a profile, supplied by Dublin, which detailed his
United Irish activities. An example of what might have happened
other witnesses if they had appeared for Fr Coigly is the case of
James O'Neill[67] of the townland of Ballyriff, parish of Ardtrea, Co

Derry who was subpoenaed to give evidence on his behalf (perhaps to counteract his neighbour Charles McFillin). He was a former United Irishman who had come forward for a pardon after a proclamation by the Lord Lieutenant and Council. He attended the trial but gave no evidence, nor was he called. On his return home he found his house and property and that of his sisters burned by the yeomanry of Magherafelt. After going on the run from their persecution, he was arrested by the yeomanry, jailed for forty-eight hours, and bailed on condition he left 'her majesty's dominions in a short time'. Whitehall and Dublin kept in touch throughout the trial. John Pollock,[68] political adviser to Lord Downshire and Irish observer at the trial, briefed the prosecutor with disreputable details about the Irish witnesses. James McGuckin,[69] solicitor for the Ulster Directory and the National Directory, went to England to give evidence on behalf of Coigly and O'Connor but, as Pollock says in a letter to Dublin from London, 28 May 1798, he 'was not produced because he knew that I knew him'. McGuckin subsequently became an informer. Leonard McNally sought out their line of defence from the lawyers acting for the accused. The informers Watty Cox and Leonard Howard (McNally's illegitimate son) attended the trial to scout and report.[70] Somewhere in the advisory background too was Samuel Turner; he had come to London on 15 May.

On 22 May Judge Buller summed up in favour of all the accused except Fr Coigly. He outlined the different journeys of Coigly, especially to France, evident from his passport (his handwriting there based on Dutton's testimony), as circumstanial evidence of a suspect person; Alexander Stewart's character reference in court he regarded as very slender (he knocked back Stewart's reason for Fr Coigly leaving Ireland, namely the wrecking of his father's house by Orangemen, saying that what happened 'twelve years ago' was not relevant); he accepted the evidence of one person, the master of the hoy from London to Whitstable, that the greatcoat, in which the Address was found, was that of Coigly (there could be no other similar greatcoat?); he dismissed the idea that the greatcoat could have been in the breakfast room overnight and therefore open to tampering; he ignored the inconsistency of Fugion as to the place of the Address in the greatcoat; he accepted that the Address was found in this coat and that Fr Coigly was the bearer of this treasonable Address from the Secret Committee of England to the Executive Directory of France. Did possession prove he was the bearer? Did possession prove approbation of the contents of the Address? The procuring and obtaining of the Address and conspiracy as an overt act, as set out in the indictment, were not proved. The judge did not attend to the fact that it was not proved that Coigly had a guilty knowledge of the Address which was in its substance treasonable. The jury retired for thirty-five minutes and returned with a verdict finding James Coigly guilty and the four others not guilty.

The trial ended as it began, with a sensation. When two Bow Street Runners attempted to seize O'Connor to rearrest him on a warrant of the Duke of Portland on a new charge of high treason, he rushed into the body of the court and a minor riot ensued before he was seized. Coigly remained perfectly calm during the tumult.

Late on the morning of 22 May, John Binns had an opportunity to see Fr Coigly, when he was leaving the prison.[71] He relates, 'On my way to the front door of the Maidstone prison, accompanied by the jailer, the passage from the room in which I had been confined to the outer door of the prison took me past the room in which O'Coigley was confined. All the rooms in that prison that I ever saw were small. The door of Coigley's room as we were passing was open, and there were three or four men in it, occupied about his person. They were changing his dress and putting heavier irons on him. No objection being made I entered the room and found Coigley in manner, tone of voice, and general deportment, the same I had ever found him. His language was full of hope as to the establishment of Ireland's independence, a cause for which he said he was about to suffer death. He desired friendly and affectionate greetings to his friends, more especially to my brother. He pressed my hand between both his hands, my eyes were full of tears, he prayed to God to bless me. I came out of the room and never saw him more. He was executed a few days after. I presume it is unnecessary to say he died as became a man conscious that he suffered in the cause of his Country's Freedom and Independence.'

The day before his execution Fr Coigly said farewell to the other prisoners and friends.[72] Two friends attended him on the morning of his execution, Thursday, 7 June. Valentine Derry was with him to the end. Fr Coigly had differences with his confessor, the same priest who had attempted to turn him informer, and this dispute between them was not resolved until a short time before his execution when they were reconciled. His anxiety to show that he was innocent, a vicarious sacrificial lamb slain at the feet of tyranny, is dominant in the short autobiography, his Address to the People of Ireland, letters he wrote to the attorney-general and the Duke of Portland while in prison and, of course, his scaffold speech. This was the propaganda of a skilled pamphleteer and he had able assistants in Valentine Derry, who wrote a preface to his 'Life' in the same vein, and in John Fenwick who used all his editorial skills to remove any taint or stain that might tarnish the character of the victim. All party political involvement was omitted in the propaganda. Anxious that his memory should be cherished, Coigly was pleased that a gentleman of rank had arranged for his portrait to be painted, but a local magistrate did not allow the painter entry to the prison.

On the morning of his execution he was taken chained to a seat on a hurdle drawn by horses to Penenden Heath, flanked by soldiers. The day was hot and he was covered with dust from the trampling of the horses. A large sympathetic crowd attended. He prayed earnestly, chanted a psalm, and before he died bravely he made a short oration, again professing his innocence. 'I never was the bearer of any letter, paper, writing, or address, or message either written, printed or verbal, to the Directory of France, or to any person on their behalf of which I am accused, nor has any person for me been such a bearer. I further declare, that I never was a member of the Corresponding Society, nor any other political society in Great Britain, nor did I ever attend any of their meetings public, or private. So help me God!' Considering that the Address was written by Dr Crossfield, that it was in line with consistent radical propaganda, that Coigly was bound by his oath as a United Irishman, quoted in the pamphlet by 'Observer' (of which I think he was the author), we may give the above statement a broad mental reservation. The whole import of the 'Life' and protestations of innocence was a contest with government. The United oath concludes, 'I do further declare, that neither hopes, fears, rewards, or punishments, shall ever induce me, directly or indirectly, to inform on, or give evidence against any member or members of this or similar societies, for any act or expression of theirs done or made, collectively or individually, in or out of this society, in pursuance of the spirit of this obligation.'

After the cap was drawn over his face, the priest's lips moved and his hands were lifted up in prayer to the last moment. He died apparently with little suffering. After being suspended for ten minutes, he was cut down, his head was severed from his body and the head and body were immediately buried under the gallows.

Fr Coigly's trial was taken down in shorthand by Joseph Gurney and published in 1798. Memorial cards and poems were soon issued in his memory. His friend John Fenwick, a sub-editor of the *Courier*, and sympathetic to Ireland's cause of freedom, wrote a critique of the trial.

Epilogue

On Sunday 8 July 1900, a party of some 600 Irish people travelled to Maidstone to pay tribute to the memory of Fr Coigly.[73] Mass was said in the Church of St Francis, Week Street, and afterwards they marched four deep to Penenden Heath where a meeting was held, presided over by Mr J. Vincent Taafe. Later a deputation visited Fr Le Bosquet to arrange for a fitting memorial at the church to Fr Coigly. Windows subsequently were erected in the sanctuary to his memory in honour of Naomh Pádraig, Naomh Proinsias and Naomh Brighid. A brass plaque at the back of the church reads: 'Pray for the Soul of Revd James O'Coigly, a Native of Ireland who was put to death on Pennenden Heath June 7th, 1798. Chuir daoine dá chineadh Gaedhealach féin suas an comhartha so agus na trí fuinneóga os cionn na haltóra le taisbeant fheabhas is thaithnigh leó a dhílseacht dá chreideamh agus do'n tír a bhfuair sé bás ar a son. This Memorial and the three Windows over the altar have been erected by a number of his fellow countrymen as a record of their admiration for his love of creed and country for which HE DIED.'

Notes:

1 For his trial and execution see Joseph Gurney, *The Trial of James O'Coigly, otherwise called James Quigley, otherwise called James John Fivey, Arthur O'Connor, Esq., John Binns, John Allen, and Jeremiah Leary*, London, 1798; John Fenwick, *Observations on the Trial of James Coigly for High-Treason*, London, 1798; Howell, Thomas B. and T. J. (ed.), *State Trials*, Vols 26, 27. Articles on Coigly: Samuel Simms, 'Rev. James O'Coigley, United Irishman', *The Down and Connor Historcial Society's Journal*, 1937; Brendan McEvoy, 'Father James Quigley, priest of Armagh and United Irishman', *Seanchas Ard Mhacha* (1970), Vol. 5, No. 2.

2 *The Life of The Rev. James Coigly, an Address to the People of Ireland, as written by himself during his confinement in Maidstone Gaol*. London. 1798.

3 Howell, *State Trials*.

4 *Life*, pp. 10, 31.

5 P.R.O.N.I., T426, p. 4; T636, p. 74.

6 Cf. *Seanchas Ard Mhacha* (1954), Vol. 1, No. 1, pp. 116-7.

7 Applotment Book, Parish of Kilmore, P.R.O.N.I., FIN 5A/186.

8 Cf. Seosamh Ó Duibhginn, *Séamas Mac Giolla Choille*, An Clóchomhar Tta (1972).

9 *Report from the Committee of Secrecy of the House of Lords of Ireland* (London, 1798), Appendix xxix, pp. 47-8.

10 *Life*, p. 9.

11 *Life*, p. 12.

12 Cf. Patrick Boyle, *The Irish College in Paris, 1578-1901* (1901), Liam Swords (ed), *The Irish-French Connection 1578/1978* (1978), Liam Swords, *Soldiers Scholars Priests* (1985), Liam Swords, *The Green Cockade: The Irish in the French Revolution 1789-1815* (1989).

13 For the Armagh Outrages see Patrick Tohall, 'The Diamond Fight of 1795 and the Resultant Expulsions', *Seanchas Ard Mhacha* (1958), Vol. 3, No. 1; Brendan McEvoy 'The Peep of Day Boys and Defenders in the County Armagh', *Seanchas Ard Mhacha*, Vol. 12, No. 1 (1986), Vol. 12, No. 2 (1987); David W. Miller, 'The Armagh Troubles, 1784-95', in Samuel Clark & James S. Donnelly, Jr (ed), *Irish Peasants: Violence & Political Unrest 1780-1914* (1983); David W. Miller (ed), *Peep O'Day Boys and Defenders: Selected Documents on the County Armagh Disturbances 1784-96* (1990); Kevin Whelan, *The Tree of Liberty* (1996); Louis Cullen, 'Late-Eighteenth Century Politicisation in Ireland: Problems in its Study and its French Links' in *Culture et Pratiques Politiques en France et en Irlande XVIe-XVIIIe Siècle* (1988); David W. Miller, 'Politicisation in Revolutionary Ireland: the Case of the Armagh Troubles' and Louis Cullen 'A Comment', *Irish Economic and Social History*, Vol. xxiii, 1996. Cullen in 'Late-Eighteenth Century

Politicisation in Ireland' puts forward the theory that Coigly wrote the pamphlet *Impartial account of the late disturbances in the county of Armagh ... since the year 1784 down to the year 1791 ... by an inhabitant of the town of Armagh, Dublin 1792.* I do not think it is in Coigly's style; it shows a familiarity with events that Coigly could hardly capture, being absent in France for most of them; on Armagh town affairs it has all the self-confidence of an inhabitant.

14   David W. Millar, *Peep O'Day Boys & Defenders*, p. 16.

15   *Life*, pp. 12-3.

16   Aiken McClelland, *The Formation of the Orange Order*, source not given.

17   *Life*, Preface, p. iv.

18   Both Fr Coigly in the *Life* (p. 20) and Robert Quigley in *The Morning Chronicle* (12 September 1835) assert that William Trimble was not transported but was committed to the fleet. He was in fact transported on the *Britannica*. Cf. Anne-Maree Whitaker, *Unfinished Revolution: United Irishmen in New South Wales 1800-1810* (1994), p. 70.

19   R. R. Madden, *Lives of the United Irishmen*, 3rd series, Vol. ii, p. 2.

20   *Personal Recollections of the Life and Times ... of Valentine Lord Cloncurry*, (1850), p. 53, 'Early in 1798 (as well as I recollect, some time in the month of February), I was waited upon by an Irish priest, who brought me a letter of introduction from my father's solicitor, Matt Dowling ... This person, who was one of the finest men I ever saw, was the unfortunate O'Coigly, or Quigly; and upon this occasion for the first time, I met him or knew of his existence.'

21   Nat. Arch., Rebellion Papers, 620/24/59; a letter of Coigly, 25 October 1795,
to   Thomas Story, Belfast, on a literary matter is in Russell Mss, Trinity College, Dublin, Ms 868/1. f. 9.

22   Nat. Arch., Rebellion Papers, 620/24/93A.

23   Nat. Arch., Rebellion Papers, 620/52/192. John Foster (1740-1828): last speaker of Irish House of Commons and opposed to the Union. Cf. A. P. W. Malcomson, *John Foster: The politics of the Anglo-Irish Ascendancy* (1978), 'In particular, it was Foster who in February and March 1798 strongly urged the bold (and successful) policy of arresting the known Irish leaders on suspicion', p. 72. Campbell may be William Campbell (alias McKeever), prominent Derry delegate to the Ulster Provincial Council, United Irishmen, 1798; cf. Brendan McEvoy, 'The United Irishmen in County Tyrone', *Seanchas Ard Mhacha*, Vol. 3, No. 1 (1959), p. 299.

24   Nat. Arch., Rebellion Papers, 620/36/227.

25   Cf. Marianne Elliott, *Partners in Revolution: The United Irishmen and France* (1982). For Irish dimension in Britain see also: Marianne Elliott, 'Irish Republicanism in England: The First Phase, 1797-9' in Thomas Bartlett & D. W. Hayton (ed), *Penal Era and Golden Age* (1979); Roger Wells, *The British Experience 1795-1803* (1983); Albert Goodwin, *The Friends of Liberty: The English democratic movement of the French revolution* (1979); J. Ann Hone, *For the Cause of Truth: Radicalism in London 1796-1821* (1982); Joseph O. Baylen & Norman J. Gossman, *Biographical Dictionary of Modern British Radicals*, Vol. i, 1770-1830 (1979).

26   Cf Réamonn Ó Muirí, 'The Killing of Thomas Birch, United Irishman, March 1797 & the Meeting of the Armagh Freeholders, 19 April 1797', *Seanchas Ard Mhacha*, Vol. 10, No. 2, 1982.

27 Nat. Arch., Rebellion Papers, 620/1/4/21.
28 John T. Gilbert, *Documents relating to Ireland, 1795-1804* (1970 edition),
    p. 116; *Charlemont Correspondence,* Vol. 2: Historical Mss Commission,
    xiiith Report, 1894, par. 303, 320.
29 Nat. Arch., Rebellion Papers 620/1/4/3.
30 Cf. Mary Thale ed. *Selections from the Papers of the London Corresponding
    Society, 1792-1799* (1983); Henry Collins, 'The London Corresponding
    Society' in John Saville ed., *Democracy and the Labour Movement* (1954).
31 P.R.O., PC1/42/A143, PC1/41/A136.
32 P.R.O., PC1/41/A139.
33 P.R.O., PC1/42/A143.
34 P.R.O., PC1/41/A139.
35 P.R.O., PC1/41/A139.
36 Colonel Edward Marcus Despard (1751-1803). Entered the British army at
    fifteen, captain 1779; served in Jamaica 50th Regiment, 1772; commander of
    the island of Rattan on the Spanish main, 1781; captured the Spanish
    possessions on the Black River, 1782; superintendent of his majesty's affairs
    in Yucatan, 1784-90; accused of misdemeanours and lost his position though
    no case was found against him; associated with radical movements;
    imprisoned 1798 and 1800; found guilty of high treason in a controversial
    trial, executed 1803. Cf. Marianne Elliott, 'The Despard Conspiracy
    Reconsidered', *Past and Present,* No. 35, Madden, *United Irishmen,* 3rd
    series, 2nd edition, pp. 293-305.
37 Thomas Evans 1752-1832. Born in the parish of Larbert, in Stirlingshire,
    Scotland. Dissenter. Founder and first secretary of L.C.S. Arrested 1794, tried
    for treason, acquitted. Retained his political principles but left active politics.
38 Nat. Arch., 620/1/4/2; 620/1/4/3.
39 Samuel Turner 1765-1810. Born Turner's Glen, Newry (now The Glen).
    Called to the bar. Prominent United Irishman, turned informer, reporting
    mainly from Hamburg. Cf. W. J. Fitzpatrick, *Secret Service under Pitt,* 1892.
40 *Memoirs and Correspondence of Viscount Castlereagh,* Vol. ii, pp. 3-7.
41 Cf. Liam Swords, *The Green Cockade;* Síle Ní Chinnéide, *Napper Tandy and
    the European Crisis,* (1962).
42 Cf. Goodwin, op. cit., pp. 434-5; Liam Swords, *The Green Cockade,* p. 130.
    Arthur MacMahon became a captain in the French army, cf. W. A. Maguire,
    'Arthur McMahon, United Irishman and French soldier', *The Irish Sword,*
    Vol. ix, 1970, No. 36, and note ibid, Vol. x, 1971, No. 39, p. 172. Fitzpatrick,
    op. cit., pp. 290-300 maintains he became an informer, followed by Francis
    Joseph's Bigger's article in *Ulster Journal of Archaeology,* Series II, Vol. xv,
    pp. 36-41, 134-140, but this is not proved. His brother Patrick was also in
    the French army, Elliott, op. cit., p. 269.
43 Captain Mumford (Mumphort). Cf. *Memoirs and Correspondence of
    Castlereagh* Vol. ii, 5, 359-61. 'Mumford is the Captain of an American
    vessel, who has been concerned in carrying Irish emissaries backwards and
    forwards, in the course of his trade, to a considerable degree. He has been
    lately employed confidentially' (July, 1799).
44 Cf. Elliott, op. cit., pp. 176, 232-3, 253, 275.
45 Nat. Arch., Rebellion Papers, 620/3/32/24.
46 Roger Wells, op. cit., p. 123.
47 Text, Gurney, op. cit., p. 240.

48 Fitzpatrick, op. cit., p. 127.

49 Charles Ross ed. *Correspondence of Charles, First Marquis Cornwallis*, (1859), Vol. i, pp. 348-9.

50 *Report from the Committee of Secrecy of the House of Lords of Ireland* (London,1798), Appendix xiv, p. 118.

51 Elliott, op. cit., p. 180; P.R.O., PC1/42/A143.

52 P.R.O., PC1/41/A139.

53 Perhaps John Revett and Edward Fugion who arrested him at Margate.

54 P.R.O., PC1/42/A143.

55 Goodwin, op. cit., p. 439.

56 Text in Gurney, op. cit., pp. 125-7.

57 Dudley Mills, *Francis Place 1771-1854: The Life of a remarkable radical* (1988), p. 35; cf. Mary Thale ed., *The Autobiography of Francis Place* (1972). Place was a tailor, member of L.C.S., expert on legal reform, advocate of trade unions and popuar education, helped launch the Chartist movement.

58 'Draper's assistant in Dublin afterwards a colonel in the service of France' (Fitzpatrick, *Secret Service under Pitt*, p. 15). Associate of Robert Emmet in 1803. Escaped from Kilmainham, joined the Irish Legion in the French army; joined Napoleon after Elba; handed over to the British but escaped from prison; died Caen in Normandy 1855.

59 John Binns, *Recollections of the Life of John Binns* ... Philadelphia, 1854, pp. 81-2, 92. Binns (1772-1860) became a newspaper editor in Pennsylvania and an Alderman of Philadelphia; born Dublin, emigrated with his brother Benjamin to London, plumber, member of L.C.S., tried for seditious expressions, April 1797, and acquitted. He wrote of Coigly in the 'Recollections', p. 80: 'Mr Coigley was nearly six feet high, of a large frame, gray eyes and gray hair ... The tone of his voice was mild and of a subdued character. His deportment and demeanour were grave. He was slow of speech, of respectable classical and literary acquirement and his understanding above mediocrity. His attachment to country, to principles and friends were firm and steadfast.'

60 Letter of Arthur O'Connor to Madden, *The United Irishmen*, 2nd series, 2nd edition, 1858, p. 308. O'Connor (1763-1852) was imprisoned until 1803, made a general, 1804, in French army by Napoleon; settled in Bignon, France. Cf. Frank MacDermot, 'Arthur O'Connor', *Irish Historical Studies*, Vol. xv, No. 57, March 1966.

61 Anecdote of Major Scott, son of William Scott, counsel of Jeremiah O'Leary at the trial. Cf. William John Fitzpatrick, *The Life, Times and Contemporaries of Lord Cloncurry*, (1855), pp. 602-4. The story is credible, since Coigly had brought important documents bearing on O'Connor from Dublin.

62 There is almost a regret at Coigly's conviction and the failure to convict O'Connor in John Pollock's report to Dublin, 'it was plain [*Coigly*] must be hanged – no one cared about him'.

63 Cf. Gurney, op. cit.; Fenwick, op. cit.

64 E. P. Thompson, *The Making of the English Working Class*, Penguin edition, (1982), p. 509.

65 Nat. Arch., Rebellion Papers, 620/36/66.

66 Nat. Arch., Rebellion Papers, 620/36/95.

67 Madden, *United Irishmen*, 2nd series, 2nd edition, 1858, pp. 304-5.

68 Clerk of the Crown for the Leinster Circuit in 1798. Managed informers Leonard McNally and McGuckin. Fitzpatrick, *Secret Service under Pitt*, p. 178, Cooke to Castlereagh, 'Pollock's services ought to be thought of. He managed Mac–, and MacGuicken, and did much. He received the place of Clerk of the Crown and Peace, and he has the fairest right to indemnification.'

69 Cf. Charles Dickson, *Revolt in the North, Antrim and Down in 1798*, (1960), pp. 166-8.

70 Thomas Pakenham, *The Year of Liberty*, (1969), p. 129.

71 *Recollections*, p. 83.

72 Account of execution given in Howell, op. cit., and Fenwick, op. cit.

73 *Dundalk Democrat*, 14 July 1900.

The Wexford Priests in 1798[1]

Kevin Whelan

Fr John Barry (1766–1836)

Born Poulrane (Kilmore). In the immediate aftermath of 1798, he was sent by Bishop Caulfield to help the 75 year old Fr Frank Kavanagh in the Camolin area (whose curate, Fr John Redmond, had been executed.) In June 1799, he was in his house at Frankford when a party of Gorey yeomen called. Fr Kavanagh slipped away but Barry was badly beaten and cut with swords. Subsequent to this beating, he was hunted out of the parish and fled to his home in Kilmore. He was later parish priest of Rathangan.

Fr Mark Barry (–1847)

Born Belgrove, Duncormick. He was curate in the parish of Kilrush in 1798, where he was much harrassed. He later became PP of Tagoat where he died on 17 September, 1847.

Fr John Broe OSF (1737–1803)

Born Wexford town. Educated Prague. One of six Franciscan friars in Wexford town in 1798. During the occupation of the town by the rebels, he was actively engaged in protecting Protestants. He baptised many of them (Taylor p. 96; Musgrave, Appendix, p. 144) On one occasion, with Fr Patrick Lambert, he was attempting to plead for some prisoners when he was 'threatened, pulled and desired to go about his business'. (Caulfield to Troy, D.D.A., Nov 3, 1799)

Fr John Byrne (–1799)

Birthplace unknown. A Carmelite at Goffs Bridge, when this convent was in serious decline. He played an active part in the rebellion, attending the camps in the south of the county. According to

Caulfield, he was 'a drinking, giddy man' and 'a very zealous, active rebel'. On hearing of his activities, Caulfield admonished him to quit the diocese and threatened suspension. But Byrne continued to 'quest' (seek alms) with effrontery, having obtained a protection. He met a most peculiar death at Clougheast Castle in 1799, when visiting Dr Waddy. Waddy had captured Harvey and Colclough on the Saltee Island in 1798, and had developed a persecution mania. He thought Byrne was attacking him and chased him out of the castle. In fleeing, the portcullis fell on the friar, pinning him to the ground and killing him. Barrington gives a typically exaggerated version of this macabre incident. There are two traditional accounts of his death – *People*, 26 April 1900, *People*, 9 September 1916.

Fr Thomas Clinch (–1798)

Born Oulartwick (Kilcormack). His grandfather had settled at Knockanure (Kilrush) after fighting in the Battle of the Boyne. His father moved from here to Oulartwick. His cousins at Knockanure (Michael and William Clinch) were the local leaders of the United Irishmen of the Kilrush area. (Clinch served as curate at Killaveney, in the Hook and at Killegney. He was suspended from duty in 1796 by Caulfield, allegedly because he was 'a beastly drunkard', and he went to live in Enniscorthy. At the commencement of the rebellion, his retarded nephew was brutally slain by a yeoman unit at Scarawalsh; he immediately joined the rebels. He was a man of huge stature, rendered even more conspicuous by carrying a scimitar and broad cross belt and riding a large white horse. He wore his vestments under his outer clothes. At the Battle of Vinegar Hill, he was engaged in single combat by the Earl of Roden, who, with the help of a trooper, succeeded in shooting him. Clinch rode off, seriously wounded, and died at Mye Cross, where he was hastily buried. Later he was exhumed and buried at Kilmallock.

Fr Patrick Cogley (1751–1803)

Born Coolstuff area (Taghmon, possibly at Aughremon). He was parish priest of Monageer in 1798, with Fr John Murphy as his curate, and was described by Caulfield as a 'truly loyal subject'. He took no part whatsoever in the rebellion, keeping his head low. Afterwards, he was one of Caulfield's right hand men in the north of the county. However, in October 1799, he was accosted while going on a sick call and beaten over the head with a large stone by two local Protestants, whom he knew well but was afraid to prosecute. Subsequently, he was forced to flee to Wexford town, when various plots were formed against him. Only on application to the magistrates in Enniscorthy, and on restoration of his gun in December 1799, did he return to his parochial duties. In 1802, he was transferred to Rathangan.

Fr James Collin (– 1802)

Parish priest of Duncormick. He gave a protection to Richard Grandy (a Protestant surgeon) in 1798, but is not otherwise mentioned.

Fr John Cooney

He was sent in 1799 to minister in the Kilmuckridge area (from which Fr Michael Lacy had fled). On his arrival, his new chapel was attacked and the windows broken and he was obliged to return to Wexford town (Caulfield to Troy, D.D.A., July 9, 1799).

Fr Andrew Corish (–1808)

Parish priest of Kilmore in 1798. Lived at Clongaddy. Born at Lough to a family which produced many priests. In May 1798, Bagenal Harvey (of Bargy Castle in his parish) sent John Boxwell (of Linziestown) to him to 'direct the people to keep order in the parish and not to appear in numbers but keep proper hours' (59th Report of the D.K.P.R.I., p. 47). When requested to baptise a local Protestant woman and her children, he replied that 'except for protection from the fanaticism of the ignorant multitude, the ceremony was useless; that he would be on the watch for her safety, and give her timely warning if he should find the performance of that rite necessary' (Gordon, pp. 217/218).

Fr John Currin (1750–1834)

Born Wexford town. Nephew of Coadjutor Bishop John Stafford

and grandnephew of Bishop Nicholas Sweetman. Educated on the
Continent and ordained at Louvain, 1779. Lived at Back Street in
the town, and was appointed parish priest in 1780. In 1798, he
played an especially prominent role in keeping the rebels pacified
in the town and in ensuring the safety of Protestant prisoners. On
one occasion, his personal intervention prevented an intended massacre at the goal. He signed passes and certificates of protection for
the many refugees caught in the town when it passed into rebel
control. His impassioned intervention, dressed in his priestly vestments and carrying a white cross, stopped the massacre on Wexford
Bridge, when he got down on his knees to implore them to desist.
He was the subject of universal praise (with the exception of
Musgrave) in the many post-1798 accounts of the occupation of
Wexford, although even he had to suffer harrassment in 1799, with
the windows of his house being broken. His schoolteacher nephew,
Patrick O'Brien, was a United Irish Captain in the Johnstown area
and was transported for nine years.

Fr David Cullen (–1807)

Born in Clongeen parish and succeeded his uncle Patrick as parish
priest of Blackwater just prior to 1798. He baptised Bleakney
Ormsby of Millenagh, a Protestant, but is not otherwise mentioned, although Thomas Dixon was his curate, and the parish of
Blackwater was a storm centre of the rebellion. (Musgrave, Appendix,
p. 129; *People*, 1 Feb, 1908). In November 1797, he supported
Mountnorris' campaign against the proclamation of martial law in
north Wexford.

Fr Thomas Dixon (–1798)

Born Castlebridge to a family heavily involved in the milling trade.
The Dixons were also linked to the Roches of Garrylough, a family
equally influential in the 1798 rebellion. As well as milling, the family
were also active in innkeeping, shopkeeping and mercantile activities
(especially malting, brewing and shipping). Dixon was curate of
Lady's Island for some years until his suspension in 1794 by
Caulfield for 'drinking, dancing and disorderly conduct'. When the

bishop thought him sufficiently amended in his ways, he was sent as curate to Fr David Cullen in Blackwater but 'he relapsed into his former pranks and was suspected latterly of being active in the accursed business of Uniting'. Caulfield accordingly interdicted and suspended him again in 1797, partially on the advice of his cousin Fr James Dixon. Francis Murphy later swore that Dixon had attempted to swear him in as a United Irishman in a public house in Wexford. For this Dixon was arrested in the spring of 1798, and at the Wexford assizes of 23 May he was sentenced to transportation. Elizabeth Richards in her diary noted the 'sullen melancholy' in the town of Wexford due to his banishment. Dixon contracted fever at the tender where he was imprisoned at Duncannon while awaiting transportation, and died. Captain Thomas Dixon, (his cousin) exacted a very public revenge on Francis Murphy, who was ceremoniously executed on Wexford bridge and his body thrown in the river Slaney. Dixon, with Fr Edward Synnott, is one of two priests known to have been actively involved with the United Irishmen prior to 1798. Catholic sources are very hostile to him, describing him as 'a priest some years degraded from his office and excommunicated; the dishonour and scandal of the clergy'. Caulfield described him as 'a notorious agitator' (Caulfield to Troy, 21 May, 1791).

Fr James Dixon (1758–1840)

Born Castlebridge, to the same family as Thomas Dixon. Ordained 1784 at Louvain and was sent as curate to Crossabeg. His brothers Nicholas and Thomas were active United Irishmen, with Thomas taking a prominent part in activities in Wexford town, especially the massacre on Wexford Bridge. He himself reported his cousin Fr Thomas Dixon to Bishop Caulfield, because of his involvement with the United Irishmen. After the rebellion, he fled to Wales with the local landlord family, the Le Huntes of Artramont, and was arrested at Milford. At his subsequent court martial in Waterford, it was maliciously alleged that he had been present at various battles in north Wexford, but it is likely that he was confused with his United Irish brothers, Nicholas and Thomas. He was totally innocent of any involvement and suffered for his family background. He was initially sentenced to death, but this was commuted to transportation and he was despatched to Botany Bay. Caulfield had initially thought that there might be some substance in the charge against Dixon, but subsequently altered his opinion: 'The poor man is a real object of pity for I am convinced in my conscience that he was, and is, as innocent of the rebellion and everything tending to it as any man in Ireland.' (D.D.A., Caulfield to Troy, 6 Dec, 1798). Caulfield also reports that 'he particularly abhorred and detested the uniting business and rebellion for he, to my certain knowledge, took great pains to advise and dissuade people from that wicked business and has, more than once, complained to me, with tears in his eyes, that he could get no good of them' (Cited Goodall, pp. 640/641). After his Australian exile, he was allowed return to Ireland in 1808, when he became parish priest of Crossabeg and died there in 1840.

Fr Bernard Downes (–1801)

Born Burkestown (Tintern), his family had been displaced from Garryrichard after the 1641 rebellion. Nephew of Fr Michael Downes. Lived at Taylorstown Castle. Parish priest of Tintern and Dean of the diocese (his kinsman, Nicholas Sweetman, was Bishop). He was an old man in 1798. He baptised Joseph Kelly (a Protestant) and many more in his area during the rebellion (Musgrave, Appendix, p. 139). According to Rev William Sutton, the Protestant clergyman of the area, his conduct was 'exemplary, irreproachable and loyal'.

Fr James Doyle (–1816)

Birthplace unknown. He was parish priest of Sutton parish (Whitechurch) in 1798. He advised the local Protestants of Fethard to go to Mass as a means of saving their lives while the rebellion raged and 'acted with humanity towards them' (Musgrave, Appendix, p. 133). He was sent a threatening letter on 14 June by Fr Philip Roche, who ordered him to bring his parishioners forthwith to the rebel camp at Lacken Hill on pain of having his house burnt over him. He complied with this threat, and was acquitted when court martialled later, on producing Roche's letter. After the rebellion, he conducted the rebels from Sutton parish into New Ross to surrender and receive protection. Thomas Handcock, a loyalist, considered that he was responsible for keeping his parish quiet in the rebellion. 'The simple loyalty and good conduct of their priest, Rev James Doyle, gave them an example by which they profitted.' (Shaw Mason, vol 2, p. 544).

Fr James Doyle (1752–1825)

Born Raheen (Adamstown). He was PP of Davidstown in 1798, when he lived with the Dunne family at Coolamurry. He succoured local Protestants during the rebellion, telling them 'rest assured that this beautiful island will not long remain in the hands of the rebels. King George will soon send over an army to defeat them.' Mrs Lett of Killaligan reported, 'I shouldn't omit to mention the kind and humane conduct of Fr Doyle who obligingly said that he was ready to perform any office that might contribute to our safety; he supposed we were activated only by fear to make the proposal of conversion.' (*The Past*, 1948, p. 124)

Fr Hendrick

Born Monamore (near Courtown). One of his brothers was shot at Gorey Hill in 1798 while fighting with the rebels. He said Mass in his family home when the local yeomanry came in quest of him, and he was forced to flee the area (*Free Press*, 11 June, 1938).

Fr Frank Kavanagh (1723–1805)

Born Templederry. Parish priest of Ballyoughter in 1798, when he was 75 years old. Lived at Frankford. He was on very friendly terms with Mountnorris and other Protestant gentry in the Camolin area, often dining and staying at Camolin Park, Mountnorris' home. Mountnorris had pro-Catholic sympathies in the 1790s and was convinced that he could keep north Wexford quiet. He was bitterly disappointed at the outbreak of the rebellion and was personally responsible for the execution of Kavanagh's curate, John Redmond. Fr Kavanagh also came under pressure, despite his impeccable loyalism during the course of the rebellion. In June 1799, he was attacked in his house by a party of the Gorey Yeomanry who 'abused him with the most horrid and contumelious language and with naked swords and sabres threatened the old croppy, the rebel scoundrel, that they would cut off his head' (Caulfield to Troy, 27 June, 1797). He managed to slip out but his curate, John Barry, and his servants were badly beaten. He then fled to Wexford town. The next evening, a volley of shots were fired through his door and his personal belongings stolen. According to Kavanagh's own testimony, he was 'publicly and repeatedly threatened by the rebels' and at the breakout of the rebellion was forced to flee to Gorey for safety. He had signed the Mountnorris-inspired petition against the proclamation of north Wexford in 1797 and a loyal address of his parishioners in April, 1797, again at Mountnorris' behest. (Musgrave, Appendix, pp. 79-81)

Fr John Keane

Born Ballymader, Bannow parish. Popularly known as 'the blessed priest of Bannow', he had a reputation as a healer and miracle worker, due to his sanctity. According to Musgrave (p. 482), 'The rebels had uncommon veneration for him.' He blessed them, distributed scapulars and constantly visited the rebel camps, mounted on a pony 'led by two men who cried out with a loud voice "make way for the blessed priest of Bannow"'. Caulfield, in the aftermath of the rebellion, described him as 'a weak poor fool' unworthy of notice who had been 'under ecclesiastical censure for the greater part of his life for drunkenness and other irregularities'. He is described as an 'idiot' (mentally defective) in another contemporary source. Because of this, he escaped repercussions after the rebellion.

Fr Mogue Kearns

Born at Kiltealy, on the slopes of the Blackstairs Mountains. He was a huge weighty man of powerful build and great activity. In his youth he had developed a reputation as a weight thrower and hurler in the Duffry Hall, well known patrons of popular culture. After his ordination in 1786, he had been in the mission at the Colclough family mansion at Clonard on the Kildare-Meath border, and here he came in contact with the Defenders. Because of his close ties to them, he was dismissed by Bishop Delaney and returned to the Duffry. Caulfield refused to employ him and he spent his time in various rural pursuits, such as grouse shooting. Fr John Murphy and himself teamed up in grouse shooting expeditions on the Blackstairs. According to Caulfield, he was 'notorious for drinking and fighting' and had been suspended prior to the rebellion. His mother was a near relative of John Kelly of Killann. His two brothers (Martin and Patrick) were active United Irishmen, as were his four cousins (Michael, Mogue, Roger and Stephen Kearns of Ballychrystal). He himself joined the rebels from the outset and was especially active in the first battle of Enniscorthy. He subsequently followed the rebels to Meath and Kildare, and, with Anthony Perry, was arrested and executed at Edenderry.

Fr Michael Lacy (–1800)

Born Enniscorthy. Parish priest of Litter (Kilmuckridge) since 1789. In November 1797, he signed the Mountnorris-inspired petition on the proclamation of north Wexford. In January 1798, he signed a declaration of loyalty from his parish which expressed 'horror and indignation' at the spread of the United Irishmen and assuring 'our Protestant brethren of our sincere and unfeigned love and affection' (*Freeman's Journal*, 10 February, 1798). He signed another such declaration in April 1798 at Mountnorris' behest. However, his brother William was one of the early United Irishmen in Enniscorthy, and acted as emissary during the rebellion. Lacy went to Vinegar Hill at the request of some of his Protestant parishioners to intercede successfully for local prisoners. As a result, he was arrested and made a prisoner by General Needham in Oulart but was subsequently acquitted. He is described in contemporary Catholic polemics as 'a most zealous and presevering loyalist'. In June 1799, his chapel of Litter was attacked and damaged and he himself sought the safety of Wexford town. It was only in December of that year that he could return to his parochial duties (Caulfield to Troy, 17 Dec, 1799), and he died the following year, a death hastened by his troubled existence of the previous two years (Grattan Flood, p. 77).

Fr Patrick Lambert OSF (1754–1816)

Born Gurteenminogue (Murntown). Became a Franciscan, educated Louvain, and was one of the six friars in Wexford town during the rebellion, where he attempted to keep the rebels under control. With Fr Broe, he was peremptorily threatened, pulled and desired to go about his business' when he attempted to intercede for prisoners on their trial (Caulfield to Troy, 3 Nov 1799). On another occasion, he was preaching a sermon against murder when one of the hearers shouted, 'Man, go mind your own business in the chapel, we know how to mind ours.' Similarly when engaged in haranguing them in the street, he had a blunderbuss immediately presented to his breast. (*A Vindication*, p. 63) In his subsequent career, Lambert became a bishop in St Johns, Newfoundland (1806-1816), as did his nephew and fellow Franciscan Fr Thomas Scallan.

Fr Bryan Murphy

Born Gallyhack, Ballymore. He became parish priest of Taghmon in 1789 and lived at Bricketstown. According to Caulfield, he was deprived of his parish and suspended in 1795. He was active on the rebel side during the insurrection, signing protections, attending camps, etc. Caulfield describes him as a 'reptile' and refers to the 'notoriety of his activity' (Caulfield to Troy, 19 Oct 1799). Although he also says that he exhibited 'proofs of his humanity' and exerted himself to save lives and property. According to loyalist sources, he gave the order to burn the prison barn at Scullabogue, although this has never been substantiated. After the rebellion, Murphy managed to get a protection but in 1800 he was forced to flee the county, under persecution from the local yeomanry, and became a mental wreck. According to Fr P. F. Kavanagh, he fled to Kerry where he taught Greek and Latin as a career. Musgrave (Appendix, p. 48) cites Caulfield's letter of March 1800 interdicting Murphy, after he had attempted to pursue his priestly career despite his suspension.

Fr Edan Murphy (–1802)

Birthplace unknown. PP of Kilrush 1770-1802. His curate, Fr Edward Synnott, had become a United Irishman and was suspended by Caulfield in 1796 as a result. On 28 January 1798, Fr Murphy signed a declaration of loyalty at his chapel, criticising the United Irishmen as 'rebels and traitors'. There is no evidence of his involvement in the events of 1798, although his two chapels (Kilrush and Munfin) were burned in 1799 by the local yeomanry.

Fr Edward Murphy (1759–1830)

Born New Ross. Parish priest of Bannow 1793-1830. Educated in Paris. In 1798, he wrote protections which he pinned to the gates of local Protestants. To the family of Mrs S. C. Hall he wrote in French telling them to fear nothing. In another note, he voiced his fear that 'the power is passing from all who do not go entirely with the people; the priest can now lead to evil but hardly to good.' According to Musgrave, he preached hardline sermons during the rebellion, and he was prosecuted in 1799 but was acquitted, partially because he had the backing of the influential Jonas King of Barrystown. King described Murphy as 'a most loyal man and a useful and fortunate man for the Protestants of his neighbourhood for that he saved their lives and property' (Caulfield to Troy, 26 April 1799). He subscribed to a poetic eulogy of General Johnson after the Battle of New Ross.

Fr James Murphy

Place of birth unknown. It is not known where he served in 1798 (possibly as curate in Sutton's parish). He is mentioned by Musgrave as being present at the rebel camp of Carrigbyrne. He sent Caulfield a 'very full and strong testimony of his loyalty and humane exertions on and before the rebellion, signed by nine Protestants' (Caulfield to Troy, 30 October, 1799).

Fr John Murphy (1753–1798)

Born Tincurry (Ballycarney), son of a 70 acre farmer and bacon curer, Thomas Murphy. Educated Seville, ordained 1779. Appointed curate in Boolavogue in 1785, near his birthplace. He was an active athletic individual, fond of handball, grouse shooting and a good horseman. He often hunted on the Blackstairs with Fr Mogue Kearns. He lodged with a local farmer, John Donohue of

Tomnaboley, and took breakfast every morning at the house of Tom Donovan in Boolavogue. Donovan's wife was one of the Byrnes of Kilnamanagh, a family which had early links to the United Irishmen (Peter, Morgan and Luke Byrne). Murphy was on visiting terms with Mountnorris in Camolin Park, Edward Fitzgerald of Newpark and the Hay family of Ballinkeele – the most important political families in his area. He supported Mountnorris's campaign not to have north Wexford proclaimed in November 1797 (Musgrave, Appendix, p. 79). Murphy's relationship with his bishop was strained. At the age of 45 he was still a mere curate in 1798 and Caulfield wrote that 'although he was never formally suspended or disgraced,' he was 'often reproached, reprimanded and threatened'. Caulfield's favourite word for describing him was 'giddy'. In the spring of 1798, Murphy wavered between support of or hostility to the United Irishmen. At Easter, he refused the sacrament to all United Irishmen who did not abjure their oath. On 8 April he signed a declaration of loyalty as CC of Kilcormack, at the instigation of Mountnorris but only under extreme pressure. At this stage, the overt security presence of yeomanry and militia units had intensified; rumours about Orangemen, massacre, French landings, proliferated; local United Irish organisation strengthened. Towards the end of May, and as a response to local law and order excesses, Murphy came over to the United Irishmen, with whom he already had many links. When the flashpoint arrived on 26 May, he took an active part in the incident at the Harrow, uttering the words, 'Better to die like men in the fields than to die like dogs in the ditches.' From there, he was led by events – the raid for arms at Camolin Park, the assembly at Oulart Hill, the defeat of the North Corks, the taking of Enniscorthy – and was pushed ever more prominently into a leadership role which he would not initially have envisaged for himself. He was eventually captured near Tullow in July 1798, when the campaign petered out and was brutally executed. His brothers, Mogue and Patrick, fought in the campaign as did his mother's people, the Whittys of Tomgarrow. Murphy is the subject of a fine biography by the Wexford historian, Nicholas Furlong.

Fr Michael Murphy (1760?–1798)

Born Ballinoulart, although his family were originally small farm-ers (20 acres) at Kilnew, Blackwater. Ordained in 1785, educated Bordeaux. On his return to Co Wexford in 1792, he lived at the house of James Kenny (tanner and shopkeeper) in Ballycanew and ministered there, apparently in an unofficial capacity. Caulfield tells us that he was 'never called even to a curacy on account of his incapacity and riotous temper'. In November he backed Mountnorris' efforts to get the proclamation of north Wexford re-scinded. He was involved in Mountnorris' campaign to pacify north Wexford and he signed a declaration of loyalty from Ballycanew on 18 April, 1798 (Musgrave, Appendix, pp. 74-92). However, White suspected him of involvement in the United Irishmen and as a result of harrassment he went 'on the run' in early May 1798, until the rebellion broke out. On 1 June, James Kenny (with whom he lodged) was shot, and his house burned by the Camolin Yeomanry (Wheeler and Broadley, p. 104). Murphy, hear-ing of the victory at Oulart, returned to the Ballycanew area, gath-ered the local men (including his two nephews James and John Murphy of Ballinoulart) and joined forces at Ballyorril Hill with those preparing the attack on Enniscorthy. Murphy had close con-tacts with the United Irishmen and was one himself. His nephew, Nicholas Murphy of Monaseed, was a United Irish captain, one of his sisters was married to John Prendergast of Knotstown and an-other to a Whelan of Ballymartin, both United Irishmen. Nicholas Murphy's mother, was related to Edward Roche of Garrylough, one of the most important United Irishmen in the county. His brother, Nicholas of Ballinoulart (ob. 1806), left Rev Nicholas Stafford £2 in his will. Michael Murphy was killed at the Battle of Arklow and his dead body was subjected to severe indignities.

Fr Edward Newport (1762–1801)

Born Castlebridge parish. Curate in Castlebridge/Blackwater 1789-1801. In the winter of 1799, the local yeomen made a raid on his res-idence near Ardcavan. He was forced to flee, hiding in a nearby thicket. He got a chill as a result, for which he died in February 1801. Buried at Ardcavan (*People*, 4/7/1920).

Fr Miles O'Connor

Born Dublin. PP of Ballindaggin 1775-1804. Lived at Coolycarney Cottage. In January 1798, he signed a declaration of loyalty from Ballindaggin chapel at a time when the United Irishmen were attempting to gain a footing in the Barony of Bantry. In it he describes them as 'malicious, wicked, designing men' with 'evil principles and diabolical practices'; and pledges his parishioners cooperation with the local magistrates (Colclough and James). Through his connections with the O'Connor family of Ballindaggin, he was distantly related to the Hay family of Ballinkeele. Perhaps as a result of this connection, he was visited in the spring of that year by Edward Fitzgerald and Anthony Perry, with a view to permitting the United Irishmen to organise in his parish. He refused to have anything to do with them. This suggests that it was standard United Irish policy to seek the tacit consent of the local priest, especially if deemed sympathetic, prior to organising an area.

Fr James Purcell (1718–1810)

Birthplace unknown. Educated Salamanca. PP of Clonegal on the Carlow-Wexford border 1759-1810. Lived at Johnstown on the Wexford side of the river Derry. The Clonegal area had an early United Irish cell, which was uncovered in the winter of 1797. In December 1797, Fr Purcell published a declaration of loyalty in which he dismissed the United Irishmen as 'enemies of Catholicity', deplored the 'weakness' and 'ignorance' of the 'lower orders of our communion who were misled by their wicked artifices' and pledged to 'drag such miscreants to the bar of justice and prosecute them to the utmost rigour of the law'.

Fr Edward Redmond (1740–1819)

Born Ferns. PP of Ferns 1786-1819, in succession to his uncle Andrew Cassin. He was claimed by Musgrave to have led his flock to the Battle of Bunclody on 1 June 1798. In April 1799, he was tried and acquitted by a court martial in Enniscorthy (Caulfield to Troy, 26 April, 1799). In October 1797, he fled to Dublin as a result of continued persecution. He is believed to have been uncle to Patrick

Redmond of Coolgreaney, United Irish Captain in that area (*People*, 29 Feb, 1908). In November 1797, he supported Mountnorris' orchestrated campaign against the proclamation of north Wexford and in April 1798, again at Mountnorris' behest, he signed a loyal address on behalf of the parish of Ferns (Musgrave, Appendix, pp. 79-81).

Fr John Redmond (–1798)

Born Ballinakill (Marshalstown). Curate in the Camolin area in 1798, serving under Frank Kavanagh. He was, like his parish priest, on very good terms with the local Protestant gentry, in particular Mountnorris of Camolin Park whom he idolised. In November 1797, with his PP Frank Kavanagh, he supported Mountnorris' anti-proclamation moves (Musgrave, Appendix, p. 80). In the spring of 1798, he was violently opposed to the United Irishmen, turning them away on their knees from Confession. Caulfield described him as 'a regular, zealous, attentive priest without reproach'. When Camolin Park was attacked, Redmond hastened to the scene to dissuade the rebels from damaging the property, 'doing all in his powers to restrain and prevent them' (Caulfield to Troy, 9 October, 1799). So vehemently did he oppose the rebels that he was called by them an 'orange priest' (*People*, 29 February, 1908). In the immediate aftermath of the rebellion, he was sent for by Mountnorris in Gorey and went there, totally unconscious of guilt. On his arrival in the town, 'he was treated as if manifestly guilty before trial, knocked down in the street and rudely dragged by some yeomen' (Gordon, pp. 185-186). After a brief court-martial (SPO 620/3/26/4), a halter was placed around his neck, he was rushed to Gorey Hill and peremptorily hanged. Mountnorris, according to Miles Byrne, personally fired a brace of bullets through his body (Musgrave, p. 7). During the course of the rebellion, Redmond 'was constantly hiding in Protestant houses from the rebels and many Romanists expressed great resentment against him as a traitor to the cause' (Gordon, pp. 185-86). Bishop Caulfield reported that even Mountnorris's own Protestant servants considered him to be a totally innocent man (Caulfield to Troy, 19 Oct 1799). He was a victim of the post-rebellion backlash and of Mountnorris' personal fury at what he would have seen as his betrayal by the Catholics of north Wexford, led by their priests.

Fr Michael Redmond (–1799)

Birthplace unknown. PP of Castlebridge 1795-1799. At Mountnorris' instigation, he signed a loyal address in April 1798. Other than this, he does not figure in any of the accounts of the period (Musgrave, Appendix, p. 81).

Fr Nicholas Redmond (1742–1834)

Born Donoughmore area. PP of Ballygarrett 1774-1834. He was not involved in any way in the rebellion. He signed, in November 1797, the petition got up by Mountnorris against the proclamation of north Wexford (Musgrave, Appendix, p. 79). On 1 January 1799, his home in Ballygarrett was attacked by the local yeomanry and he just had time to escape. His niece and housekeeper were, however, both murdered in this attack (letter Seán Etchingham to G. O. C. Redmond, 2 January, 1910).

Fr James Roche

Place of birth unknown. Ordained 1785. Curate in Wexford town in 1798, lodging with Bishop Caulfield. He preached a sermon in the chapel in June 1798, and addressed the converts: 'You come here more from motives of fear than sincere conversion, but I tell you that unless you are sincere, you will be murdered. (To the pikemen) For over one hundred years, you have suffered much from the cruelty and oppression of the Protestants: yet I would advise you to spare these poor people and destroy none but your enemies. Though you have suffered and are still suffering much from the Protestants you are fighting in the cause of God, of your religion, and for your rights. You have put your hand to the plow, you will not look back' (Musgrave, *A Concise Account*, p. 29; Caulfield to Troy, 23 Sept 1799). On this occasion, he also read the rebel proclamation against the notorious magistrates, Boyd, White, Jacob and Gowan. Caulfield comments that 'I know he was intimidated by a chapel full of pikemen and Capt Kieuh (Keugh) who compelled him to read the proclamation' (Caulfield to Troy, 23 Sept 1799). He was not arrested after the rebellion and continued in his parochial duties. In April 1799, he left the diocese of Ferns, at Caulfield's instigation and never returned (Caulfield to Troy, 26 April 1799).

Fr Philip Roche (1760? –1798)

Born Monasootagh (Boolavogue). Ordained 1785. He was stationed in Gorey and came in contact with the United Irishmen there in the early 1790s. Miles Byrne (p. 86) comments that, because of his Gorey stint, he knew 'of the many inhuman deeds committed by the Orange magistracy of that area'. According to Caulfield, he was 'a proper man and would be useful' but that 'he indulged in excess of drinking and began to agitate' and became 'obnoxious' and had to be removed. After 'reprimanding, admonishment and instruction' by Caulfield, he was deported to the far end of the diocese as curate to Fr Thomas Rogers in Killegney. On the outbreak of the rebellion, he immediately occupied a prominent position with the rebels, and eventually replaced Bagenal Harvey as commander-in-chief. Rev James Gordon, who knew him well, states 'he was certainly not a favourite with me, as I disliked his rough, familiar manner and his too frequent displays of ebriety' (Gordon, p. 399). Musgrave similarly refers to his drink problem and his 'rough and boisterous exterior'. Both of them, however, stress that he was personally brave, had a kind and generous streak, and was the means of saving many Protestant lives. He liberally distributed written protections or 'gospels' (to be worn about the neck) and seems to have deliberately exploited the traditional aura of power associated with priesthood to inspire his followers. After the defeat at Vinegar Hill, he surrendered himself in Wexford town, where he was summarily court-martialled and hanged. According to Plowden, he was the only priest in the diocese of Ferns who had entered into United Irish politics prior to the rebellion. (Plowden, vol 2 (2), p. 716)

Fr Redmond Roche (1742–1819)

Born Garrylough. PP of Crossabeg 1779-1819. He was brother of General Edward Roche, the rebel leader (*People*, 31 August 1912).

He was also related to Nicholas Murphy, the United Irish captain in the Monaseed area. Despite this, he did not figure in 1798, except to sign a loyal address on behalf of his parishioners in April 1798, at Mountnorris' behest (Musgrave, Appendix, p. 81), where he is incorrectly given as Redmond Rooke).

Fr Thomas Rogers (–1815)

Birthplace unknown. PP of Killegney (Rathnure-Cloughbawn) 1793-1815. He was highly praised by Rev James Gordon for his exertions during the rebellion. 'No Protestant was killed, nor house burned due to the laudable conduct of Fr Thomas Rogers, who encouraged his flock to believe that all the Protestants of the area had voluntarily converted to Catholicism' (Gordon, p. 142) In particular, he succoured Rev Samuel Francis, the Protestant clergyman and his family, and the Whitney family of Gurrawn (Kennedy, *Banks of the Boro*, p. 359).

Fr William Ryan (1728–1798)

Born Kilninor area. PP of Arklow 1772-1798. Lived at Cooladangan on the Wicklow-Wexford border. He was murdered by a contingent of the Castletown yeoman cavalry, on 14 December, 1798 – the only death in the pogrom against Catholic priests in north Wexford in the aftermath of the rebellion.

Fr Thomas Scallan (1763-1830)

Born Churchtown (Ballymore). One of six Franciscan friars in Wexford town during its occupation by the United Irishmen. Like Broe and Lambert, he used his influence to intercede for the prisoners. On one occasion, when visiting the goal, he 'was grossly insulted and turned away'. (*Vindication,* p. 63) He succeeded his uncle, Patrick Lambert, as Bishop of St John's, Newfoundland, in 1816.

Fr John Shallow (–1831)

Born Park (Old Ross) Parish Priest of Adamstown-Newbawn 1795-1817. Lived at Ballyshannon. According to his own testimony, he strongly opposed the spread of the United Irishmen in his parish in the spring of 1798. He considered their philosophy 'analogous to and flowing from French atheistical revolutionary principles, derogating from and repugnant to the established laws of the land.' Subsequent to the rebellion, he was charged with being involved in the massacre at Scullabogue barn, which was in his parish, but was able to call numerous witnesses to show that he was only present there to rescue local Protestants.

Fr Mun Stafford (–1806)

Born Baldwinstown Castle. PP of Lady's Island 1763-1806. He had a crowded congregation during the rebellion as all the local Protestants flocked to the chapel to be baptised (Taylor, p. 97). He was the only priest in the extreme south of the county to be harrassed with intimidatory visits after 1798 (Caulfield to Troy, 16 Sept 1799) possibly because he was uncle of Fr Patrick Stafford, the curate in Gorey who was forced to flee his parish and return to his home in Baldwinstown.

Fr Nicholas Stafford (1753–1811)

Born Ballyvoodock (Blackwater). CC of Riverchapel (Ballygarrett). The Stafford family had been landholders here in the mid-seventeenth century. In November 1797, along with his parish priest, Nicholas Redmond, he signed the remonstrance (inspired by Mountnorris) against the proclamation of martial law in north Wexford, and on 18 April 1797, he signed a declaration of loyalty of the congregation of Ardamine (Riverchapel), again at the instigation of Mountnorris. However, his name is on the list of United Irish officers, found in Matthew Keugh's house and which dates to late 1797. Stafford was at this early stage a committed United Irishman. Musgrave accuses him of being a 'notorious rebel' (*Concise Account*, p. 67) and he became a fugitive immediately after the rebellion. Caulfield suspended him as soon as information of his pro-rebel stance reached him. After 1798, Stafford returned to Ballyvoodock, and never again ministered openly as a priest. He had contracted T.B. while 'on the run' and his suspension was never lifted. The fact that he was still a curate in 1798, although aged 45, suggests that Caulfield disapproved of his political opinions.

Fr Patrick Stafford (–1823)

Born Little Graigue (Duncormick). He was initially a chaplain in the French navy and subsequently curate in Gorey, serving in the Kilanerin district until 1803, when he became parish priest of Kilmuckridge. In the winter of 1798, he was harrassed so much that he left the area, returning to his family home in Little Graigue for a period of eighteen months (*People*, 19 Dec 1914).

Fr John Sutton (–1832)

Born Ryane (Oylegate). Curate in Enniscorthy 1789-1801. He was bitterly opposed to the United Irishmen in 1798. Thomas Handcock (who lived in Enniscorthy) comments of him that he screened as many Protestants as he could (*Narrative*, p. 125) He was the sole witness at the court-martial of Patrick Beaghan on 16 July 1799 for the murder of Samuel Heydon. On Sutton's evidence, Beaghan was convicted and executed (SPO, 620/6/70/28). According to family tradition, he was so opposed to the popular side in 1798 that no member of the Sutton families ever became a priest afterwards (Mrs Seán T. O Kelly).

Fr Edward Synnott (–1797)

Birthplace unknown. Appointed curate in Kilrush parish in 1793, where he joined the United Irish movement. It is possible that he was related to Thomas Sinnott of Kilbride, an important local figure in the north-east, who was married to an aunt of Thomas Cloney. On a list of United Irish leaders found in Matthew Keugh's home (and possibly dating to late 1797), he is listed as captain in the Kilrush area (Musgrave, Appendix, p. 162). His fellow curate, Nicholas Stafford, is listed as an officer in the Riverchapel area. His activities soon came to the attention of Caulfield, who considered him a 'notorious agitator' who did 'much mischief' by 'agitating and uniting' (Caulfield to Troy, 21 May 1799, ibid., 23 Sept 1799). He was suspended as a result in 1796 and died in 1797, as a result of pneumonia, contracted, Caulfield claimed, by 'an excessive use of spirits'.

Fr John Synnott (–1814)

Born Blackwater area. PP of Gorey 1784-1814. He took no part in the rebellion, but was harrassed by the yeomanry to such an extent that he fled the parish in the summer of 1799, not returning to it until early 1800 (Caulfield to Troy, 28 July, 1799). His chapel at Kilanerin was twice burnt in this period. He signed the Mountnorris' inspired address of loyalty in April 1798.

Fr Nicholas Synnott (1725–1823)

Born Kilbride (Oulart). PP of Oulart 1760-1823. Lived at Kilbride. He was considered a loyalist in 1798. In November 1797 he signed the petition against the proclamation. In April 1798, he signed the Mountnorris' inspired declaration of loyalty for the Catholics of Oulart (*Freeman's Journal*, 1 May 1798). He was brother to Tom Synnott, a prominent United Irish leader, and uncle to Miles and Richard Doran, who were also prominent.

Fr William Synnott (–1805)

Born Glynn. PP of Enniscorthy 1784-1801. He became a priest after his wife's death and his son John was also ordained. During the rebellion, he provided shelter to many of the local Protestant gentry women, and to the Protestant clergyman, Rev Joshua Nunn. According to Mrs Pounden of Daphne 'the priests of Enniscorthy, taking no part in the rebellion, were afraid to remain in the town' (*Irish Ancestor*, vol 8, 1976, p. 6) Partially as a result of his experiences in 1798, he resigned the parish, and retired to Wexford town.

Note:

1   This article is a prosopography of the Co Wexford priests in 1798. The general background is covered in my article, 'The role of the Catholic priest in the 1798 Rebellion in County Wexford', in K. Whelan (ed.), *Wexford: History and Society* (Dublin, 1987), pp. 296-315, which also provides full bibliographic details.

The Church and Fr John Murphy
of Boolavogue 1753-1798

Nicholas Furlong

We should always be aware that what now lies in the past once lay in the future. — F.W. Maitland

That Fr John Murphy of Boolavogue remains a major figure in the 1798 United Irish revolt is inescapable. Folk memory and perception has placed him in a dominant position. The reputation surviving him was expanded in the Franciscan Patrick Kavanagh's account of 1798 in Co Wexford (Dublin, 1874), while P. J. McCall's words of the song 'Boolavogue', using a traditional air, has given his name recognition at home and abroad wherever the Irish sing.

John Murphy was not a major participant in the United Irish movement since that society was inaugurated in Gorey in 1792. Nor had he a role of any consequence whatever in revolutionary strategies until late in the month of May in 1798 toward the end of which hostilities broke out. His public notoriety, personality, qualities, leadership in war and ultimate stoicism became observed and recorded for only the last two months of his life. Prior to that he lived and worked in rural obscurity.

The man, John Murphy, who engaged in the hazard of war in May of 1798, was a man noted by his later admirer Miles Byrne[1] as 'one of the priests who had used their pious assiduity and earnest endeavours to keep the people in thraldom'.

The question, or questions, to be addressed accumulate around the basic query, how did the obscure curate of Boolavogue arrive at the point or decision of revolt in arms, taking a leadership role? What background influences propelled him there? To what extent, if any, did his rigid background training and education influence him? What local and family conditions moulded him? Since he became a Catholic priest, what policies in the church influenced him

– if they influenced him? Finally, what caused him to turn uncharacteristically against his bishop, Dr James Caulfield, and the deliberate denunciations Caulfield reiterated throughout the decade against the United Irishmen and the revolutionary 'French poison'?

In John Murphy's choice of role there occurred a family business upheaval. His brother James, one of five brothers, had been undergoing preliminary studies for the priesthood but withdrew because of ill health. At this time John Murphy was the horseman on the family farm at Tincurry, parish of Ferns, five miles north of Enniscorthy. The family, despite legal and penal restrictions, was comfortable. His father, Thomas, was a bacon curer and this profession, buying, killing, curing and supplying the huge Dublin market, lent fiscal stability. It also provided a more than usual network of social and business contacts in the fairs in Co Wexford and through the carmen transporting bacon to Dublin. The upheaval took place when John Murphy took a decision to take his brother James's place and declared for the priesthood. In every moderately sized farm, of any size between twenty and two hundred acres, the horseman so denominated is the horse breeder, the horse trainer, the ploughman, sower and cultivator. He is, and in most cases has been to the 1950s, the farm work manager. It was a skilled, sophisticated profession, and we know that John Murphy was a superb horseman. We are left with no other detail except that of John Murphy taking leave of his home position to undertake study and training for the priesthood. It was probably during his twenty-sixth year.[2]

The Murphy farmstead at Tincurry on the east bank of the River Slaney is identified today only by the presence of an earthworks called the Raheen, or small rath, denoting long human occupation. No trace of the farmstead remains above ground. John Murphy's father, the bacon curer, was named Thomas. His mother, Johanna, was a Whitty from a farm in Tomgarrow on the west side of the Slaney almost opposite the low hill land of Tincurry. The Murphys had four other sons, Moses, the eldest, Philip, James and Patrick. They had one daughter, Katherine. They actively farmed between thirty and forty acres and very likely paid rent for more.

The soils in the Tincurry area and in north Wexford generally are amongst the best multi-purpose soils in the world, free draining, fertile, easily worked. These soils, referred to by agronomists as 'Clonroche series soils', have a particular facility for growing top quality malting barley. So great was the output and so excellent the quality (which still obtains) that an eighteenth-century writer defined the county as 'the granary of the kingdom'.

Irish, the spoken tongue in the rural areas, declined towards west Wexford by the close of the century but its use in the post-Cromwellian and Williamite plantation period rendered unmistakable the identification of colonists on confiscated lands. The Murphy name had been predominant in this area of north Wexford as far back as records extended, but the Gaelic regime, with its recognised heads, was drastically altered by the Elizabethan Plantations, followed by Cromwell's thorough purge of 'Irish Papists' in the 1650s. The planting of colonists on the farmlands of north Wexford had been so thorough that in the townland of Tincurry the Murphy family were surrounded by ten farming families of English descent, all members of the Church of England, Protestant and reformed.

The Murphys of Tincurry, were they not diligent rent payers, were in a precarious position being tenants at whim. The children attended a hedge school in their parish. The name of the hedge school master was Martin Gunn. Little is known of John Murphy's early life and adolescence anymore than any other of his fellow pupils. He enjoyed one advantage in that he had an aptitude for languages, a facility common in bi-lingual societies. It was recorded that he became the equal of his teacher Martin Gunn at Latin and Greek, a facility which must have been of great benefit during his years in Spain.

In common with most of the old Irish families on the land, the Murphys dealt with the status quo as best they could. Conditions had certainly improved since Thomas and Johanna Murphy's childhood. There were however two annual irritants. The first was the rent due to a landlord for land which had been confiscated in the lifetime of Thomas Murphy's grandfather. The second was the payment of tithes to the minister of the Established Church, the church identified as that of the colonist and English establishment loyalist. These were the normal conditions obtaining, conditions to which the majority in Co Wexford had made adjustment and not without some gratifying success.

The choice of role in life taken by John Murphy introduces us, however, to an ecclesiastical milieu in the diocese of Ferns which, though known to historians and researchers of the period, must appear baffling to readers of today. The boyhood years of John Murphy and the years of his subsequent training for the priesthood were dominated in the diocese of Ferns by one of the most flamboyant figures in the Irish church, a man of whom it was (perilously) said, 'Had he lived in the days of the Confederation (of Kilkenny) he would have been chosen unanimously general of the Northern Army'.[3] The name of this prelate, the Bishop of Ferns, was Nicholas Sweetman.

Sweetman was a member of a powerful eighteenth-century Catholic mercantile family. From a large and very secluded family home at rural Newbawn in South Wexford, they wielded remarkable commercial as well as ecclesiastical power. The loyalty and respect they commanded from their fellow countrymen suffering penal deprivation was extraordinary, while they themselves, using the talent which they could legally exploit, had merchant and shipping bases extending from Placentia in Newfoundland to Cadiz in Spain. Nicholas Sweetman, brilliant and energetic churchman, who was compelled to walk a tightrope of suspect legality and taut discretion all his life, was more than a bishop. He was the undeclared figurehead, inspiration and stabiliser of a native stock still recovering from the humiliations of the previous one hundred years.

Nicholas Sweetman's life spanned most of the century. He was born in the memory of Cromwell's campaign, he ruled the diocese of Ferns from 1744 to 1786, the longest span ever enjoyed by any prelate. Born in the seventeenth century, decisions he took, prelates he consecrated, priests he ordained, were still effective well into the nineteenth century.

Nicholas Sweetman's flock was suffering constant deprivation under the penal system. The Mass Rock, the temporary movable altar in a field, the mud-walled thatched chapel, half hidden, were factors of life, and yet conditions had so improved in Sweetman's day, his years held the promise of better days to come.

The Roman Catholic Church recognised the monarch of England as the rightful monarch of Ireland as well. In the eighteenth century, however, this presented an additional hazard because there were two active monarchs, two royal families, in contention. Following the Williamite Revolution in 1688 which deposed the reigning monarch, James II, the issue, instead of being settled, was compounded, for there were those in England and more especially predominantly Catholic Ireland who in conscience, whether they liked it or not, maintained allegiance to and recognition of the rightful, anointed King, James II and his Stuart Succession. William of Orange was succeeded by Queen Anne in London. In exile the rightful Stuart monarch, James II, was succeeded by his son, the Prince of Wales, who assumed the title of James III. In Ireland's case the problem was rendered more acute when the Williamite succession was consolidated at Queen Anne's death. She was succeeded by the closest related Protestant male heir, the Elector of Hanover, a German who could speak no English, George I.

Meanwhile in Pontifical Rome, James III held court, recognised as rightful King of England, Scotland and Ireland by the Pope and most European Courts, by an uncomfortable number in England and Scotland, the vast majority in Ireland, but most rigidly in fact and conscience by the Roman Catholic bishops and clergy. Political as well as religious persecution was invited.

The king in exile (the 'Old Pretender') James III, held England in a state of paranoid suspense for sixty years. He launched three civil wars with the aim of restoring the House of Stuart. His most famous campaign was commanded in 1745 by the Prince of Wales ('Bonnie Prince Charlie'). This situation had specific effect in Ireland while in Co Wexford it was of active significance for the entire lifetime of Nicholas Sweetman, i.e. until 1786. Although James III's de facto political power declined, he was by no means powerless. He maintained the right to nominate the bishop or archbishop of any See in Ireland. James III nominated the Irish Catholic bishops, which nominations were ratified by the Holy See.[4]

Nicholas Sweetman's predecessor, Dr Ambrose Callaghan, was a Franciscan for whom was procured the preferment of James III before three secular priests.

On the death of Dr Ambrose Callaghan in the Friary, Wexford, Nicholas Sweetman was postulated for bishop by the secular clergy of the diocese. A Franciscan, Fr James Nugent, was, however, ably proposed to James III. Realising the conditions obtaining, it is remarkable to record that, despite the lobby in Rome against him, Nicholas Sweetman was nominated for the See of Ferns by James III on 20 September 1744. His nomination was ratified by the Holy See on 25 January 1745 and faculties bestowed on him on 9 May 1745. That nomination process and the Franciscan sponsorship of an opponent were matters he never forgot.

Nicholas Sweetman was born in 1696 at Newbawn, Co Wexford, an area with which he maintained close contact all his life. After ordination he completed his studies at the college of St Iago, Salamanca, in Spain. He returned and entered with vigour into the duties of the home mission. He was brave to the point of foolishness, a fearless, outspoken and noted Stuart supporter, which he remained until his death in 1786.

His unambiguous support of the Stuart claimants to the throne resulted in a situation of great peril. A priest guilty of inflicting grievous bodily harm on his parish priest was suspended by Bishop Sweetman. The curate, Fr James Doyle, went promptly to Dublin Castle where he laid the mortal charge before the authorities that Bishop Sweetman was engaged in recruiting soldiers for 'The Pretender', James III. Bishop Sweetman was arrested twice on this charge but in his examination in Dublin Castle before the Privy Council so impressed the Viceroy, Lord Chesterfield, with his bearing, learning and urbane manners that he was released. *Walkers Magazine* recorded 'the production of all his papers and correspondence with the court of Rome proved highly honourable to himself and singularly advantageous to the Catholics of Ireland.'

From that crisis onwards strict discipline in the diocese of Ferns, at least amongst the secular clergy, was the rule. Candidates for the priesthood were carefully scrutinised. His liberation by the Viceroy apart, back in Co Wexford his inflexible support of the Stuart monarch, with its emphasis on Roman Catholicism as an antagonistic though low profile factor, was made particularly acute. Implicit in this situation was the unspoken conviction that the Hanoverian King George III was a usurper without moral right to his jurisdiction and certainly no divine right. The further taint of heresy in that monarch and all his supporters was thereby also held, but in Christian and benign forbearance.

This serious situation was the one obtaining in the diocese of Ferns when John Murphy submitted himself to the training programme for the priesthood. The situation would undoubtedly have provoked open turbulence had not the political status quo and confiscations consolidated to such an extent that '... if their public quarrels did not discover them (the Catholic clergy) the Government would wink at them.'

In or around the time John Murphy considered the road toward the priesthood, the Stuart restoration was no longer politically practical. The sting began to leave the penal laws. In 1774 a harmless oath of political allegiance to the Hanoverian monarch in London was drawn up. It was to be regarded as a step toward Catholic emancipation and was drawn up with such cunning that a Roman Catholic could take it without any religious scruple. Catholics, clergy and bishops, took this oath. Bishop Sweetman was urged tirelessly by Bishop John Troy of Ossory, an insistent Hanoverian loyalist, to come to terms with the political realities but Nicholas Sweetman refused with equal vigour and persistence, becoming one of the very few who matched that awesome Dominican prelate.[5]

The man with whom John Murphy commenced his training was one of Bishop Sweetman's special appointments. He was Dr Andrew Cassin, parish priest of Ferns, Vicar General of the diocese. Significantly he was a Jesuit, the first and only member of that Society to serve in such a role in the Diocese of Ferns. The remarkable coincidence of his involvement with John Murphy has been explained in that Bishop Sweetman gave support and sustenance to the Jesuits before and after their suppression by Pope Clement XIV in 1773. It has been pointed out that Pope Clement was a Franciscan, an Order which Nicholas Sweetman regarded with distaste. Whatever of that as speculation, nothing could be more calculated to offer Rome a studied rebuff than the promotion of a Jesuit to a premier position in the diocese ahead of all the secular clergy. His place of appointment itself, Ferns, the old Gaelic capital of Uí Chennselaig and Leinster, gave emphasis to Cassin's authority even though his formidable talents had to be contained in a secluded thatched chapel at Newtown, half a mile outside Ferns with its venerable ecclesiastical remains.

This then was the man responsible for the formation of John Murphy's character, education and discipline as a Roman Catholic priest. It was a most serious responsibility in all cases because priests were ordained only as a result of the considered recommendations of their parish priest and before they completed their studies in theology and philosophy in one of the mainland European colleges. John Murphy's training under Cassin included pastoral work, the rubrics, the broad issues confronting a candidate for the priesthood, along with consideration of the political issues obtaining. However the influences impinged upon John Murphy there is no doubt but that the ecclesiastical conditions of his life were managed by two of the most dominant, independent and fearless intellectuals of that century in Co Wexford. In fact Bishop Sweetman gave a delicious pen picture of Dr Cassin in an earlier parish visitation report:

> 'July 23rd. At Newbawn with Rev Laurence Doyle where Rev Andrew Cassin gave a sermon above ye capacitie of ye auditory tho' intelligible exhortations are much wanting there as Rev Mr Doyle never gives any.'

John Murphy was ordained priest by Bishop Nicholas Sweetman in June 1780 behind closed doors in his chambers at High Street, Wexford. All the minor and major orders were conferred throughout that week on the candidates present who had lodged in premises all over the town.[6] At the approach of Autumn 1780 Fr John Murphy was sent by Bishop Sweetman to the Dominican College of St Thomas Aquinas in Seville in Southern Spain for five years to undertake his studies in theology and philosophy. The contrast between Seville and the Irish rural parish of Ferns must have made an impression bordering on shock upon John Murphy. Visitors to Seville from rural Ireland, even today, can repeat the impression. Seville demonstrated a Roman Catholic Church overwhelmingly triumphant in 1780, not merely in atmosphere, dogma, learning, and dispute and public displays such as the famed Passiontide processions, but in its massive cathedral and churches filled with gold, silver and precious stone alongside religious artefacts from massive to small proportions. The single creation which inspired most awe was the cathedral, one of the wonders of Christendom. Its decorations, madonnas, saints and tabernacles were without remote precedent in Ireland. The high altar and its reredos was constructed of a mass of solid silver. In an interior of blazing candles the tabernacle was more than twelve feet high and was supported by forty eight columns. These visual extravagances were trifling when compared with the gold and precious stones which had been deposited in the cathedral and churches all over Seville by zealous Catholics when the riches of the Americas flowed into this great city.

The baking climate was such that John Murphy saw an abundant Irish commodity, water, being sold for such a price that the vendors lived well for the winter on the proceeds. He was not without Irish faces and contacts. His cousin, Edward Murphy, married to Josepha Langton from Kilkenny, was a prosperous wine merchant in Cadiz where Bishop Sweetman's brother Patrick's business also thrived. Many of the Irish exiles in Seville and Cadiz, down river, were merchants who had brought Irish people over to work with them.

John Murphy's lodgings in Seville consisted of a residential house for 'worthy priests, poor and infirm', an indication of the meagre resources which sustained his education. His scholastic superior was the Dominican Don Francisco Aquilar y Ribon, a man of major significance in church and Seville university life for almost half a century. An enthusiastic reformer, he is still noted as one of the most accomplished alumni of Seville University.[7] The characteristic of determination in John Murphy became evident as two references to Bishop Sweetman suggest:

'... Reverend John Murphy from the diocese of Ferns did earnestly and diligently and without noticeable interruption attend the philosophy lectures of Melchior Cano for a period of three full years in our public schools.'

'... he did reside and accept maintenance in this house piously attending the spiritual exercises and showing good example and obedience. From here he attended with permission the philosophical and theological studies at the major college of St Thomas Aquinas of the Order of Preachers. In virtue of this we adjudge the said Reverend John Murphy to be fit and worthy to return to his own country so that he may assume his sacred mission and his spiritual duties.'

John Murphy's academic accomplishments were modest. Nevertheless the ecclesiastical and dogmatic disputes between, for example, the Franciscan and Dominican Orders, ranging from the Immaculate Conception tradition to matters trivial, were well suited to perplex a student in whose home country Masses were in some places still celebrated on a movable altar in open fields.

An event which horrified Seville in 1782 and undoubtedly every overseas church student including John Murphy, was the sentencing by the Inquisition and the burning at the stake of a mentally disturbed semi-religious, a BEATA. She was charged with corrupting her confessor and followed by '... corrupting the priesthood and either from passion or from vanity extended daily over the servants of the altar the dominion of her charms. (She) ... foolishly imagined she was acting under divine authority. She pretended to have seen an angel. This being a crime within the cognisance of the Inquisitors she was brought to trial and burnt.'[8]

Strict orthodoxy prevailed in the Spanish Dominicans' teaching of theology and philosophy. Passive obedience was the theological fashion at the time of John Murphy's residence and, like all students for the priesthood in France or Spain, John Murphy was indoctrinated in 'the Divine Right of Kings'. One aim was clear. The Dominicans in Seville did not intend to train or export radicals.

The service of 'the Sacred Mission' in whatever country or political climate was the target of their zeal.

BACK TO COUNTY WEXFORD

Fr John Murphy returned to Co Wexford in the summer of 1785. Bishop Nicholas Sweetman still controlled church affairs with an alert mind which belied his ninetieth year. He had a coadjutor bishop, parish priest of New Ross, an alumnus of the Dominican University in Seville, Dr James Caulfield. Bishop Sweetman appointed Fr John Murphy to the curacy of Boolavogue convenient to his family members and convenient to his mentor, Dr Andrew Cassin SJ in Ferns. Sweetman though, urged by Bishop Thomas Troy OP of Ossory to see the futility of supporting the Stuart claimant in Rome, 'Charles III', still resolutely persisted and could not be persuaded to join the moving flow of adherents, clerical and lay, to the Hannoverian monarchy in London, George III. Throughout John Murphy's first year of pastoral work in Boolavogue the situation was still simple if abrasive. Protestants supported the Hannoverian Protestant monarch in London. Catholics, through their bishop, recognised the rival monarchy in Rome.

John Murphy was established as a good pastoral priest, noted in help to parishioners in trouble where he employed his earlier skills in farm management. He was an experienced horseman and huntsman, a lover of sport excelling in the game of handball. His travels and education saw him welcomed, as the continentally trained priests were, to the houses of the influential, whether Cromwellian, Williamite or old Irish. The people in his curacy were of mixed loyalties, Catholic and Protestant, of planter descent and old Irish. Things had changed but little. However, as 1786 progressed changes took place which were abrupt and unsettling in a radical course alteration.

John Murphy's bishop, Nicholas Sweetman, and John Murphy's mentor, the Jesuit Dr Andrew Cassin, both died in 1786. With Nicholas Sweetman's death there followed revolution in Catholic Church policy in the diocese of Ferns.

The new Bishop, Dr James Caulfield, succinctly defined the change:

'Loyalty and fidelity to our gracious good King George the
Third (not to the Pope in Temporals), submission to his
Majesty's government and to the constituted authorities; obedience and observance of the laws, were considered and established as far as such meetings could establish, to be of religious,
conscientious, indispensable duty to every Catholic.'[9]

These instructions and orders were given, as Bishop Caulfield
recorded, to the pastors and clergy accordingly. In Fr John Murphy's
case they were issued and reiterated unceasingly at the monthly conferences for the Catholic clergy of the Enniscorthy deanery. The
conferences were held in the inn at Enniscorthy Bridge belonging to
John Rudd, a Protestant, a loyalist and later a yeoman, throughout
the 'fair weather months'. The notices convening the conferences
were printed by a Protestant printer. Bishop and clergy dined in the
inn. They met at 11 am, dined at 2 pm and all left for home at 5 pm.
The Seville and Dominican background in both the new bishop and
John Murphy's careers must have established an early bond. In the
later maelstrom, Bishop Caulfield had great difficulty in believing
badly about his curate in Boolavogue. But the clarity and direction
of Bishop Caulfield's strict instructions created immediate antagonisms and the first to bear the brunt of the antagonisms were the
priests themselves, especially when they were on the traditional
Sunday meal visit to their families. The priests' families were Co
Wexford based and in most cases were Wexford based for centuries.
Broadly speaking they were respected, they were rural mostly and a
great many were from the dispossessed and evicted families of the
previous one hundred years.[10]

Whatever about humouring a delicate bishop, as Caulfield was,
in the matter of royal loyalties, it was quite another matter indeed
when the same prelate advocated recognition of the legal rectitude
of the Cromwellian and Williamite confiscations. A modest price,
it was argued, for civil liberties. To the families of proud background who had endured humiliation as well as dispossession
Bishop Caulfield's urgings bred contempt. By contrast with his
greatly admired predecessor, Sweetman, he was regarded with hostility. In John Murphy's own family the ultimate verdict on

Caulfield's writ was provided in the 1790s when two of his brothers, Mogue and Patrick, along with his first cousin James Whitty, became United Irishmen. Fr John Murphy, however, remained loyal to Bishop Caulfield and followed his instructions with determination down to Easter of 1798 which took place toward the end of April.

The personal characteristics of Fr John Murphy were well identified. He was a well-built man of medium height, well fleshed, light complexioned with a high forehead and receding hair over regular features. His amiable manner made him popular but he was not an easy going curate. He was 'terribly active'. The adjective 'terrible' is repeated in an observation made by a 1798 veteran. 'He was terrible when opposed.' Again, 'He was a right sort of a man, but could be hot.' He gave his considered opinion freely but his inflexibility was also observed. His education and travel gave him entry to many houses including that of Lord Mountnorris of Camolin Park where his conversation was found admirable, 'even by Cromwellian and Williamite'.

Mountnorris's practice of entertaining Fr John Murphy and other mainland European trained Catholic priests was regarded as foolhardy by the extremists of his class, but Mountnorris, like a growing number of the ascendancy party, was a liberal who courted Catholic support. The Boolavogue curate was also in touch with the old Irish Catholic families who maintained the substance of county gentry, the Hay family of Ballinkeele and the Fitzgeralds of Newpark. These contacts, and his popularity amongst his own parishioners and family connections, afforded him comprehensive information throughout his twelve years of residence in Boolavogue.

The American War of Independence was well reported while the return of one of Washington's veterans, Jeremiah Kavanagh, to prominence in Wexford complemented local perceptions. It was the French Revolution, however, in its unprecedented magnitude and violence which caused continual effect in Co Wexford. The news of its aims and expansion percolated rapidly throughout Wexford because of the many mercantile, shipping and smuggling connections. Moreover, a member of an influential Co Wexford landlord family, Colclough of Tintern Abbey, was in Paris for the outbreak while an exiled Ferns bootmaker, Kavanagh, was engaged in active provocation at the attack on the Bastille.

The shock sustained by churchmen in the expansion of the French Revolution cannot be overemphasised. The foundation and then the spread of the United Irish Society into every corner of Co Wexford, following the first branch inauguration in Gorey in November 1792, created great unease amongst the Catholic and Established Church leaders. It was not merely the spectre of French Revolution excesses which inspired disquiet, it was the remarkable mix of Protestants and Catholics together in the early Co Wexford United Irish ranks, all committed to reform of parliament and the ideals of liberty, equality, fraternity. These were the 'levelling principles' which Bishop Caulfield found repugnant as well as sinister.

The earliest members of the United Irish Society in Co Wexford included Protestants like Beauchamp Bagenal Harvey of Bargy Castle, his brother James, William Hatton of Clonard House, Samuel Cooper, John Grogan of Healthfield, Anthony Perry of Inch, George Sparks, Blackwater, Capt Matthew Keugh, Wexford, a former British army officer, Henry Hughes of Ballytrent, Robert Graham of Inch and John Boxwell of Sarshill. The old Irish Catholic families were represented by their younger and very impatient members, John Hay, a former French army officer, and his brother Edward of Ballinkeele, Nicholas Murphy of Monaseed, Edward Fitzgerald of Newpark, Edward Roche of Garrylough, Nicholas Sweetman, a nephew of Bishop Sweetman, Esmond Kyan of Mount Howard and James Edward Devereaux of Carrigmannon.

This fusion of the prominent, who preferred the common identity of Irishmen to the bitter sectarianism clearly observed in the general elections of 1791 (and 1797) in Co Wexford, was nevertheless viewed with grave suspicion by Bishop Caulfield. The Society of the United Irishmen, he noted, had sinister flavours, French revolutionary, Free Masonic and Protestant. The United Irishmen's oaths were noted by him 'as they ought to be', and emphasised as unlawful, perjurious and wicked. There was not the slightest room for leniency. 'I tell you,' Caulfield declared, 'that every action, every attempt to conspire or join with the United Irishmen or any agreement or consent to any measure which tends towards turbulence, to disturbing the public peace and good order or opposing the King's Government and legislation must be marked with detestation and reprobation.' Such activities, he declared, 'are contrary to the doctrine of Jesus Christ and his Apostles and to all social and good order, loyalty and fidelity to our gracious good King George the Third'.

Convenient though Bishop Caulfield's interpretation of Christ's doctrine was, it must be argued in his defence that he was motivated by concern for his flock's immortal souls and the continued freedom of his church recently emerged from penal severity, a church not yet fully emancipated in law.

Fr John Murphy was under direct orders from his bishop to make clear that submission to his Majesty's government was the indispensable duty of every Roman Catholic. In common with all the parish priests of the diocese, this policy was reiterated in Boolavogue chapel. It had little effect. The independent self-confidence bred by the old Bishop Sweetman survived amongst 'the faithful' all over Co Wexford particularly amongst the young. In no place were the bishop's ceaseless instructions ignored more blatantly than in Boolavogue. It was a district well politicised and in the final analysis unrepentantly United Irish.

If one's companions are a judge of character John Murphy may be said to have at least lived dangerously. His daily breakfast companion was Thomas (Tom) Donovan on whose rented land Boolavogue chapel was situated. Tom Donovan's wife and son, Jerry, the latter lame since birth, were outspoken critics of the government and the Established Church. Tom Donovan knew a lot and feared nothing. In a previous generation the Donovans had forsaken their own culture and become members of the English speaking Established Church. Tom Donovan reverted to the Roman Catholic Church. His first cousins, the Donovans of Tobergal, remained in the Established Church and between the two branches of the same old Irish family there prospered an awful antagonism to which Tom Donovan contributed lustily. Fr John Murphy had his breakfast each day of his sojourn in Boolavogue in the nearby Tom Donovan's, after daily Mass. They were in effect his sacristans. Because of that the Donovans had the ear of the priest, a factor of certain significance.

John Murphy's other sporting companion was a priest in ecclesiastical disgrace, Fr Mogue Kearns, of whom Bishop Caulfield was to note in his obituary dismissal as follows: 'Rev Mogue Kearns of the Duffry had been employed by Dr Delaney (Bishop of Kildare and Leighlin) for some time but latterly dismissed. He was notorious for drinking and fighting and joined the rebels among whom he made a gigantic figure and was hanged at Edenderry.' Kearns had been sacked by Bishop Delaney for his zeal in political agitation. Both John Murphy and Mogue Kearns were enthusiastic huntsmen and spent many weekends together after game in the Blackstairs Mountain range on the Wexford and Carlow side, a home terrain which Mogue Kearns knew intimately and which John Murphy quickly learned.

While England and France were once more at war, the United Irishmen veered sharply toward armed revolt. John Murphy's frail but agitated bishop was possessed of such complete detail of every situation in his diocese whether political, personal or of church provenance, that its sum even today commands respect. Nothing escaped him. He knew in fine detail of the escalation of the United Irish movement along with the spread in his diocese of the 'French poison'. His admonitions, read today, have a shrill ring to them, though that may well have been due to the terror of the time. John Murphy continued to follow Bishop Caulfield's instructions and repeated them unremittingly in Boolavogue chapel. Despite that, political agitation by United Irish agents found ready acceptance all around him and it was not merely the young who became embroiled in the oath-bound organisation. His closest adjacent friend, Tom Donovan, became the leading figure in the movement along with his wife's brother, Patrick Roche. Both men owned and concealed guns.

In the development of what has been described as 'the Boolavogue cocktail' it would seem that the unobtrusive schemer was the senior United Irish officer, Tom Donovan. It was Tom

Donovan who orchestrated events, gathered what intelligence was available and it becomes somewhat pitiful to note Fr John Murphy's insistence on his church's alarmed instructions while his parishioners were seeping away in an opposite direction. The developing situation seems to have been one allowed by Tom Donovan to develop without disturbing the conscience or program of the priest. There can be little doubt, however, that Tom Donovan was influencing the priest, if his constant rages against his Protestant cousin John Donovan is any yardstick by which he may be measured.

John Murphy persisted with Caulfield's policy throughout the catastrophic fall in malting barley prices and bankruptcies of 1797.[11] That grain price collapse was a most effective United Irish recruiting agent, when the spring 1797 price of 26 shillings a barrel fell to 6 and 5 shillings at harvest. Martial law was about to be proclaimed since the county was on the brink of revolt by November of 1797. To add to the alarm, Napoleon Bonaparte was appointed General Officer commanding the French armies being assembled on the Atlantic coast. At the bishop's insistence and Lord Mountnorris's collaboration, an oath of loyalty to King George III and the constitution was submitted to north Wexford's Catholic parishes.

This oath was taken under protest in Boolavogue chapel where Lord Mountnorris himself presented the words. There were angry exchanges unlike the seeming docility met with in other chapels. The refusal to sign at first brought a furious outburst from Mountnorris, who threatened to quarter the military in their countryside so that 'they would demean themselves as peaceable subjects through fear if they would not now take the oath for love'. United Irish recruitment proceeded at a pace most satisfactory. 'Incendiaries were sent down from Dublin to fan the disaffection. A visible change took place in the temper and manner of the lower classes'.[12] This episode in Boolavogue chapel may have been the one for which Fr John Murphy was reprimanded and finally threatened by Bishop Caulfield. If so, it had the effect of tightening him even more into church discipline. The fears of the Catholic Church at that precise time approached crescendo. Rome was declared a free republic on February the tenth when the French army entered. The cardinals were arrested and the Pope was expelled. All the churches were plundered. At the approach of Easter, Monsignor Erskine, the Papal Envoy in London, wrote to Thomas Troy OP, now Archbishop of Dublin and Primate of Ireland.

'The "Pastor" is stricken, the flock is scattered. I hope the Irish bishops are recalling the Irish people to a sense of duty and devotion so that they may be recalled from that precipice into which I hear with horror they are plunging themselves. It is dreadful to think that Irish Catholics who suffered so much for so long for religion should now think of joining with the enemies of religion at the behest of a few intent on their own views and slaves of their own passions. If the Pope knew it would add to his afflictions.'[13]

At Eastertide Fr John Murphy refused the sacraments to all United Irishmen who refused to abjure their oaths and business.[14]

On Easter Monday, Fr John Murphy, in an urgent manoeuvre to avert martial law, succeeded in getting the signatures of seven hundred and fifty-four of his parishioners to an address of loyalty to the Lord Lieutenant, the Earl of Camden. This remarkable total is in sharp contrast to the 154 signatures in Castlebridge chapel and indicates a damage limitation exercise at all cost in the United Irish organised stronghold of Boolavogue.

From that day to the outbreak of hostilities the involvement of Fr John Murphy assumes a quality of inevitability. Intimate parochial antagonisms beyond his control played a decisive role. Tom Donovan's Protestant first cousin, John Donovan, had married a younger Catholic girl, a parishioner of Fr John Murphy's. They had four children. John Donovan made a pathetic figure. He was an alcoholic. He became a loyalist member of the Camolin Yeoman Cavalry and thereby a target of contempt amongst his neighbours while his ascendancy 'betters' must have barely tolerated him.

John Donovan employed a young yardman, a Catholic and a United Irishman named Boyne. Because of John Donovan's alcoholism, Boyne became an indispensable support to his wife and children. John Donovan was possessed of a deep-rooted hatred of

Boyne stimulated no doubt by ravages of his illness. This family misery, exploited in a village hostelry situation, as frequently occurred in Redmond's of The Harrow, created numerous opportunities for old Irish neighbours to vent their fury at John Donovan.

In the week before the outbreak of revolt, Fr John Murphy became embroiled by association when his own helper at his lodgings, in Donoghue's of Tomnaboley near Boolavogue, shot a Protestant neighbour, Clement Goff. He claimed that Goff was stealing the cows but the most significant item in that tragedy was that the priest's man was able to lay hands on a concealed gun. The killing of the respected Goff would have had severe repercussions were the following days' events not to overwhelm it.

As a policy of widespread brutalisation by a well-informed and rightly fearful government continued, the fever of war, of hatred, revenge and opportunity combined with fear to grip an entire population. In this culture the final strands to restraint were broken. John Donovan, the Yeoman, had been drinking heavily all week and uttering threats of well-recognised violence to neighbours. Eventually, in Redmond's of The Harrow on Thursday evening, 24 May, when drinking amongst neighbours, he was baited. As the temperature rose he was offered 'terrible' insult. He became hysterical. He threatened, as a Yeoman, three men from Ballyorley with pitch caps but, on his abrupt leaving, he swore that the following night there would be 'more blood spilled than in Cromwell's war'. Those were significant words in any part of Co Wexford. He next descended on his next door neighbour, James Gahan, accusing him of United Irish membership and promising to return to pitch cap him. All developments were reported to Fr John Murphy and Tom Donovan. Tom Donovan saw to it that the forty-five-year-old curate was well informed. On receipt of the reports which included information from an ascendancy source, Buckys of Rockspring, Fr John Murphy was recorded as saying, 'It is their turn tonight. It may be our turn tomorrow night.' It was the first public hint of a change in his thought process. Conditions worsened on the following days. The executions of well-known men suspected of United Irish membership in Carnew (28) and Dunlavin (34) created near panic. Whether John Murphy was aware of the arrests of the United Irish leaders in Dublin and the betrayal under torture of the United leadership in Co Wexford or not, he carried on with one last gesture of amelioration or, as some would have it, deception. He persuaded those of his parishioners he deemed in need of safe-conduct permits to surrender their weapons in Ferns on Saturday morning 26 May. Whatever about the quality of those weapons (there are conflicting accounts), they were surrendered to two mag-istrates, Captain Isaac Cornock, a liberal whom Fr Murphy knew and trusted and Reverend Francis Turner.

Having surrendered their weapons, the Boolavogue contingent were abused and herded out of Ferns toward Boolavogue by a unit of the North Cork Militia and the Ferns Yeomanry, referred to at this time as 'The Black Mob'. In their precipitate flight they were fired on at will. It was this spectacle of retreat that Fr John Murphy witnessed as he rode across to meet those he had sent to Ferns. He met the rout at Coolatore and apparently put a halt to it. However, when called upon for his opinion, his recorded words demonstrate a drastic reversal of his previous outspoken position.

'I know they have me marked out. Look to the inhuman slaughter in Carnew and if the report of the butchery in Dunlavin is true it is worse. Our jails are full of the best of our people and it may be our lot to be in company with them before tomorrow night.' He then admitted that it would be better to die like men defending themselves than to fall with folded arms under their enemies' swords. The process was almost complete. It was completed be-yond redemption that night near The Harrow when the focus on Boyne brought the Camolin Yeoman Cavalry and a badly armed Boolavogue vigilante group headed by Tom Donovan and Fr John Murphy into abrupt conflict at dusk. Tom Donovan shot his Protestant Yeoman cousin, John Donovan, dead and the ascendancy extremist, Lieutenant Thomas Boocky of Rockspring, was piked to death.

The subsequent military career of Fr John Murphy is well docu-mented. Whatever may be said of it, it must be conceded that it was a remarkable one for a man untrained in war strategies or leadership of large bodies of fighting men. As a priest in good standing he would have known that by taking the role that he did he would have effectively suspended himself. Nonetheless, the evidence is that he acted in good conscience and said Mass in the camps daily. In one recorded incident he gave the last rites to a dying villager at Rahanna, Co Carlow, while engaged in a rapid march. He said his last Mass in Jordan's of Coolnasneachta, Co Carlow, on or about July first, 1798.

His suffering and harsh end on 2 July, 1798 following a court-martial in Tullow, gave evidence of a stoicism rarely met in those whose execution is inevitable. Nevertheless it was surpassed by his aide, James Gallagher of Tomahurra, Co Wexford, on the same occasion. The military had not succeeded in identifying John Murphy as the then notorious rebel commander he had become. They identified him as a Catholic priest because they found a stole and a phial for blessed oils in his coat. The two fugitives were handed over for interrogation before execution, the details of which are horrifying indeed. In the prolonged questioning, firstly of James Gallagher, neither man betrayed the other or betrayed their United Irish comrades, plans or situation. Their final hanging came as a mercy.

AFTERMATH

There does remain one final area of query, and that lies in the relationship between Bishop Caulfield and the curate of Boolavogue. The letters which suggest a relationship different from that employed with the other priests in open revolt, are those written to Archbishop Thomas Troy of Dublin from the Bishop of Ferns, James Caulfield. In the aftermath of the insurrection, there was initiated stern ecclesiastical enquiry. The extent of the insurrection in Ireland, particularly in predominantly Catholic Wexford, was regarded with dismay in the upper Roman Catholic Church echelons. The exaggerated reports that a Catholic priest was one of the leaders of the insurrection, indeed the cause of it, and its chief general, led to enquiry from astounded Papal representatives. The news of murders of loyalists, priests' open involvement, massacres and burnings was well circulated. Caulfield denounced the clergy involved as 'renegade, abandoned, reprobate priests'. On 29 July 1798 Monsignor Erskine, the Papal Envoy in London, wrote to Archbishop Troy. He demanded to know who started, who prompted and who instigated the rebellion – *and their religion*. Troy pounced on Bishop Caulfield. The inquisition was conducted by mail, sometimes sent on vessels plying between Wexford and Dublin. Troy's letters do not survive but the replies, in Caulfield's painstaking hand, indicate a prelate reeling on the defensive. The interesting aspect of Caulfield's replies are, however, his efforts to shield the memory of the prominent priest and rebel leader from his own diocese, Fr John Murphy. It was public knowledge in Co Wexford and in government circles in June of 1798 that at least half a dozen priests of Dr Caulfield's diocese, and one Carmelite friar, were involved to a great or less degree in the hostilities, just as there was a number of Anglican clergymen active participants on the government side. Nevertheless, Dr Caulfield in detailed replies to Archbishop Troy from the end of June made no mention whatever of John Murphy or any of the priests involved, for a long time. In his first replies to Troy, Bishop Caulfield is at pains to detail every issue except the most notorious of them all. He defends his and the clergy's helplessness in preventing the execution of loyalists on Wexford Bridge for, 'It soon became treason for us all to plead for protection (i.e. for the loyalists) for *they* were all Orangemen and would destroy us all'. He declared to Troy that his conduct and language had graduated him the equal of an Orangeman. 'My house must be "pulled down, or burnt and my head knocked off"'! – this last sentence was boldly pronounced to my face, surrounded as I was in the public square (The Bullring) by four or five thousand pikes, spears and muskets, when I was striving to save Lord Kingsborough's life. There were other priests there too from the county but dared not show themselves or speak for fear of the pikes. I remained till the King's army began to come in ... I sat with Lord Kingsborough and some others at his place of confinement to a bit of salt beef at the fall of night and got a Captain Bourke of the North Corks, a worthy fellow, to escort me home.' Bishop

Caulfield reassured Troy of his own impeccable loyal credentials. 'The Government,' he declared, 'well knew my loyalty.' He described introducing himself to General Gerard Lake and Lake's polite and kind attention to him. An English officer, General Hunter, had called upon him in High Street to confer; but to his clergy in the fray, Bishop Caulfield makes not a remote allusion.

These details and expressions were all very fine but it was not the information which Troy required or which Erskine had demanded. Indeed Troy himself was more than likely taxed trying to explain to the Papal Envoy in London the events of the summer. More letters, more queries were dispatched to James Caulfield. The months of July and August of 1798, with a shoal of letters from Caulfield to Troy, passed. In them all there was evident a resistance to give any explanation, expansion or information concerning John Murphy.

The first letter to give individual details of the diocese of Ferns priests who joined the United Irish ranks is dated 2 September 1798.

'Rev Thomas Dixon of Castlebridge, curate at the Lady's Island for some years, but for drinking, dancing and disorderly conduct was suspended about four years ago … sent as assistant to Rev David Cullen, Blackwater … active in the cursed business of uniting … interdicted and suspended.'

'Rev Thomas Clinch, … appointed curate to Rev Thomas Rogers in Bantry but turning out a most beastly drunkard and unfit for duty … suspended two years ago…'

'Rev Bryan Murphy … another reptile …'

'Rev Philip Roche alias General Roche … had been a proper man and would be useful but indulging in excess of drinking and beginning to agitate became obnoxious…'[15]

Rev Michael Murphy, killed at the Battle of Arklow, is not mentioned at all but Fr John Murphy is given the following pen picture which is benign by comparison with Dr Caulfield's literary lacerations:

'Rev John Murphy, curate to Rev Patrick Cogly of Boolavogue, ever giddy but not noted for immorality, was the first to com-

mence the rebellion and became a signal general in it. He had
been apparently, but not really, dutiful to his superior. He was
whipped, hanged, beheaded, and his body burnt in the County
Carlow at Tullow.'

This particular letter did not satisfy Archbishop Troy. More letters
from his Metropolitan arrived at Dr Caulfield's High Street residence
in Wexford. Repeated questions to the Bishop of Ferns indicate either
confusion or dissatisfaction with the information or evasions supplied to that date. By October Bishop Caulfield was reporting that
reprisal outrages still continued. On November third he had still not
satisfied John Thomas Troy but another shift of attention was created.
James Caulfield blamed the rebels for the continuing church burning
– 'in order to put the blame on the Yeomen'. He reported the burning of the elegant chapel of Caim and added that but for the regular
English military they would all be massacred by the Yeomen. He detailed his dining with generals and officers.

The year 1799 arrived and by February of that year Archbishop
Troy was armed with facts. This time he had John Murphy's name
isolated but, unfortunately for the chess game in which they had
indulged, Troy had his titles and clergy slightly mixed up. It gave
James Caulfield room to manoeuvre again. His reply to Archbishop
Troy on 27 March 1799 is the most remarkable evidence of his defensive agility. 'I never heard,' Bishop Caulfield wrote, 'of Rev John
or Friar Murphy mentioned in yours ... I have made due enquiry
... He cannot be of this county, nor as a clergyman he could not
make any stay, much less officiated, without my knowing, except
he disguised himself ... I wish I may never hear of any of their
cast'.[16]

This letter may have worn James Caulfield's inquisitor out, for
on 10 April the Bishop of Ferns complained anxiously to him that
he, Bishop Caulfield, had received no reply from Troy to three previous letters. A further reply from Caulfield to Troy of 26 April,
1799, while brimful of incident, had nothing of solid fact about the
now notorious priests of his diocese, two of whom had commanded
armies of rebels in the field.

Father Murphy of Bannow was discussed and may have provided

James Caulfield with another delaying tactic. But Thomas Troy was
made of stern stuff and he returned again with persistent vigour. It
is clear that James Caulfield was submitted to a cross examination
which after almost one full year he could no longer resist. In his
reply of 21 May, 1799, one year after the insurrection, James
Caulfield gives his Metropolitan bare details.

'I enclose a list, first such as I thought inexcusable, the others I
think honest and excusable, most of them innocent, even in ap-
pearance as well as in fact; nay, meritorious. They are as follows:
Reprimanded: John Murphy, killed
Ml. Murphy, not empl./suspended
Philip Roche, removed, reprimanded, suspended
Bryan Murphy, suspended
John Cane, an idiot
Fr Byrne, suspended, post rebellion
Nich. Stafford, suspended post rebellion
Mogue Kearne, (Kearns), killed
Thomas Clinch, killed
Edward Sinnott and Thomas Dixon as noted mischief men died
before the rebellion
Honourably Acquitted: Kavanagh, Jn. Redmond, Edw. James
Murphy, James Roche, John Shalloe, James Dixon, Edw.
Redmond
Massacre on Bridge: 45 in all killed. From jail 16. From Market
House 26. From prison ship 3.
Protestants *per se* not the target else they would all have been
wiped out.'

The brevity of this dispatch may have inspired a blast of rage from
Troy. In a reply of 2 June 1799, James Caulfield essays at placation in
words which should have reduced any churchman to benevolence.
Having informed his Metropolitan of an attempt to burn his house
in High Street, the burning of his neighbour's house, his rescue at 1
am by the Midlothian Regiment and the Militia, he concluded with
a verdict upon his superior: 'St Peter's Chair,' wrote James Caulfield,
'would not be an extravagant reward for Your Grace.'

This silenced Troy for a while and James Caulfield was compelled in glowing terms to chide his archbishop again in that he had not replied to two or three of his previous epistles. Caulfield's reports continued and they dealt with matters as disparate as the comparison of straw with slates for church roofing, the gratitude owed by the whole people to the Midlothians, and the anxiety of Edward Hay to visit Troy. Archbishop Troy was not to be put off. The mighty wave that a simple country curate had allegedly put into motion and which could well have, as Sir John Moore wrote, 'finished the country had the French landed', was not a matter to be glossed over. Caulfield acknowledged the now 'famous Boolavogue (chapel)' and 'this acknowledged notoriety' in his reply of 10 September 1799. It was not until 30 September 1799 that he responded to Troy in a manner which indicated that he had more than a suspicion of John Murphy's revolutionary career. In that reply he did not refer to him as Fr Murphy. He referred to him as 'General Murphy'. That, at last, was enough for Troy. It was clear to him that James Caulfield, for whatever reason, had minimised the role of John Murphy for a year and a half in letters padded with less consequential material. Questions Troy hitherto considered evaded were dispatched to the Bishop's House in Wexford. Question number five demanded that the curate of Boolavogue be explained.

On 23 September 1799, Bishop Caulfield responded with brevity. He gave his archbishop information which he could have well supplied in July of 1798.

> 'General Murphy never was formally suspended or disgraced, but often reproached, reprimanded and threatened. He refused sacraments to all United Irishmen who refused to abjure their oaths and business the Easter immediately before the rebellion. Poor, giddy mortal!'

The last phrase of pity was the last written of John Murphy by his bishop. It is succinct. It was written in the knowledge that it could become the property of more eyes than Troy's, and in that light, what little it does convey may be amplified. By comparison with the violent language Caulfield used when describing other curates

involved in the hostilities, his definitions of John Murphy are de-
void of malignance. It is evident that Bishop Caulfield regarded Fr
John Murphy kindly.

APPENDIX

On 13 September 1798, James Caulfield, Bishop of Ferns, issued from his house in High Street, Wexford, a pastoral letter. It was sent to all the clergy of the diocese. Accompanying it were the following instructions:

'Note Well – the letter is to be read distinctly from the Altar and its purport to be enlarged and explained to the Congregation, the Sunday after the receipt of it, and elsewhere, as occasion may offer or require, by all the Pastors and officiating Catholic Clergy of the Diocese of Ferns.'

Wexford,
September 13th, 1798

'Some short time ago a Report was industriously, but most maliciously and wickedly, propagated in this Town, and through this part of the Country, that the Roman Catholics intended an immediate Rising and general Massacre of the Protestants. Time having now given the Lie to that mischievous Story, the Devil and his Imps come forward with the Reverse; telling the Roman Catholics, or insidiously insinuating to them, that there is an Intention existing among the Protestants of putting the Roman Catholics to death. Tis, alas! too well known, that these fabricated Stories have been alternately most sedulously and viciously given out, and believed, or affected to be believed, by many, since or before the Commencement of the late un-natural and shocking Rebellion. And for what purpose or end? Evidently to set the Protestant and Catholic by the Ears in the beginning, and to work upon each, to consider the other as a most dangerous and sanguinary enemy. Now thanks, and thanks, for ever to kind Providence, that unfortunate (and to us disgraceful and scandalous) Rebellion is crushed and extinct: Why still keep up and give out those abominable, diabolical Reports? Why, merely to endeavour to continue the intended Enmity, to create alarm, to cherish distrust, to do away all confidence, and to bar every social, neighbourly, and friendly intercourse between a people, who, by the Law of God and Nature, as well as by their situation, ought to consider and treat each other as Neighbours and Friends. But by whom are these stories fabricated, whispered, and given out? By infernal Agents who, either of themselves or instigated by other poor wretches who wish to keep up an implacable hatred, a vindictive spirit of resentment, to plunge the country into disorder and confusion, to fish in troubled waters themselves, with the hope of gaining something, having nothing to lose. But will any Man in his cool sober senses suffer such a death-dealing viper to bite him, or open his ear to the plausible, fascinating voice of such an Asp, that promises everything and secures nothing but ruin and destruction, sin and shame? No; the man of common sense will shun and avoid him as a most dangerous pest, as I said before; he will consult his own safety and peace; he will, by his industry, procure bread and comfort for himself and his family; as a man and member of society, he will listen to the voice of nature. 'Do as you would be done by'; as a Christian subject, he will listen to the voice, and attend to the example of Jesus Christ; he will give Caesar his due; he will pay due deference and obedience to the Laws and constituted authorities, he will fear God and honour the King, in a word, he will love his neighbour as himself, and owe no man any thing but good will.

The uniting of Irishmen for the late Rebellion was hatched in the dark, it was communicated by private Whispers, it was recommended by specious promises, impressed by flattering prospects, enforced by threats and menaces; denouncing death and destruction on the persons and properties of those who refused to unite and co-operate; and the Union was secured and sanctioned by a solemn oath. The people in general, more credulous than wise or virtuous, swallowed the bait, and joined in the diabolical confederacy, adhering to their perjurious oaths more strictly than to their baptismal Vows, or the most sacred ties of conscience, religion, and the express word of God. In vain did their Pastors repeatedly explain to them the sinfulness of their conduct, and the perjury and nullity of their Oaths, which were only Bonds of Iniquity, their object being unlawful and wicked; that it is exceedingly sinful to take the Oath, but infinitely more so to observe or fulfil it. But the Bishop, the Priest, the Preacher, would not be attended to, but become obnoxious, threatened and endangered for explaining their Duty to them in the discharge of his own.

And how will the infatuated, the deluded, or the designing men of that confederacy account now for their Oaths? How many of them are now observed? Very few. They have been generally broken, and so they ought: they have been renounced and abjured by a solemn Oath of Allegiance to the King, (the best of Kings) and his Government; which is a laudable, lawful Oath, a conscientious religious bond, which cannot be broken or violated without incurring the guilt of mortal sin, the forfeiture of their title in heaven and their very existence here. But it is a most lamentable circumstance to consider the disrepute and discredit into which they have brought Oaths, the most sacred pledge that can bind Man to Man, or to his God, by their prevarications, swearing backwards and forwards as occasion or their caprice led them. What degree of credit can they expect to be given to their Oath in a Court of Justice, or in any case to be decided by an Oath? How will the authors of the Oaths, or those who tendered them, answer to God, or to man, for the multitude of evils and injuries done to the country by their means and destructive agency? How will they answer to God or the world for the numbers of widows and orphans, or for the number of families left without a cow to give them a sup of milk or a horse to till their little holding; without means of paying rent or debt; in a word, without fuel, food, or raiment? And all this accumulation of misfortunes brought on the country by the machinations of crazy, ambitious, revolutionary adventurers, through the credulity of the incautious and ignorant multitude. What of plunder and robberies, of cursing, swearing and blaspheming, of lives lost in battle, and above all, of Massacres, of murders in cold blood? Oh! how horrible to the recollection! but how flagitious, how atrocious must be the commission of sins crying to heaven for vengeance? They must have tarnished and blacked the Catholic name, and the credit of its ministers. And let me ask who have they served by this great measure! I apprehend, nobody. Who have they injured? Many thousands, in manifold ways. Oh! what cogent cause, what imperious indispensable necessity for a long and lasting repentance, for a most pungent sorrow and sincere contrition! May God of His infinite mercy grant them that Grace, with a real conversion of Heart, and an amendment of their mortal lives.

They have injured their Protestant neighbours, it is too true, and must expect that they naturally feel and resent it; but they are not to imagine or apprehend that there exists in the Protestants any intention to massacre them; nor are they to believe any officious insidious, or ill-designing wretches, who came to them with such malignant stories; they should drive them away as enemies to the peace and tranquillity of the country, and to the desirable return of confidence, good neighbourhood, and social order of it. Our most gracious sovereign has stretched out his strong arm to crush and chastise them for their Rebellion: but he has also extended the other lenient Hand with Mercy and Pardon of all their political crimes, on their repentance, and return to their duty and allegiance, the people who rely on it, that his Commanders and Officers here, actuated with the same Spirit of Humanity, will take care to see that Protection has its due effect.

Let them, then, continue peaceably and orderly their honest industrious pursuits, and they will have nothing to apprehend from their Protestant neighbours, or from his Majesty's Government, but safety and protection. They have got a strong and severe lesson; but with a mitigation which they did not expect or deserve. The Mercy of God, and the clemency of their Prince, have spared them, and saved their existence and property too, as far as the ravages of the unnatural war would allow. They should now, with Hearts overflowing with the most lively gratitude and sincere thanksgiving, return to their lawful occupations, and by their industry and diligence, endeavour to repair the losses they have sustained by their folly and madness.

You are to call on them in the name of Almighty God, the lawful Judge of Heaven and Earth, who will reward and punish them according to their deserts or demerits; you are to conjure them by the Passion of Jesus Christ, and the Bowels of his Mercy, to return seriously and sincerely to their duty; to set aside all strife, contention, sedition and turbulence; to refrain from all cursing, swearing, Oaths, except in truth, in justice, and in judgement; to avoid detraction, calumny, and lies, to obey their rulers, not so much from necessity, as for conscience sake (for it is impossible for them to be good Christians, if they are not good subjects); with meekness and humility to submit themselves to the Laws of God, and of his holy church, to enter speedily on a due Course of Penance, and to endeavour, by all means in their power, to repair all the injuries they have done, and to atone for all their transgressions against God and their neighbour; and with true compunction of Heart beseech the God of Mercy to grant them a full pardon of their sins, the grace of a perfect reconciliation and perseverance in the Love and Fear of the Lord, in piety and good works to the end of their lives. That the Lord may vouchsafe to grant them these graces, and every desirable Blessing, is the fervent and daily prayer of,
Your faithful and humble Servant in Christ,
James Caulfield.

Notes:
1   *Memoirs*, Paris, 1863 vol. 1, pp. 53-59
2   Furlong, N., *Fr John Murphy of Boolavogue 1753-1798*, Second Edition, Dublin 1997.
3   Renehan, *Collections on Irish Church History*, vol. 2, Dublin, 1873.
4   Fenning, Hugh, 'Some Problems of the Irish Mission 1733-74 in *Collectanea Hibernica*, No. 8, Benignus Millet (ed), Dublin 1965.
5   Furlong, 'The Times and Life of Nicholas Sweetman, Bishop of Ferns 1744-1786', *Journal of the Wexford Historical Society*, No. 9, 1983-84, Brendan Culleton (ed).
6   Letters of John Kavanagh, Archives Passionist Fathers, Mount Argus, Dublin.
7   Ribon Mss., Library, University of Seville. *Catholic Encyclopaedia*, New York 1913.

8 Townsend, Joseph, *A Journey Through Spain,* London 1791. Don
  Leucadio Doblado, *Letters from Spain,* London 1822.
9 Caulfield, Reply, Dublin, 1801. Veritas, Dublin 1798.
10 List of RC Ferns Clergy of 1798, in 'The Catholic Priest in the 1798
  Rebellion', Kevin Whelan, *Wexford History and Society,* K. Whelan, (ed), p.
  314.
11 Powell,T., in *Studia Hibernica* XVI (1976) pp. 144-70.
12 Hancock, T., Rev., Rector of Kilcormack, Mss. N.L.L mic. 1,044.
13 Letters to Archbishop Troy from Luke Concannon 24 Feb. 1798 and Mons.
  Charles Erskine, 16 April 1798. Dublin Archdiocesan Archives.
14 Letter, Caulfield to Troy, 23 September 1799, Dublin Archdiocesan Archives.
15 This man of exceptional qualities has not yet received the attention which is
  his due. See Dickson, *The Wexford Rising in 1798,* pp. 192-4, Tralee, 1955, and
  de Val, 'Priests of '98', in *The Past,* No. 20, 1997, pp. 12-25 *et al.*
16 Caulfield to Troy, 27 March 1799, I.S.P.O.

Church of Ireland Clergy and the 1798 Rising

Patrick Comerford

INTRODUCTION

When the former Bishop of Cashel and Ossory, the Right Rev Noel Willoughby, was being conferred with the Freedom of Wexford in St Iberius' Church in January 1997, he recalled the prominent role played in the 1798 rising by members of the Church of Ireland, including: Matthew Keugh, Beauchamp Bagenal Harvey and Cornelius Grogan, who were executed on Wexford Bridge in June 1798, as well as Anthony Perry, John Boxwell, William Hughes, William Hatton and George Sparks .[1]

The 1798 rising is still fresh in the memories of many Wexford families. My grandfather could recall the stories handed down from his grandfather, Edmund Comerford; as a boy, according to my late aunts, he had witnessed the massacre of the men of Bunclody in John Street, Wexford in 1793; five years later, he saw the executions on Wexford Bridge; and family lore says he barely escaped with his life near Bunclody.

However, myth and memory can be selective. My family folklore failed to pass on to me the memory of James Comerford, one of the four Protestant yeomen killed in Kyle Glebe after the Rev Robert Burrowes was murdered there prior to the Battle of Oulart Hill on 27 May, 1798. And yet, the names James and Robert, along with Edmund, were handed on with pride to the children of successive generations in our family.[2]

Myth and folklore are the memories that form present perceptions and prejudices. It is a common myth that because members of the Church of Ireland were prominent in the leadership of the United Irishmen in Co Wexford, the rising had a different flavour in the south-east than that given to it by Presbyterians in the north-east. On the other hand, some still argue that members of the Church of Ireland would have been too closely identified with the establishment to be considered potential supporters of the rising, or even as neutrals, as was the case with Quakers.[3]

But not all inherited myths about 1798 help members of the Church of Ireland today to recall the rising as a struggle for democracy and human rights. Many have inherited memories of the massacre of Protestants in the Scullabogue Barn on 5 June, 1798;[4] some still claim Father John Murphy reneged on his undertaking and allowed Robert Burrowes to be piked to death in Kyle;[5] others talk of the vandalism with which Bishop Euseby Cleaver's library was plundered in Ferns.

In the years immediately after 1798, the Church of Ireland contribution to the rising was quickly forgotten in the loyalist triumph, and in New Ross and Enniscorthy liberty trees were burned in loyalist parades for years. Those who wrote their own accounts influenced how many members of the church would recall the rising in later years. Musgrave laboured the assertion that the real aim of the revolt was to exterminate Protestants;[6] and George Cruickshank's illustrations added racism to Maxwell's sectarian interpretations. Those sectarian assertions were strengthened by the reinterpretation of 1798 by Patrick Kavanagh's 1870 history, and the very Catholic emphasis of the 1898, 1938 and 1948 commemorations .[7]

There is a real danger of one-sided, sectarian interpretations of the rising once again: in Belfast, the negative myths are being recycled by, for example, a new edition of George Ogle's sectarian, Orange account of the rising, complete with Cruickshank's cartoons.[8] In the prevailing political climate in the first half of the last century, the recollections of Orangemen and loyalists such as Hunter Gowan and Hawtrey White were heard, while the contribution of Protestants like Harvey, Boxwell and Hatton were forgotten, and not only by Wexford Protestants.

The consequences of these past interpretations, in denominational terms, have been two-fold. Firstly, the commemoration of 1798 was often left to those who wished to identify the cause of Irish nationalism with the claims of a narrow form of Irish

Catholicism, reinforcing the assertion that the main aim of the rising was the extermination of Protestants. Secondly, the claims of Ogle and others have allowed many to slip into simple clichés about the place and contribution of Wexford Protestants over the generations. Some authors refer to Anglicans in the diocese of Ferns in 1798 as members of the Church of England rather than the Church of Ireland, and they use words like 'planters' and 'loyalists' without examining the family background or political ties of the 1798 clergy.[9] Few historians have asked either about the state of the Church of Ireland in the diocese of Ferns in 1798, or to what degree the Protestant leaders of the rising in Wexford were integrated into the life of the Church of Ireland.

It is worth taking a fresh look at the Church of Ireland clergy in the diocese of Ferns and in Co Wexford at the time of the 1798 rising, examining their family backgrounds, their education, their connections (if any) with both the United Irishmen and the political establishment, their place in the rising, how the rising affected their parishes, their later lives and careers, and their relations with neighbouring Roman Catholics. And indeed, it is worth taking a new look at the Protestant leaders of the rising in Co Wexford and their backgrounds, asking whether they were alienated from the everyday life of the Church of Ireland, and if so, then to ask whether this explains their role in 1798? Or to ask whether they were closely tied to the life of the Church of Ireland in Co Wexford.

THE DIOCESE OF FERNS IN 1798

From Grattan-Flood's history of the diocese of Ferns, published in 1916, to the latest studies by distinguished historians such as Monsignor Patrick Corish and Dr Kevin Whelan, we have a very detailed picture of the Roman Catholic Church and clergy in Co Wexford at the time of the Rising. From Grattan-Flood's book and Professor Whelan's essay on the clergy of 1798, we can see how many Roman Catholic clergy were living in Co Wexford at that time: there was one bishop (James Caulfield) living in Wexford; 36 parishes in the diocese of Ferns with 64 parochial clergy, with an additional six suspended or unemployed priests, and 12 friars,

Augustinians, Carmelites and Franciscans; in addition, there was one parish each in both the diocese of Kildare and Leighlin and the archdiocese of Dublin whose parochial boundaries crossed into Co Wexford, and these were served by one priest each. This gives us a total of one bishop and 84 Roman Catholic clergy spread throughout 38 parishes in Co Wexford in 1798.[10]

Of those 85 men, a maximum of eleven can be said to have been actively engaged in the rising. But the overwhelming majority, 74, were either active loyalists or kept a low profile – they included priests like John Shallow of Adamstown, who was vehemently opposed to the United Irishmen, refused to hear a rebel's confession, and co-operated closely with the local magistrates and yeomanry; and John Redmond of Camolin, who deliberately turned away United Irishmen on their knees for their Easter communion a month before the rising, and was identified as an 'orange priest'.[11] Of the eleven priests actively engaged in the rising, Caulfield was disparaging in dismissing their motives: he described John Keane of Bannow as an 'idiot' and a 'weak poor fool', the Carmelite John Byrne as 'a drinking giddy man', and Bryan Murphy as a 'reptile'.[12] And so, we have very complete, and often contrasting, assessments of those 85 men, and comprehensive studies of the state of the Catholic Church in Co Wexford in 1798.

Unfortunately, so far, no similar studies have been done of the Church of Ireland and its clergy in Co Wexford at the time of the rising. Canon Leslie's list for the diocese of Ferns is simply that, a listing of parishes and their clergy; but it gives us little insight into the attitudes and values of the clergy and, of course, it does not take account of those parts of the county in the dioceses of Leighlin and Glendalough. To compare like with like, I have followed Kevin Whelan's method of looking at the clergy, not just in the diocese of Ferns, but in all Church of Ireland parishes in the county at the time. The parishes or united parishes in the diocese of Ferns were all, either totally or in part, in Co Wexford, and portions of three additional parishes from the neighbouring dioceses were in Co Wexford too. And so, at the outbreak of the rising, excluding military chaplains, there were 57 Church of Ireland clergymen working

in Co Wexford: Bishop Euseby Cleaver of Ferns; 51 other clergymen in 40 parishes or united parishes in the diocese of Ferns, and a
clergyman who was a schoolmaster in New Ross; one clergyman
(Rev John Cliffe of New Ross) without appointment;[13] one (Rev
Thomas Trocke) whose appointment is difficult to determine;[14]
two clergymen with parishes in the dioceses of Leighlin (of whom
one also served as a curate in a parish in the diocese of Ferns); and
one in a parish in the diocese of Glendalough but partly in Co
Wexford.

It is interesting that – with the notable exceptions of Dudley
Colclough, Walter Hore, who was a grandson of the Earl of
Courtown, and John Kennedy who was closely related to the
Carew family – none of these clergymen came from the great landed,
aristocratic families who held political and social power in Co
Wexford – the Annesley, Chichester, Gore, Leigh, Loftus-Tottenham,
Barry-Maxwell, Stopford, Ram and Wallop families.[15]

While clergymen from those families held appointments outside Co Wexford, most of the Church of Ireland clergy in Co
Wexford in 1798 came from families that were part of the middle-
rank of merchants and landowners, or were from clerical or lower
middle class families, and in some instances even from families
with working class backgrounds. In other words, by and large, they
shared similar social backgrounds to their Roman Catholic coun-
terparts.

Contrary to the claims that those clergy were mainly 'loyalists'
and 'planters', research shows that of the 57 only three were
English-born. On the other hand, more than half (31) had strong
Wexford family connections – many with old Wexford names like
Browne, Colclough, Hore and Sutton.

No more than four had an Oxbridge education – Cleaver,
Palmer and Swanne at Oxford and Naylor at Cambridge. But for
any who might doubt they were an educated and cultured collection of men, at least 42 – almost 74 per cent – were graduates of
Trinity College Dublin. They mixed in cultured circles – Palmer
was a nephew of the painter Joshua Reynolds;[16] and many of them
were writers too: Archdeacon Burrowes wrote the preface to the

transactions of the Royal Irish Academy; Chartres wrote a poem on the rising, 'Vinegar Hill';[17] books on the rising were penned by Gordon, Handcock, and by Jane Adams, sister of Roger Owen. James Bentley Gordon's history challenged the prevailing sectarian interpretations of the rising, and although it upset Cleaver his history won wide respect. Handcock also wrote a 'Statistical Survey of Whitechurch Parish' for Mason's *Parochial Survey,* and other contributors to that work included Bevan (Carne), Eastwood (Tacumshane) and Radcliff (Enniscorthy).[18]

In addition, at a time of strong corruption and clientelism in the Church of Ireland, relatively few of the Wexford clergy, as we shall see, were pluralists holding appointments in other dioceses.

FAMILY BACKGROUNDS

At least eleven of the clergy appear to have been born in Co Wexford: John Browne, Dudley Colclough, Thomas Hore and William Sutton came from what might be classified as old Wexford families – families settled in the county long before the Cromwellian era;[19] and John Cliffe, Samuel Heydon, Ulysses Jacob, Joseph Miller and Joshua Nunn came from families that had been settled in the county for a century or more. In addition, Ralph Boyd was born in Co Wexford, and received his early education in the county,[20] and John Kennedy of Fethard also came from a Co Wexford family.[21] William Glascott's grandfather was from the county, a member of one of the seven closely-knit merchant families that controlled the commercial and civic life of New Ross;[22] and Oliver Cary, although he was born in Co Roscommon, came to Co Wexford as a child, attended a school run by Heydon, and his family was settled in Co Wexford for generations.[23]

The names of three of those clergymen – Browne, Hore and Sutton – are of interest because of their associations with prominent Roman Catholic families of the area at the time. According to Bernard Browne and Kevin Whelan, 'The Brownes were a quintessential Catholic family.'[24] According to Hilary Murphy, 'The Hores are noted for their contribution to the service of the (Roman Catholic) Church in the diocese of Ferns – possibly greater than any of the other priestly families of Wexford.'[25] And there is a tradition in the Suttons that no member of the family ever became a Catholic priest after John Sutton of Enniscorthy provided the evidence that convicted Patrick Beaghan for the murder of Heydon.[26] It may well be that Protestant and Catholic family identities were not as clearly defined before the 1798 rising as they came to be in the nineteenth century.

Hilary Murphy appears to be of the opinion also that Francis Turner may have been from the old Wexford family of that name;[27] Turner was born in Dublin, however, although he did marry into the De Renzy family.[28] Similarly, Peter Browne, despite his name, was not from Wexford, but was born into a Co Mayo family. He had strong Co Wexford family connections, through his father-in-law, George Howse of Inch, but although he had enrolled as a Freeman of Wexford, through the benefit of his pluralities he maintained strong connections in the west of Ireland throughout his clerical career.[29] And, despite his Wexford-sounding name, John Davis was born in Co Armagh, and came from a Drogheda family.[30]

Nevertheless, many of the clergy who came to the diocese of Ferns by way of appointment married into Wexford families, or their children regarded themselves as Wexford people, with their descendants continuing to live in the county for a number of generations after. The best-known of these families may be the descendants of Elgee, but others included the families of Alexander, Burrowes of Kyle, Chartres, Coates, Corvan, Gordon, Hawkshaw, Hinson, Howse, Little, Owen, Pentland, Radcliff, James and Richard Symes, Thomas and, of course, Wynne. Hawkshaw's family even gave their name to a bridge near Horetown Church. And so, the overwhelming majority of the clergy were either members of Wexford families, or formed strong family connections with the county.

NON-RESIDENTS AND PLURALISTS

It appears that at least seven of the clergy were not resident in their parishes: Adams, Bond, Archdeacon Burrowes, Davis, Hore, Palmer and James Symes of Castle Ellis.

Although Burrowes as archdeacon was rector of Adamstown,

and although he did not have a curate, he was also rector of
Cappagh in the diocese of Derry from 1796 to 1807. He was
Archdeacon of Ferns and rector of Adamstown for little more than
two years, resigning in the midst of the rising on 1 June, 1798; he
continued to hold Cappagh, and was appointed headmaster of
Portora Royal School, Enniskillen (1798-1819), and later rector of
Drumragh (1807-1841) and Dean of Cork.[31] Despite his pluralism,
he was a highly-regarded scholar: he wrote the preface to the first
volume of transactions of the Royal Irish Academy. Cotton says he
was 'an accomplished scholar and most eloquent preacher, a man of
great talent, sparkling wit and instructive conversation,' and he was
the teacher and patron of the hymn writer, Henry Francis Lyte,
later curate of Taghmon.[32]

Palmer, who became Chancellor of Ferns in 1779, was made
Dean of Cashel in 1787. When he resigned his posts in Ferns for the
more lucrative post of Precentor of Waterford, he remained Dean
of Cashel. Even then, he appears to have continued to divide his
time between Ireland and his native England, and when he died in
Bath in 1829 at the age of 80 he was buried in the family vault in
Exeter Cathedral.[33]

Palmer does not appear to have employed a curate to attend to
parochial duties in Tacumshane. On the other hand, Bond, who as
treasurer also held the parish of Ballycanew, employed three curates
to carry out his duties: Colley in Ballycanew, Gordon in Leskinfere,
and Little in Monamolin.[34]

Although Peter Browne remained Dean of Ferns after 1798, he
became rector of Ahascragh in the diocese of Clonfert in 1799, and
appears to have spent much of the rest of his career in Co Galway:
in 1809 he was living in Ahascragh, and two or three of his children
appear to have been born in Co Galway. In 1823, Chartres was acting as his sub-dean. However, Browne returned dutifully to Gorey
at intervals: his youngest son, Rev Matthew Cassan Browne, was
born in Co Wexford c.1814, his younger daughter Elizabeth married Dr Richard Carey of Newtownbarry, and the dean died in
Gorey on 21 July, 1842.[35]

At least ten other clergymen in the diocese of Ferns were holding clerical appointments in other dioceses in 1798, namely: Adams, Cane, Davis, Draffen, Gordon, Hawkshaw, Hore, Stephens, James Symes and Wynne.

Of these, Henry Wynne, with three, held the largest number of appointments outside the diocese. He had become Precentor of Ferns and rector and vicar of Templeshanbo in 1797, resigning as vicar of Athboy in the diocese of Meath that year, but he remained vicar of Killucan in Co Westmeath (diocese of Meath) from 1784 to 1828, and briefly was rector and vicar of Annagh (diocese of Kilmore) from 1797 to 1798.[36]

Adams held Killinick (1779-1810) and the parish of Ashfield in Kilmore diocese (1795-1808) at the same time. Although he may have had a town house in Wexford, since there was no clerical accommodation in Killinick, it is unlikely that he spent very much time in the diocese apart from checking on the curate he employed, Richard Bevan. He certainly spent a lot more time in his native Cavan, and died there in 1840.[37]

Cane, who became rector of Kilnamanagh only in the month before the outbreak of the rising, was, at the same time, rector and vicar of Tullagh and Creagh in the diocese of Ross.[38] John Davis held appointments in the diocese of Tuam throughout his time as Prebendary of Kilrush, but must have been resident in Co Wexford as he was appointed a JP for the county in 1799.[39] Frederick Draffen was treasurer of Leighlin at the same time as he was incumbent of Ardcolm.[40]

Gordon, who was Bond's curate at Leskinfere was also vicar of Barragh, outside Bunclody, in the diocese of Leighlin; he was rector and vicar of Carnaway in Cork, where he employed a curate, but he lived in Co Wexford throughout that time.[41]

Hawkshaw, while serving as Prebendary of Taghmon and rector of Ballycormick and Ballymitty, was a member of the cathedral chapters in both Kilmacduagh (Islandeddy, 1777-1813) and Clonfert (Fenore, 1784-1813) – not very demanding, but lucrative sinecures in dioceses with very few members of the Church of Ireland and even fewer demands for cathedral services[42] – but he remained resident in Co Wexford, and was related by marriage to a number of other clerical families: his son, Rev Samuel Hawkshaw, later vicar of St Mullins, married a daughter of Captain Francis King, who owned the barn at Scullabogue.[43]

Hore, while he was rector of Kiltennel (1787-1803), was rector of Ballymoney in Cork (1796-1798) and then vicar choral of Ross.[44] The post of vicar choral carried responsibility for the daily round of cathedral services, and so despite his strong family connections and his claim for £55 compensation after the rising, it is unlikely that he spent much time in Kiltennel, secured through his cousin, Lord Courtown. Shortly after the rising, Hore's wife, 22-year-old Lady Mary Howard, died at York on her way to Scarborough; five years later, he resigned from Kiltennel and moved to Surrey, and he died in London in 1841.[45]

Stephens held a number of parishes in the neighbouring dioceses of Ossory and Cashel while holding Kilrane and Bannow in the diocese of Ferns.[46]

Although James Symes had strong family links with the county, he does not appear to have lived in Wexford either. It was said that while he was vicar of Castle Ellis, he also held a chaplaincy in England, and in 1802 he was deprived of the living of Castle Ellis after being cited before the Diocesan Consistorial Court for non-residence. That decision was reversed on appeal, but eventually he resigned the parish in 1812 and left the diocese.[47]

And so in all, thirteen of the clergy – less than a quarter – either were non-resident in Co Wexford or held appointments in other dioceses that demanded absences of some length from their parishes in Co Wexford.

PLURALISTS IN CO WEXFORD

A number of parishes in Co Wexford maintained their separate identities and names from medieval times, but had effectively been amalgamated with neighbouring parishes, forming one consolidated parochial unit or union. But apart from the incumbents of those unions, very few clergymen were pluralists within the diocese, holding more than one parochial appointment.

Chartres was rector of Kilpipe and curate of Ferns, Clone and

Kilbride, but these were neighbouring parishes and for all intents this was one parochial appointment.[48] Little, Bond's curate in Monamolin, was also rector of Killanne, but he appears to have spent most of his time working in Monamolin, and employed Simon Pentland as a curate in John Kelly's home parish.[49] Heydon employed Boyd for his parish in Carne while he served as vicar of Ferns and Clone, where he also employed Chartres as a curate.[50] Hinson held Coulstuffe while working as Nunn's curate in Enniscorthy, but Coulstuffe was a nominal appointment to go with his prebendal stall, and so his curacy in Enniscorthy shows he was resident in the diocese rather than a corrupt pluralist.[51] Naylor was rector of Rossdroit and Templescobin and of neighbouring New Ross from 1797 to 1804; but he employed at least three curates, including McNeill in Old Ross and both Nicholson and Radcliff in New Ross.[52]

Radcliff too was a pluralist. As well as being one of Naylor's two curates in New Ross, as Prebendary of Whitechurch he held the parishes of Whitechurch and Kilnehue at opposite ends of the county. He appears to have made a career of pluralism: later as rector and vicar of Enniscorthy (1802-1836), he also held the parish of Fenagh, Co Carlow, in the diocese of Leighlin. His net income was then estimated at £1,371, and he also had £548 from Fenagh, but he paid his curate in Enniscorthy £92. He lived in splendid style, kept hunters in his stables, and his wife gambled the family into such debt that 'the living was sequestered for debt, and the incumbent confined to his house, except on Sundays'.[53]

And so we have identified 13 clergy as non-residents or men who held so many appointments outside the diocese that they could have spent little time living in Co Wexford. But the vast majority of the clergy – 42 out of the 55 with appointments, or almost three-quarters – appear to have devoted themselves sincerely to their parishes: men like Nunn who worked hard to consolidate his parishes and to reform the antiquated parochial structures he had inherited in Enniscorthy. That the majority of the clergy lived in Co Wexford while holding parochial appointments is borne out by the high number who applied to be enrolled as Freemen of

Wexford; we know that Miller, Elgee and Eastwood lived in Wexford town at the time of the rising, but it appears that Adams (like his successor at Killinick, Rev William Hughes), Hawkshaw, Owen and Sutton also had town houses in Wexford.[54]

II

Links with the establishment

In so far as they benefitted from the collection of tithes, all Church of Ireland clergy were perceived as members of the establishment that bound church and state together at the end of the eighteenth century. In many instances, the actual tithe incomes had already passed out of the hands of the parishes, and into the hands of rich landlords, so that some parishes did not have enough income to employ parochial clergy; other clergy who came from long-established landed families may have had an income secure enough to allow them not to be vigorous in collecting the tithes. And in some instances the tithes benefited the tithe proctors more than the clergy. Nevertheless, tithes were a highly emotive issue at the time of the rising, leading eventually, for example, to the brutal killings at the Battle of the Pound in Bunclody in 1831.[55] In Father Murphy's own Kilcormick, where Handcock succeeded Edward Tottenham as rector in 1793, the tithes were collected on behalf of the rector in Monageer and Boolavogue by two Catholics; Nicholas Furlong says: 'Both were inevitably seen by their fellow Catholics as poachers turned gamekeepers.'[56] On the other hand, the tithes for James Symes in Castle Ellis were collected by the Hay family, closely associated with the leadership of the United Irishmen.[57]

Apart from the tithes, three other areas of public life are pointers to the degree with which clergy might be identified with the establishment: political, military and judicial appointments.

Political: Three, possibly four, of the 57 clergymen being considered in this paper were elected Mayors of Wexford: Joseph Miller, his father Joseph Miller, or both men, held the office of mayor in 1788, 1805, 1808 and 1811; John Elgee was mayor in 1802; and Ralph Boyd was mayor in 1815.[58] In addition, William Sutton had been Portreeve (Mayor) of Enniscorthy in 1774, and Charles Naylor of Rossdroit and New Ross became a burger of New Ross in 1793. And nine of the 57 enrolled as Freemen of Wexford: Bevan (1799), Dickson (1781), Draffen (1830), Heydon (1776), Kennedy (1781), Nunn (1782), Owen (1782), Palmer (1782) and Sutton (1782).[59] The close links between church and politics were to be found in many clerical families: for example, Bond's brother, Sir James Bond, had been MP for Naas 1790-1797, and Robert Burrowes' brother became MP for Enniscorthy.[60]

Military: Surprisingly few of the clergy had direct connections with the military: Cane was the son of an army major and the grandson of an admiral; Elgee had a son who became an army major; and Wynne had two sons who became lieutenant colonels.[61] But apart from army chaplains who followed army regiments to Wexford, the formal links with the military are surprisingly few.[62]

Judicial: At a time when it was common for the clergy along with the other professions to be magistrates, only six of the 1798 clergy in Co Wexford – 10.5 per cent – were Justices of the Peace. Adams of Killinick was a JP for Co Cavan.[63] Cope was appointed a JP for Co Wexford in 1771, and it is said that he presided over the massacre of 28 prisoners in the Ball Alley in Carnew on the eve of rising on 25 May. These prisoners, who included a Protestant, William Young, had been flogged and pitch-capped in the town prior to their slaughter. Cope's reputation as a pitch-capping clerical magistrate was surpassed only by Owen.[64]

On the other hand, Handcock, appointed a JP in 1797, was 'negatively neutral' in his attitude to the United Irishmen, according to Whelan.[65] Glascott, who was appointed a JP in 1791, may even have been positively neutral.[66] And Turner may even have been regarded in a more positive way as John Murphy encouraged his parishioners to hand over their pikes in Ferns to Turner and Isaac Cornock, a liberal magistrate suspected of being a United Irishman, perhaps in the knowledge that the pikes were safe and in the hope of recovering them when the rising began. We know many of the leading United Irishmen were magistrates, so Cope and Owen may well have been exceptional men. Certainly, as

Kevin Whelan points out, the illiberal magistrates, both clerical and lay, tended to be socially marginal or outsiders, despised by members of long-established Protestant families in the county whose profile remained liberal.[67]

III

Clergy sufferings during the rising
From the ranks of the 57 clergy, five (less than 9 per cent) were killed during the rising: Robert Burrowes at Kyle Glebe, Samuel Heydon and Francis Turner a day later; and a day after that, John Pentland, the young 22-year-old curate of Killanne, and Thomas Trocke on Vinegar Hill on 29 May.

Robert Burrowes, the rector of Kilmuckridge, was killed at Kyle Glebe on the morning of 27 May in the search for arms before the Battle of Oulart Hill. Research by Brian Cleary shows that the murder of Burrowes may have been precipitated by a shot at the rebels from the yeomen in the upper floor of Kyle Glebe, and he hints strongly that Father Murphy and his men may have been present not to attack the house but to collect pikes and weapons. The murder was used by later partisan historians to promote the theory that the rising was a sectarian, anti-Protestant tumult, but Cleary's paper does much to redress the balance. Certainly Burrowes was not a sectarian man – his brother Peter was a United Irishman and a friend of Wolfe Tone, his mother was a Roman Catholic, and Robert was a close friend of the local parish priest, Nicholas Sinnott. In the aftermath of the rising, Peter Burrowes was elected MP for Enniscorthy and was a strong opponent of the Act of Union; in 1803, he was Robert Emmet's lawyer. The treatment of the Burrowes family in the awful moments after the attack on Kyle Glebe certainly indicate that Father Murphy's motives were anything but sectarian.[68]

A day after the murder of Burrowes, Heydon and Turner were killed. Samuel Heydon, vicar of Ferns, was murdered in front of his wife on the streets in Enniscorthy by a local butcher, Patrick Beaghan, on 28 May 1798. The murder may have been sectarian, and caused revulsion among the local Catholic clergy, and Beaghan was convicted of murder on the evidence of a Catholic priest named Sutton.[69]

Francis Turner, rector of Edermine, who lived at Ballingale House or Woodview, was killed a day after the Battle of Oulart Hill. Leslie says he was killed on the streets of Enniscorthy, but most other accounts agree he was killed in a search for arms at his home on 28 May. Turner was trusted by John Murphy and worked closely with Cornock, a sympathiser of the United Irishmen, and as I have indicated, it may be that this was less of a search party and more of a collecting party. When the group arrived, however, things went badly wrong. Turner, who was engaged in the baptism of a neighbour's child, had the side of his face blown off, and nine other people were murdered, including the baptised infant's father and two sponsors. Turner's 'mangled body' was 'consumed' in the burning ruins of his own home.[70]

John Pentland, the young 22-year-old curate of Killanne, was piked to death on Vinegar Hill the following day, 29 May, along with Thomas Trocke.[71] According to the Rev George Taylor of Ballywalter, a cousin of Henry Hatton, Portreeve of Enniscorthy, 400 Protestants were massacred at Vinegar Hill,[72] but I think further research is needed into those claims, and into the circumstances surrounding the murder of Pentland, Trocke and others.

Apart from these murders, a number of other clergy suffered during the rising. The bishop's palace at Ferns was plundered and Euseby Cleaver's library and much of his property were destroyed; the raiders helped themselves from the episcopal cellar and left the building a smoking ruin. It is said that the vellum was ripped from his books and the leather bindings used by some of the rebels as saddles for their horses, but that the house itself was saved with the suggestion that it would make a good home for Father John Murphy after the rising. Maxwell claimed the leader of the marauders was an orphan boy who had been found naked and starving at the age of seven by Cleaver and had been fed and clothed by the bishop.[73]

Later, Cleaver suffered psychiatrically as a consequence of his experiences in the rising. He was appointed Archbishop of Dublin in 1809, but his mind was so impaired that it was found necessary to appoint Archbishop Charles Brodrick of Cashel as his co-adjutor, the only example of such an appointment in the history of the Church of Ireland. Cleaver moved to Tunbridge Wells, and died in 1819, although his children continued to live in Ireland.[74]

In addition, seventeen other clergy were imprisoned by the rebels or lost some of their property.

Roger Owen of Camolin, who narrowly escaped execution first in Gorey and later on Wexford Bridge, probably suffered the most and later became unhinged in his mind, according to his sister, Mrs Jane Adams. He was ill-treated, abused and pitch-capped – a punishment handed out to him because he was a pitch-capping magistrate himself. And yet he was the 'most fortunate of provocateurs' – after his arrest he was held first in the Market House in Gorey, where he was the butt of anger and ridicule, publicly displayed before parading rebels with his coned pitch-cap fixed to his head. He refused offers to secure his release from Francis Kavanagh, parish priest of Camolin, knowing that 'Owen released was Owen lynched.' Later he was taken by the John Street Volunteers to Wexford jail, but there he escaped the attention of Thomas Dixon; and once again, as he was about to be executed on Wexford Bridge, he was saved by the timely arrival of General Edward Roche. Pakenham paints a sympathetic profile of him, giving credence to Jane Adams' depiction of him as 'an Old Testament figure at the prison grating'. But his reputation for cruelty was so strong that it endured for generations. Nicholas Furlong charitably questions his sanity, but has described him as 'one of the most demonic wretches ever to disgrace his cloth'. Later, Owen claimed he had lost property valued at £248 during the rising. He continued to hold office until his death in 1844, but Mrs Adams, in her account of the rising, claims that owing to his treatment at the hands of the rebels he became slightly unhinged in his mind.[75]

Henry Wilson of Mulrankin was imprisoned too during the rising, and his church was badly damaged. But the only reference to the rising in the vestry minutes is in 1799, when £1.10s.0d was paid for repairing the church windows, broken during the rising. In the same year, £80 was spent in repairs and reslating. A new church was built in 1843.[76] At least three church buildings were destroyed or damaged during the rising: The church in Old Ross was burned down and a new church was built after the rising. In Gorey, according to Ogle Gowan (never a reliable source for historians), the church windows were smashed, the prayer books were torn to shreds, the Bibles were made into saddles, and two Protestant prisoners were piked to death in the aisle. And in 1799, the Easter Vestry at Rathaspeck voted £3 to repair damage to the church during the rising. But the number of Protestant churches damaged during the rising is markedly low when compared to the burning of Roman Catholic churches and chapels, which continued long after 1798.[77]

Morgan claimed he had been forced to leave the county with his family, and Radcliff said his house had been plundered. In addition, fourteen other clergy claimed the loss of property as suffering loyalists during the rising: Dean Browne, who had been briefly detained by the rebels, £95; Colley (named as Conolly by Musgrave) lost his house and property; Cope, £40; Draffen, £107; Eastwood, £113 in Wexford; Handcock, £747; Hinson was deprived of the means of subsistence; Hore, £55; Howse, who fled his house with his wife and six children, claimed £400; Jacob said he had been forced to flee at the beginning of the rising and claimed £24; Lendrum, £40; Little was reduced to the 'utmost want and indigence', and claimed losses to the value of £73 in Monamolin; McNeill, £64; Nunn, £2,952; and Swann, £345.[79]

Many of these monetary claims may have arisen through the loss of earnings as a consequence of tithes not being collected. In all, 19 of the 57 clergymen suffered directly as a consequence of the rising, either through murder, imprisonment, or assault. But while others lost property or suffered indirectly as a consequence of the rising, many were unmolested and were left undisturbed by the events of 1798.

Claims of massacres

Among the laity, three events have been claimed as evidence that the rising was a sectarian pogrom: the murders at Vinegar Hill, the massacre at Scullabogue, and the executions on Wexford Bridge.

Musgrave put the number of Protestants killed in Scullabogue Barn at over 200. But according to Ogle Gowan's account, 84 people were burned to death in the barn, and 37 others shot. The dead included Hawkshaw's butler, Robert Cooke of Taghmon, but also included Protestants with strong connections with the United Irishmen, such as members of the Lett family, three Quakers, and a large proportion of Catholics. As Daniel Gahan points out, of the seventeen rebels directly linked to the slaughter, three were Protestants, John Ellard, Robert Mills and John Turner, and Mills admitted hacking with his pike at prisoners trying to escape from the barn and striking a woman prisoner so hard that the weapon bent. According to Gahan, no atrocity 'can match Scullabogue in terms of raw brutality. It was the single largest case of mass murder by either side, and, very significantly, it was the only case in which rebels killed women and children.' But Sean Cloney says, 'Calling Scullabogue a sectarian massacre appears to be excessively simplistic if not altogether erroneous.'[80]

According to a Methodist minister quoted by Ogle Gowan, 97 Protestants were 'cruelly butchered on [Wexford] Bridge, martyrs to conscience and Britain'.[81] But it is hardly likely that any one of those Protestants saw themselves either as martyrs or as dying for Britain. As Sean Cloney points out, the massacres at Scullabogue, Wexford and Enniscorthy have been used to give sectarian interpretations to the events of 1798, but unlike the massacres of Carnew and Dunlavin they were not carried out with official sanction – on the contrary they were condemned outright by the leadership of the United Irishmen.

IV

Links with the United Irishmen

Henry Wilson of Mulrankin admitted taking the oath of the United Irishmen, saying it was administered to him in Wexford by Harvey, but later claimed he only took the oath as a pretext to secure the release of parishioners from Mulrankin being held in Wexford gaol.[82]

However, if none of the clergy openly admitted to being sup-

porters of the United Irishmen – and Burrowes is a clear example
that some if not many had sympathies at least for the cause of the
United Irishmen – then, as Kevin Whelan points out, of the 85
Roman Catholic priests in Co Wexford, only 11 (less than 13 per
cent) 'became actively involved in the rebellion', and for most of
those 11, close family links with committed United Irishmen was a
major factor explaining their participation in the rising.

Burrowes may well have been a United Irishman. He held part
of his parochial responsibilities through the patronage of the
Hatton family of Clonard, it is reported that he told Mountnorris
shortly before the rising that he would as soon become a United
Irishman as agree with Mountnorris in his idea for a solution to
Ireland's ills. His brother Peter was a prominent United Irishman,
and his son was engaged to Dorah Lett, Bagenal Harvey's niece and
one of the three 'Rebel Angels' of the Wexford Republic. There is a
distinct possibility that he used his steward to get the message to
the Dublin Directory that the rising was about to begin in
Wexford, and his family later suffered delay and obtuseness on the
part of the government when it came to compensation for his
death.[83]

Dudley Colclough, curate of Templeshanbo, was related to
many of the leaders of the rising. He was licensed as curate in 1793,
but appears to have resigned soon after the rising, perhaps because
of questions about his loyalty, and he was succeeded as curate of
Templeshanbo by George Law. He never held another church appointment, but he continued to live in the area and later returned
to Enniscorthy Castle, which had been leased to the family by the
Earls of Portsmouth, and died there in 1830.[84]

The Colclough family were patrons also of two parishes, nominating the incumbents of Owenduff and Tintern in the diocese of
Ferns and of St Mullins in the diocese of Leighlin. And the Grogan
family were patrons of the living of Ardamine. So did Ulysses Jacob
of Ardamine, William Sutton of Owenduff and Tintern, and
Francis Thomas of St Mullins share the political views of those who
had nominated them to their parishes? Ulysses Jacob claimed as a
suffering loyalist to have lost property valued at £24 during the ris-

ing, but it is worth noting that he was nominated twice to Ardamine, first by John Grogan in 1759, and once again by Cornelius Grogan soon after 1790 when John Allen left for America. It is hard to imagine with two successive nominations like those that he did not share the political outlook of his patrons.[85]

Francis Thomas from Co Carlow was presented to the living of St Mullins by Sir Vesey Colclough in 1783, in succession to Thomas Colclough, son of Caesar Colclough of Tintern Abbey. Obviously, the Colclough family would have ensured that someone to their own liking was placed in that parish.[86] William Sutton of Longraigue was presented to the parish of Owenduff, Tintern and Clonmines by Sir Vesey Colclough in 1785. Three years earlier he had enrolled as a Freeman of Wexford, and in 1794 he was Portreeve of Enniscorthy.[87] I would be interested in learning more about his political affiliations, but once again I suspect that he might have been sympathetic to the cause of the United Irishmen.

V

Ecumenical relations

Furlong says Handcock appeared to treat the Catholic clergy as if they did not exist, and where they did exist he regarded them as in-flamatory demagogues.[88] But many of the clergy had good working relations with their local Roman Catholic neighbours. Burrowes was friendly with Nicholas Sinnott, and perhaps with John Murphy.[89] John Sutton gave evidence to convict Turner's murderer. William Synnott, parish priest of Enniscorthy, protected the rector, Joshua Nunn, by taking him and his valuables into his own house.[90] John Sutton of Enniscorthy and Michael Lacy of Kilmuckridge went to Vinegar Hill at the behest of local Protestants to see if they could get members of their families re-leased, and John Shallow went to Scullabogue barn at the request of the Lett family on a similar rescue mission. On the other hand, John Redmond of Camolin was in constant hiding in Protestant homes for fear of his life at the hands of the rebels in 1798, and his parish priest, Francis Kavanagh, who had tried to secure Owen's freedom in Gorey, had to flee to Gorey for his own safety.[91]

VI

Consequences for post 1798 clergy

If there is any one clear indicator that the majority of Church of Ireland clergy did not feel threatened by the events of 1798, or feel that the rising was symptomatic of an underlying and dangerous current of violent sectarianism, then it is the fact that so many of them remained on in the county after the rising, leaving only when promotion was offered in other dioceses or when they died.

Wexford became a more acceptable place for clerical appointments after the rising than it had been before 1798, attracting members of the landed aristocracy who had heretofore spurned the diocese of Ferns: Lord Robert Ponsonby Tottenham, of Tottenham Green, returned as Bishop of Ferns; and the Rev Richard Ponsonby, from the Bessborough family, succeeded Cope as rector of Carnew.[92] The clergy felt politically safe, as we see with the election of John Elgee as Mayor of Wexford in 1802, Joseph Miller in 1805 and 1808, and Ralph Boyd in 1815. Francis King, proprietor of Scullabogue barn in 1798, was the father of Rev Richard King, who returned to Co Wexford in that politically safe climate, relatively free of sectarian bitterness, as curate of Kilturk (1826), curate of Kilscoran (1830), rector and vicar of Tomhaggard (1834 to 1861), and vicar of Killurin (1866 to 1876); he died in Dublin in 1878.[93]

Evidence of this low level of sectarianism in the aftermath of the rising, and the contribution of the clergy to ensuring that such a climate continued is seen in the will of Canon Nicholas Devereux of Kilrush, a former chaplain to Ely's militia, who left a quarter of the residue of his estate to be divided equally between the Church of Ireland and Roman Catholic parishioners of Kilrush.[94] We even know that the clergy grew more prosperous in the decades after the rising: Draffen, who lost property valued at £107 in 1798, felt secure enough to build a new glebe house close to Castlebridge at a cost of £1,303 in 1805.[95]

VII

The Protestant leaders of 1798 in Wexford

Can it be argued that the Protestant leaders of the rising were marginalised in the Church of Ireland or alienated from it?

The founding and prominent leaders of the United Irishmen in Co Wexford who were members of the Church of Ireland included Beauchamp Bagenal Harvey of Bargy Castle, who became President of the Wexford Council; his brother, James Harvey; their cousin, John Boxwell of Sarshill, Kilmore; Henry and William Hughes of Ballytrent; William Hatton of Clonard; John Grogan of Healthfield; Cornelius Grogan of Johnstown Castle; Anthony Perry and Robert Graham of Inch; George Sparks of Blackwater; Samuel Cooper; and of course Matthew Keugh, Governor of Wexford Town.

Four of the eight members of the government of Wexford town were Protestants – Nicholas Grey, Bagenal Harvey, William Hatton, and Matthew Keugh – and all three colonels for the Baronies of Forth and Bargy were members of the Church of Ireland (Harvey, Hatton and Cornelius Grogan).[96] A brief look at the family backgrounds of some of these men will show that the Protestant leaders of the United Irishmen in Wexford were totally integrated into the life of the Church of Ireland in these dioceses in 1798.

Bagenal Harvey's two grandfathers were clergymen: his paternal grandfather was Rev William Harvey (1682-1765) of Bargy Castle, at one time Mayor of Wexford and rector and vicar of Mulrankin. His maternal grandfather was Rev James Harvey of Killiane Castle, near Piercestown. He had two paternal uncles who were clergymen: Rev Christopher Harvey of Kyle, Prebendary of Edermine; and Rev Ambrose Harvey, curate of Killinick, who was disinherited in William Harvey's will. And a first cousin, William Harvey of Kyle, was son-in-law of Maurice Crosbie, Dean of Limerick.[97]

His cousin, John Boxwell of Sarshill, was the grandson of Rev Ambrose Harvey of Killinick and great-grandson of both Rev William Harvey of Mulrankin and Rev Pierce Hughes of Slade.[98]

Nicholas Grey, secretary of the Rebel Council in Wexford and aide de camp to Bagenal Harvey, married a daughter of Henry Hughes of Ballytrent, a cousin of Canon Lambert Hughes, Chancellor of Christ Church Cathedral, Dublin.[99]

William Hatton was descended from Rev Henry Hatton, Prebendary of Clone. In addition, a cousin was married to George

Gore, Dean of Killala, and he was a great-uncle of Charles Gore, the editor of *Lux Mundi* and a leading figure in the movement that radicalised the Anglo-Catholic movement in these islands in the century after the rising. And the Hattons of Clonard were patrons of portion of the living held by Robert Burrowes of Kyle.[100]

The Colclough family, who provided two of the leaders of the United Irishmen, were patrons of at least two parishes in Co Wexford, Tintern and Owenduff in the diocese of Ferns, and St Mullins in the diocese of Leighlin.

The Grogans were patrons of Ardamine, nominating the vicars and paying their salaries. Cornelius Grogan of Johnstown Castle was churchwarden of Rathaspeck in 1796; as he went to his death on Wexford Bridge in 1798, 'the sailors of the Royal Navy who hanged him were amazed when ... they heard him recite "Protestant prayers"'.[101] John Grogan of Healthfield and Johnstown had married Ann Coote, the niece of two clergymen and the cousin of many more.[102]

Matthew Keugh, Governor of Wexford during the rising, was executed with Father Philip Roche on Wexford Bridge, sharing his last moments in prayer with the rector of Wexford, John Elgee.[103] The heads of Harvey and Grogan were paraded through the town and along with Keugh's head were displayed on pikes outside Wexford Courthouse for weeks after.[104] According to Daniel Gahan, 'Protestant rebels were clearly to be made an example of.'

But harsh lessons are usually devised not to teach the dead a lesson, for they need no further deterring, but to deter the living! If the living Protestants needed deterring, then it can only be that the authorities, aware of the extent to which the leaders of the rising were integrated into the daily life and structures of the Church of Ireland in this county, feared they could not trust the loyalty of Protestants in South Wexford, and perhaps throughout the county.

VIII

Conclusions

In the immediate aftermath of the rising, Peter Burrowes was a strongly nationalist MP for Enniscorthy. But in the political climate after the rising, liberal Protestants, generally speaking, were muted for a number of decades. There was substantial emigration to Canada by Protestants with loyalist sympathies in the 1820s, and the political climate stabilised by the mid-nineteenth century;[105] nevertheless, in the time that lapsed, Protestant memories had been formed by Scullabogue and Musgrave's history, and any pride in Keugh, Grogan, Harvey, Boxwell and others that remained was beneath the surface.

As Kevin Whelan points out, an honest and accurate understanding of the rising is important because of the implications for current political and cultural thinking. But it is important too for members of the Church of Ireland in Co Wexford in coming to grips with the real story of the church in the county, in putting aside the legacy of those who wanted to misrepresent the vision of a non-sectarian, democratic and inclusive Ireland.

A new approach and fresh understanding of the role of members of the clergy and laity of Church of Ireland in Co Wexford at the time of the rising might even allow us to repeat the words printed on quarter-pint jugs in Wexford's public houses in 1798, honouring three leaders of the rising, two of whom were loyal members of the Church of Ireland:

Long live Grogan, Harvey and Ned Hay,
As long as the Slaney flows into the sea.[106]

Acknowledgments

I wish to thank: The committee of Comóradh, Rev Canon Norman Ruddock and the Select Vestry of St Iberius Parish, Wexford, Bunclody Historical Society, and Mr Rory Murphy, for their invitations to present this research in 1996 and 1997. The former Bishop of Cashel and Ossory, Right Rev Noel Willoughby, for chairing the first lecture in St Iberius's and for his encouragement. Dr Raymond Refaussé and Ms Heather Smith of the Representative Church Body (RCB) Library, Dublin, and the Dean of Ferns, Very Rev Leslie Forrest, for access to church, diocesan, parochial and individual records and papers, and advice on reading; Dr Refaussé also compiled a list of Euseby Cleaver's papers. Mr Clive Allen, Mr Dominic Berridge, Mr Bernard Browne, Rev Peter Barret, Ms Gloria Binnions, Mr Nicholas Furlong, Dr Kenneth Milne, Mr King Milne, Mr Hilary Murphy and Mrs Helen Skrine; Mr Alan Dalton, editor of Parish Chimes (Glenageary), Rev Canon Nigel Waugh, editor of the Diocesan Magazine (Cashel and Ossory), and the Very Rev Stephen Ross White, editor of Search; and many others, particularly my wife Barbara, for information, assistance and encouragement.

Sources:

Bowen, Desmond, *The Protestant Crusade in Ireland, 1800-1870*, Gill & Macmillan, Dublin, 1978, xiv + 412 pp.

Browne, Bernard, and Whelan, Kevin, 'The Browne Families of County Wexford', pp. 467-489, Whelan, 1987.

Cleary, Brian, 'The Battle of Oulart Hill: Context and Strategy', pp. 4-66, in *The Past*, Uí Chennsellaig Historical Society, 1995.

Burke's Irish Family Records, Burke's Landed Gentry of Ireland (BLGI), *Burke's Peerage*, various editions.

Cloney, Sean, 'South-West Wexford in 1798', pp. 74-97, *Journal of the Wexford Historical Society*, No 15, 1994-1995.

Collier, Patrick, *The Castle Museum Enniscorthy*, Enniscorthy: Castle Museum, n.d., 32 pp.

Corish, Patrick, 'Two Centuries of Catholicism in County Wexford', pp. 222-237, Whelan, 1987.

Cullen, Louis M., 'The 1798 rebellion in Wexford: United Irishmen organisation, membership, leadership', pp. 248-295, in Whelan, 1987b.

Culleton, Edward, Furlong, Nicholas, and Sills, Patrick (eds), *By Bishop's Rath and Norman Fort*, Drinagh Enterprises, Wexford, 1994, 285 pp.

Dictionary of National Biography (DNB), vols. iii and iv.

Furlong, Nicholas, *Fr John Murphy of Boolavogue 1753-1798*, Geography Publications, Dublin, 1991, viii + 206 pp.

Gahan, Daniel, *The People's Rising: Wexford 1798*, Gill & Macmillan, Dublin, 1995, xv + 367 pp.

'The Scullabogue Massacre', pp. 27-31, *History Ireland*, Vol 4, No 3, Autumn 1996.

Goodall, David, 'A Divided Family in 1798: The Grays of Whitefort and Jamestown', pp. 52-66 in *Journal of the Wexford Historical Society*, No 15, 1994-1995.

Gordon, James, *History of the Rebellion in 1798*, Dublin, 1801.

Grattan-Flood, W.H., *History of the Diocese of Ferns*, Downey, Waterford, 1916, xxiv + 246 pp.

Handcock, William Domville, *The History and Antiquities of Tallaght*, Anna Livia Press, Dun Laoghaire, 1991 (199? ed. reprint), 160 pp.

Keogh, Daire, *The French Disease: The Catholic Church and Irish Radicalism, 1790-1800*, Four Courts Press, Dublin, 1993, 297 pp.

Keogh, Daire, and Furlong, Nicholas (eds), *The Mighty Wave: The 1798 Rebellion in Wexford*, Four Courts Press, Dublin, 187 pp.

Kinsella, Anna, '1798 Claimed for Catholics: Father Kavanagh, Fenians and the Centenary Celebrations', pp. 139-155 in Keogh and Furlong.

Leslie, J.B., *Dublin Clergy and Parishes*, Ts, RCB Library, Dublin.

Ferns Clergy and Parishes, Dublin, 1936.

Leighlin Clergy and Parishes, Ts, 2 vols, RCB Library, Dublin.

Mannion, John, 'A Transatlantic Merchant fishery: Richard Welsh of New Ross and the Sweetmans of Newbawn in Newfoundland 1734-1862', pp. 373-421, Whelan, 1987.

Maxwell, William, *History of the Irish Rebellion in 1798*, 6th ed, H.G. Bohn, London, 1864, viii + 477 pp.

Murphy, Hilary, *Families of County Wexford*, Geography Publications, Dublin, 1986, ix + 263 pp.

Musgrave, Richard, *Memories of the Rebellion in Ireland*, 4th ed (eds Steven W. Myers, Delores E. McKnight), Duffry Press, Enniscorthy, 1995, xxv + 982 pp.

Pakenham, Thomas, *The Year of Liberty: The History of the Great Irish Rebellion of 1798*, Orion, London, 1992, 416 pp.

Reck, Padge, *Wexford – A Municipal History*, Mulgannon Publications, Wexford, 1987, 251 pp.

Power, T.P., and Whelan, Kevin (eds), *Endurance and Emergence, Catholics in Ireland in the Eighteenth Century*, Irish Academic Press, Dublin, 1990, x + 204 pp.

Roche, Richard, 'Forth and Bargy – a place apart', pp. 102-121, Whelan, 1987.

Skinner, B.G, *Henry Francis Lyte*, University of Exeter, Exeter, 1974, x + 164 pp.

Whelan, Kevin (ed), *A History of Newbawn*, Macra na Feirme, Newbawn, 1986.

'Politicisation in County Wexford and the Origins of the 1798 Rebellion', pp. 156-178, in Hugh Gough and David Dickson (eds), *Ireland and the French Revolution*, Irish Academic Press, Dublin, 1990, xii + 255 pp.

'Reinterpreting the 1798 Rebellion in County Wexford', pp. 9-36, in Keogh and Furlong (eds).

'The religious factor in the 1798 rebellion in County Wexford', pp. 62-85 in Patrick O'Flanagan, Paul Ferguson and Kevin Whelan (eds), *Rural Ireland, Modernisation and Change, 1600-1900*, Cork University Press, Cork, 1987, xiv + 187 pp. (Whelan, 1987a).

'The role of the Catholic Priest on the 1798 Rebellion in county Wexford', pp. 296-319, Whelan, 1987. (Whelan, 1987b) (ed.), *History and Society, Wexford*, Geography Publications, Dublin, 1987 xvi + 564 pp.

Whitten, J.B. (ed), *Murder Without Sin, The Rebellion of 1798*, Grand Orange Lodge of Ireland, Belfast, 1996, 105 pp.

Notes:

1   *The Wexford Echo*, 8 February, 1997.
2   James Comerford was killed along with Samuel Judd, Thomas Earl and
     Joseph Aston; Musgrave indicates James Comerford was a parishioner of
     Burrowes, but Cleary states he was also a yeoman; Elizabeth Comerford and
     their five children, who were at Kyle, survived. (See Musgrave, p. 743; Cleary
     1995, pp. 22-23.) Sifting of family memories from 1798 was common in the
     last century: see Nicholas Furlong, p. 186, n 34; Anna Kinsella, *passim*; L.M.
     Cullen, 'The United Irishmen in Wexford', p. 54, in Keogh and Furlong
     (eds).
3   Louis Cullen writes, 'there was little danger ever in highly politicised
     Wexford of anyone confusing Anglicans, with their emotive and political
     attachment to the establishment, with other Protestants' (Cullen, p. 277).
4   Musgrave gave the figure as over 221 (Musgrave, pp. 398-408, 734-754);
     Maxwell put it at 230 (p. 123); but more sober assessments are given in both
     Cloney and Whelan, 1986, pp. 45-52.
5   See Leslie, *Ferns*, p. 120.
6   See Musgrave, pp. 347 ff.
7   See Kinsella, *passim*.
8   See Whitten, *passim*.
9   For examples, see Furlong, 1991, pp. 1, 9.
10   See Grattan-Flood, *passim*; Corish, 1987, passim; Whelan, 1987b, p. 314;
     Whelan, 1990, pp. 159-164.
11   Whelan, 1987b, pp. 296-298, 310-311.
12   ibid., pp. 309, 315.
13   See *Burke's Landed Gentry of Ireland* (Hereafter *B.L.G.I.*), sv Cliffe, and
     Leslie, Ferns, *passim*.
14   Trocke is described by Musgrave as a curate, but is not listed by Leslie;
     see Musgrave, pp. 346, 735, 762-763; however, I have not been able to ident-
     ify his parish or curacy (for Enniscorthy curates, see Leslie, Ferns, p. 151).
     He may have been the father of Rev William Trocke, born in Co Wexford
     c.1796, educated by Rev Jospeh Miller in Wexford, and Vicar of Tallaght,
     Co Dublin, 1822-1830 (Handcock, p. 27; Leslie, Dublin Ts, s. v. Tallaght, f
     570).
15   Members of those families who had become clergymen in the Church of
     Ireland had found more rewarding positions in 1798, including Charles
     Tottenham's son-in-law, Sir James Hutchinson, who was Archdeacon of
     Achonry; Henry Maxwell, who was Bishop of Meath, and who died only
     weeks after the Rising, on 7 October, 1798; and James Stopford, Thomas
     Stopford and Digby Joseph Stopford Ram, who had found more
     comfortable parishes in Co Cork – Thomas Stopford had been Dean of
     Ferns until 1794 and a JP for Co Wexford, but became Bishop of Cork in
     1798.
16   Leslie, *Ferns*, p. 40.
17   I wish to thank Bernard Browne for a copy of Vinegar Hill by Chartres.
18   Leslie, *Ferns*, pp. 99, 126, 180; see Cleaver Mss, RCB Library, Dublin, Ms
     328, 3.1 dated 6 August 1802 and 3.2 dated 10 August 1802.
19   See Hilary Murphy, *passim*, particularly pp. 20ff, 126ff and 238ff.
20   Leslie, *Ferns*, p. 78.
21   ibid., p. 126.

22   ibid., p. 184; Mannion, p. 376.
23   Leslie, *Ferns*, p. 218.
24   Browne and Whelan, p. 471.
25   Murphy, p. 130.
26   Whelan, 1987b, p. 311.
27   Murphy, p. 245.
28   Leslie, *Ferns*, p. 73.
29   See ibid, p. 26.
30   ibid., p. 85.
31   ibid., p. 53.
32   Cotton, quoted by Leslie, *Ferns*, p. 54; Skinner, pp. 7-21.
33   Leslie, *Ferns*, p. 40.
34   ibid., pp. 115, 211, 213; Leslie, Leighlin Ts, ii, f 362.
35   Leslie, Ferns, pp. 26, 59.
36   ibid., p. 34.
37   ibid., pp. 188-189.
38   ibid., pp. 194, 233.
39   ibid., p. 85.
40   ibid., p. 110.
41   ibid., pp. 147, 182; Leslie, *Leighlin* Ts, i, f 144.
42   Leslie, *Ferns*, pp. 92-93.
43   ibid., pp. 190, 270.
44   ibid., p. 208.
45   do.
46   Leslie, *Ferns*, pp. 82.
47   ibid., p. 133.
48   ibid., pp. 59, 129.
49   ibid., pp. 73, 93, 180-181, 213.
50   ibid., pp. 59, 126.
51   ibid., p. 234.
52   ibid., pp. 150, 222, 224, 233.
53   Bowen, p. 70, p. 335 n. 187; Leslie, *Ferns*, pp. 98, 150.
54   Leslie, *Ferns*, pp. 99, 180, 188, 250-251; for example, Hawkshaw's son Samuel
     was born in Wexford town in 1782 (Leslie, *Ferns*, p. 93); Peter Fannin's 1800
     map shows Miller's house on the east side of South Main Street, almost
     opposite Keyser's Lane (see map facing p. 349, Musgave, op. cit., and
     Pakenham, p. 5).
55   Bowen, pp. 156ff.
56   Furlong, 1991, p. 17.
57   ibid., p. 178, n 11.
58   Reck, p. 14.
59   ibid., pp. 118-133.
60   *B.L.G.I.*, s.v. Bond; DNB iii, p. 450.
61   Leslie, *Ferns*, pp. 34, 233, 250-251.
62   I have excluded from this study military chaplains, as their presence in the
     county was transient and was boosted by the events surrounding the rising;
     to include them in this study would distort any analysis of the diocesan clergy.
63   *B.L.G.I.*, sv Adams of Northland.
64   Leslie, *Ferns*, p. 128; Furlong, 1991, pp. 48-49.
65   Whelan, 1990, p. 162; Leslie, p. 98.
66   Leslie, *Ferns*, p. 184.
67   Furlong, 1991, pp. 48-50; Whelan, 1996, p. 18.

68   Cleary, *passim*; Musgrave, pp. 743; DNB iii, p. 450.

69   Musgrave, p. 744; Diocesan Registry; Leslie, *Ferns,* p. 59; Furlong, p. 69; Whelan, 1987b, p. 311.

70   Leslie, *Ferns,* p. 73; Whitten, p. 55.

71   Musgrave, pp. 346, 735, 762-763; Leslie, *Ferns,* p. 181; although Musgrave also suggests 1 June as the date of their murder, pp. 89-90.

72   Whitten, p. 37.

73   Leslie, *Ferns,* pp. 17-18; Furlong, 1991, p. 64; Maxwell, pp. 89-90; Pakenham, p. 155.

74   Leslie, *Ferns,* pp. 17-18; DNB iv, p 478.

75   Musgrave, pp. 314, 438, 737, 772-775, 807; Furlong, 1991, pp. 43, 107-112, 120; Leslie, *Ferns,* p. 96; Nicholas Furlong, Letter to the Editor, *The Irish Times,* 23 August, 1996; Pakenham, p. 252.

76   Leslie, *Ferns,* p. 292; Musgrave, pp. 477, 809.

77   Leslie, *Ferns,* p. 228; Whitten, p. 75; Culleton *et al,* p. 86. See Whelan 1987a, p. 81 and p. 80 figure 4:4; Whelan 1987b, p. 312;

78   Leslie, *Ferns,* p. 222; Musgrave, p. 403.

79   Leslie, *Ferns, passim*; Musgrave, pp. 734-737.

80   Gahan, 1996, pp. 26-27; Musgrave, pp. 734ff; Whelan, 1986, pp. 45-52; Cloney, pp. 74-97; Whitten, pp. 68-69.

81   Whitten, pp. 80-85.

82   Musgrave, p. 477.

83   Cleary, pp. 19-22; DNB iii, p. 450.

84   *Burke's Irish Family Records,* s.v. Colclough; Collier, p. 11; Leslie, *Ferns,* p. 244.

85   See Leslie, *Ferns,* p. 106.

86   Leslie, *Leighlin* Ts, i f 330.

87   Leslie, *Ferns,* p. 229; Reck, p. 133.

88   Furlong, 1991, p. 17.

89   Cleary, pp. 19-22.

90   Whelan, 1987b, p. 309.

91   ibid., p. 310.

92   See *Burke's Peerage,* various editions, s.v. Bessborough and Ely.

93   Leslie, *Ferns,* pp. 190, 270.

94   ibid., p. 86.

95   ibid., p. 110.

96   Whelan, 1990, p. 158; Gahan, p. 8.

97   Leslie, *Ferns,* pp. 73, 201, 216, 266, 271; BLGI, s.v. Harvey.

98   Leslie, *Ferns, passim*; BLGI, s.v. Boxwell, Harvey and Hughes.

99   Goodall, *passim*; *B.L.G.I.,* s.v. Hughes.

100   *B.L.G.I.,* s.v. Hatton of Clonard; Burke's Peerage, s.v. Arran.

101   Culleton *et al,* p. 84; Nicholas Furlong, in Culleton *et al,* pp. 59-60.

102   *Burke's Peerage,* s.v. Coote.

103   Musgrave, pp. 473-474; Musgrave does not name the clergyman, but John Elgee's descendants and Nicholas Furlong (*The Echo,* 13 September, 1996) believe he was Elgee.

104   Gahan, 1995, pp. 241-242.

105   ibid., pp. 299-300.

106   Whelan, 1990, p. 172.

107   Whelan, 1996, p. 9.

APPENDIX 1

Clergy of the Diocese of Ferns, 1798
Bishop: Euseby Cleaver

CHAPTER

Dean: Peter Browne (Gorey)
Precentor: Henry Wynne (Templeshanbo)
Chancellor: Joseph Palmer (also Dean of Cashel)
Treasurer: Wensley Bond (Ballycanew)
Archdeacon: Robert Burrowes (Adamstown)

Prebendaries (in order of precdence)
Kilrane: Thomas Stephens (Bannow)
Coulstuffe: William Hinson (Coulstuffe)
Fethard: John Kennedy (Fethard)
Edermine: Francis Turner (Edermine)
Taghmon: Robert Hawkshaw (Taghmon)
Kilrush: John Davis (Kilrush)
Tombe: Roger Owen (Tombe)
Clone: Samuel Heydon (Clone, Ferns, Carne)
Whitechurch: Richard Radcliff (Whitechurch, New Ross)
Crosspatrick: Richard Henry Symes (Crosspatrick)

PARISHES AND BENEFICES

Adamstown: Robert Burrowes (Archdeacon)
Ardamine: Ulysses Jacob
Ardcolm: Frederick Draffen.
Ballycanew: Wensley Bond (Treasurer)
                  Arthur Colley (curate, Ballycanew)
                  James Bentley Gordon (curate, Leskinfere,
                  Vicar of Barragh, Diocese of Leighlin) [1]
                  Simon Little (curate, Monamolin) [2]
Bannow: Thomas Stephens (Preb of Kilrane),
                  Joseph Miller (curate, Duncormick)
Carne: Samuel Heydon (Preb of Clone) [3]
                  Ralph Boyd, curate
Carnew: Charles Cope
                  Joseph Lendrum (curate)
Castle Ellis: James Symes
Clonegal: John Browne
Coulstuffe: William Hinson (Preb of Coulstuffe) [4]
Crosspatrick: Richard Henry Symes (Preb of Crosspatrick)
                  ? Charles Spencer Coates, curate
Edermine: Francis Turner (Preb of Edermine)
Enniscorthy: Joshua Nunn
                  William Hinson, curate (see Coulstuffe) [4]
Ferns & Clone: Samuel Heydon (vicar, Preb of Clone) [3]
                  Mark Chartres (curate) [7]
Fethard: John Kennedy (Preb of Fethard)

Gorey:	Peter Browne (Dean of Ferns)
	John Corvan, curate
Horetown:	James Morgan
Kilcormick:	Thomas Handcock
Killanne:	Simon Little (curate of Monamolin) [2]
	John Pentland, curate
Killegney:	Samuel Francis
Killesk:	William Glascott
Killinick:	Benjamin Adams
	Richard Bevan, curate
Killurin:	Abraham Swann
Kilmuckridge:	Robert Burrowes
Kilnamanagh:	Robert Erskine Cane
Kilpipe:	Mark Chartres [7]
Kilrush:	John Davis
Kiltennel:	Thomas Hore
Mulrankin:	Henry Wilson
New Ross:	Charles Naylor [5]
	Daniel McNeill, curate
	? Andrew Nicholson curate
	? Richard Radcliff curate [6]
	Robert Alexander, schoolmaster
Newtownbarry:	Oliver Cary
Owneduff and Tintern:	William Sutton
Rathmacnee:	Matthew Russell
Rossdroit:	Charles Naylor (see New Ross) [5]
Tacumshane:	Joseph Palmer (Chancellor)
Taghmon:	Robert Hawkshaw (Preb of Taghmon)
Templeshanbo:	Henry Wynne (Precentor)
	? Dudley Colclough curate
Tombe:	Roger Owen (Preb of Tombe)
Wexford:	John Elgee
	William Eastwood, curate
Whitechurch:	Richard Radcliff (Preb of Whitechurch) [6]

Resident without appointment:	John Cliffe (ex New Ross)
Appointment unknown:	Thomas Trocke

Diocese of Leighlin

Barragh:	James Bentley Gordon [1]
St Mullins:	Francis Thomas

Diocese of Glendalough:

Inch and Kilgorman:	George Howse

Notes:

1, 2, 3, 4, 5, 6, 7:	Refer to the same people.

APPENDIX 2

Clergy holding appointments in Co Wexford, 1798:

Adams, Benjamin, Killinick.

Alexander, Robert: schoolmaster, New Ross.

Bevan, Richard: curate of Killinick.

Bond, Wensley:Treasurer; Ballycanew.

Boyd, Ralph: curate, Carne.

Browne, John: Clonegal.

Browne, Peter: Dean of Ferns; Gorey.

Burrowes, Robert: Archdeacon of Ferns; Adamstown.

Burrowes, Robert: Kilmuckridge:

Cane, Robert Erskine: Kilnamanagh.

Cary, Oliver: Newtownbarry.

Chartres, Mark: Kilpipe; curate, Ferns and Clone.

Cleaver, Euseby: Bishop of Ferns.

Cliffe, John, former curate of New Ross.

Coates, Charles Spencer: ? curate, Crosspatrick.

Colclough, Dudley: ?curate, Templeshanbo:

Colley, Arthur: curate, Ballycanew.

Cope, Charles: Carnew.

Corvan, John: curate, Gorey.

Davis, John: Prebendary of Kilrush; Kilrush.

Draffen, Frederick: Ardcolm.

Eastwood, William: curate, Wexford.

Elgee, John: Wexford.

Francis, Samuel: Killegney.

Glascott, William: Killesk.

Gordon, James Bentley: curate, Leskinfere; vicar of Barragh, diocese of Leighlin.

Handcock, Thomas: Kilcormick.

Hawkshaw, Robert: Prebendary of Taghmon; Taghmon.

Heydon, Samuel: Prebendary of Clone; Vicar of Ferns and Clone; and Carne.

Hinson, William: Prebendary of Coulstuffe; Coulstuffe; curate, Enniscorthy.

Hore, Thomas: Kiltennel.

Howse, George: Inch and Kilgorman (Diocese of Glendalough).

Jacob, Ulysses: Ardamine.

Kennedy, John: Prebendary of Fethard; Fethard.

Lendrum, Joseph: curate, Carnew.

Little, Simon: Killanne; curate, Monamolin and Killanne.

Miller, Joseph: curate, Duncormick.

McNeill, Daniel: curate, New Ross.

Morgan, James: Horetown.

Naylor, Charles: Rossdroit; New Ross.

Nicholson, Andrew curate, New Ross.

Nunn, Joshua: Enniscorthy.

Owen, Roger: Prebendary of Tombe; Tombe.

Palmer, Joseph: Chancellor of Ferns; Tacumshane; also Dean of Cashel.

Pentland, John: curate, Killanne.

Radcliff, Richard: Prebendary of Whitechurch; Whitechurch, New Ross; ? curate, New Ross.

Russell, Matthew: Rathmacnee:

Stephens, Thomas: Prebendary of Kilrane; Bannow.
Sutton, William: Owneduff and Tintern.
Swann, Abraham: Killurin.
Symes, James: Castle Ellis.
Symes, Richard Henry: Prebendary of Crosspatrick; Crosspatrick.
Thomas, Francis: St Mullins (Diocese of Leighlin)
Trocke, Thomas, appointment unknown.
Turner, Francis: Prebendary of Edermine; Edermine.
Wilson, Henry: Mulrankin.
Wynne, Henry: Precentor of Ferns; Templeshanbo.

The Clergy and the Connacht Rebellion

Sheila Mulloy

One of the more intriguing aspects of the 1798 Rebellion is the quite distinct form it assumed in the three theatres of conflict. In the northern Leinster counties, where the United Ireland movement was highly organised, the arrest of the leaders and the brutality of the soldiery had resulted in a sullen calm which was broken by some fourteen disorganised but courageous attacks by large numbers of rebels, which were defeated in all but two cases by a much smaller number of professional troops. But farther south, first in Wicklow and Carlow, and later in Wexford, vast numbers of 'the men of no property' were to rise out under the leadership of their priests and a few men of property and pit themselves against the whole might of state and Established Church, government and opposition, against the bulk of the respectable class of wealthy landowners and successful businessmen, against trained soldiers, militia and yeomanry. Unfortunately, religious animosities were to animate the reckless courage of the mainly Catholic rebels and the vindictive fury of the outraged loyalists, and resulted in some savagery on both sides the memory of which was to fester in men's minds for another hundred years.

In Ulster, Belfast had been the political centre of the United movement, and the American and French Revolutions had profoundly influenced the mainly Presbyterian population. They suffered religious discrimination and were eager for social justice and political power. They were imbued with republican principles, but the brutality of the disarmament campaign by the government had cowed many of them. Furthermore, the growth of religious tension with the rise of the Orange Order on the one hand and Defenderism on the other, and a virtual land war in Armagh proving just how fragile were the chances of unity within the United movement, combined with what many saw as the mob rule of the Catholic rebels in Wexford, made many hesitate and pull back from the brink when the time for action arrived. The colonels were arrested or failed to appear, leaving a dearth of leaders, while the Defenders failed to play their allotted role. Only those deeply committed to the cause played their part with northern tenacity but notable restraint. Among these were a number of Presbyterian clerics whose number varies from 'more than a score' according to Stewart and forty-eight according to Holmes, quoting Miller.[1] Some of them paid the ultimate penalty, but, although they were leaders in their community, they were not versed in military matters.

When we turn to Connacht, the picture is very different. Here all was calm on the surface and apparently the pacification measures of Lord Carhampton had cowed the people and left them with no desire to join the United movement. The province was the least politicised of the four provinces, although some efforts had been made to spread the United movement, and Defenderism had also begun to make some progress, some of this sedition being attributed to the northern refugees who had fled to the province in 1796.

The Earl of Altamont and his brother, the Honourable Denis Browne, had welcomed the northern refugees to their estates, thinking that their weaving skills and habits of sobriety could not fail to have a good influence on their more easy-going Mayo tenants. Denis Browne described them as 'acting quietly and inoffensively', and convinced himself that the local inhabitants feared that the northern Presbyterians and their French allies would 'drive them from their habitations and propertys and *so strongly* does this operate that I am persuaded they would beat the French out of this Country with stones.' He continues to report on the loyalty of the county in January 1797, and hopes piously that the evidence of loyalty given by the country will convince England, and lead to gracious measures of 'commercial arrangement and internal regulation'. The northern immigrants have now 'been obliged to come forward and take the oaths of allegiance', which would indicate that suspicions are beginning to form in the Honourable Denis's mind.[2]

The northern refugees are now as numerous as the natives in his area, and he fears that 'want will lead them to depredation and almost justify it,' a surprisingly reasonable statement to come from the pen of the most active and extreme of the Mayo loyalists. He writes further in the same letter:

I am informed by several letters that *private swearing* has made its way into Mayo. If it takes root in a mountainous country containing as I think *200,000 inhabitants exclusive of strangers,* it will be difficult if not impossible to eradicate it, and it will, I should hope, be easy to put it down now. Sligo, that borders Mayo, is disturbed and proclaimed. Roscommon and Leitrim are countys from circumstances of interior policy, easily worked up to disturbance.

He makes two proposals for preserving the peace in Connacht. The first is to station a troop of 'good cavalry' at Westport where there is accommodation for them, and they can be sent to any part of the province where they are needed. The other proposal is to station a press gang of six men and an officer in the revenue barge of Westport. Any person found to have taken a United oath would then be faced with banishment 'which is a greater object of fear to them than death'.[3] In June he writes to Dublin Castle that he now knows 'that the Northern emigrants here are United Irishmen and that they are poisoning the minds of the inhabitants of this place'.[4]

By March 1798 the ever-alert Denis has discovered the methods used by the United men to spread their movement in Connacht.

The moment a gentleman from this country goes to Dublin, he is invited by some of the *Dublin Iluminati* to diner. There he meets with Iluminators who make use of their eloquence to work on his mind, by proving to them that the country is ill-governed, that the Catholicks are persecuted (of which class the invited generaly belongs), that a revolution is certain, that property will only be endangered by resisting it.

It is the young Catholic gentry who have been seduced and especially those of the 'middling gentry'. He writes of the 'great misery' being suffered from want of fuel and falling prices for agricultural produce.[5]

His more cautious brother, the Earl of Altamont, writes in May 1798 that 'everything in every part of the province is peace, tranquility, good order, obedience to the laws and prosperity unequal'd.' He wants no measures of severity by the military. Unless their numbers are increased 'the people will rise upon them infallibly, and the gentry disapproving the measure entirely and having only *one opinion* upon it, will not cooperate in the execution of it with that zeal that will enable the garrisons to make any stand.' Altamont shows surprisingly good judgement here, and the same must be said of Denis Browne when he writes to Altamont in June:

> This county *continues quiet*. The continuance of the Wexford Rebellion has *not yet operated on us*. Without going at length into the subject, in my opinion never did a Rebellion begin with such courage and address on the part of the rebels, nor was there ever a Rebellion so unwisely treated by a Government.[6]

These letters of Lord Altamont and his brother, coming as they do from the pens of the most powerful of the loyalist Protestant landlords in Mayo, reflect the feelings of their co-religionists in the entire province. They are nervous of their position in a province where the vast majority of the population is Catholic and smouldering with discontent. With wishful thinking, perhaps, they report that the province is peaceful, because they are the guardians of law and order and want to give the impression of a situation under control. Above all, they want no 'severity' on the part of the military, unless their numbers are sufficient to overcome the inevitable reaction on the part of the people. They realise the seriousness of the rebellion in those parts of the country where it has already broken out, but feel that it can be avoided in Connacht by less severe measures.

To a certain extent these are also the feelings of the comparatively large number of Catholic landowners. They also are anxious to preserve the *status quo* in the province. They are fearful lest their hardwon relaxation of some of the harsher clauses of the Penal Laws would be rescinded should they be seen to oppose the Dublin government. Only by good behaviour can they hope to attain the political and social equality with their fellow-countrymen of another faith to which they feel entitled. However, there is an added dimension to these feelings in the hearts of the Old Irish Connacht families and of those other Catholic families who had been transplanted there in Cromwellian times, in that they continue to harbour the hope that perhaps one day they will come into their own. There is a certain homogeneity in the Connacht population which is missing from the other provinces. They are the most traditional with regard to faith and language, and live under the harshest conditions where the necessities of life are concerned. They are, as a result, less politicised, and remain firmly focused on their local grievances of tithes, rents and payments to their clergy. Their life is a continual struggle for survival, and it takes a very small additional burden to drive them over the brink.

When we examine the participation of the clergy in the rebellion, there is also great diversity as between the provinces. Members of the majority Presbyterian Church were prominent in the United Irish organisation in Ulster from the beginning. Nancy Curtin estimates that seventy-one Presbyterian ministers, six Church of Ireland clergy and twelve Catholic priests were members of the Society.[7] By far the most important of the Catholic priests was the Reverend James Coigly, who was executed in London on 7 June 1798 prior to the rebellion, but Catholic or Church of Ireland priests do not appear to have been involved in the actual insurrection.

The involvement of Presbyterian ministers, on the other hand, was quite considerable. Most of the ministers had been trained in Edinburgh or Glasgow where they had been exposed to radical ideas. They belonged to a faith where there was no hierarchy, and each man followed his own conscience within certain limits. This created a sturdy independence which was difficult to shake. Their community had suffered under the Penal Laws, and some 300,000 of them had emigrated to the United States between 1718 and 1775, where they had supported the Americans in the War of Independence. John Barkley writes that by 1784, when there were only twenty Catholic priests in the whole of the United States, there were over two hundred Ulster Presbyterian ministers there. Barkley writes further that they were ecumenical 'but probably in the sense that they looked forward to the day when all would be Presbyterians'.[8]

Although seven per cent of the ministers, according to Nancy Curtin's figures, were involved in the United movement from the beginning,[9] there were many more who were sympathetic to its aims, but who wanted to achieve those aims by constitutional means. The much-vaunted union of Catholic and Dissenter was never really achieved at ground level, and agrarian strife, which resulted in hostilities between Peep-o-Day-Boys and Defenders, with the subsequent formation of the Orange Order and the yeomanry, had weakened that union still further. In the event, some two to five per cent of the Presbyterian clergy actively supported the rebellion according to the conflicting figures given us by the authorities.

Outside the province of Ulster, the clerical involvement in the rebellion was restricted to the majority Catholic Church, apart from those unfortunate Church of Ireland clergymen who found themselves in the wrong place at the wrong time. The Catholic priests were suspected of United Irish sympathies in Dublin, especially the regular clergy, but since the rebellion had not broken out there as planned, it is difficult to estimate how many of them would actually have taken up arms. William Corbet lists thirty-six priests as 'Democrats' out of a total of 113 in 1796, and Keogh writes that eleven priests were implicated in United Irish activities, which gives us a rather high involvement rate of ten per cent. In Kildare and Leighlin one priest was hanged for his part in the conflict while another was sentenced to death but later released.[10] A clerical student was hanged in Waterford, but it was mainly in Wexford that the Catholic clergy became embroiled in the insurrection. This is not surprising since greater numbers of men were involved there than in any other Irish county.

Many of the Wexford rebel priests proved to be natural leaders, and the best known of them, Fr John Murphy, was acknowledged to be a skillful military commander, where strategy and the handling of men were concerned. He and three other priests were hanged after the rebellion, while others were killed in the course of the struggle. Kevin Whelan estimates that there was a total of eighty-five priests working in Co Wexford at the time, and of these 'ten can clearly be demonstrated to be rebels'.[11] This gives a twelve per cent involvement, which is considerably higher than five per cent, the higher of the two figures quoted for the involvement of Presbyterian clerics in Ulster.

Richard Hayes, in his study of priests in the independence movement of 1798, comes to the conclusion that there is no evidence that any member of the episcopacy supported the United organisation, although the authorities would have dearly loved to have been able to procure such evidence.[12] The bishops would naturally have taken a broader view of the welfare of their church, and felt that the aftermath of the French Revolution posed a threat to the Catholic Church in Europe. They were also conscious that full religious freedom would not be granted by the British government, as long as members of their church represented a threat to British authority in Ireland. They felt strongly that the wisest policy was to be seen to be loyal at all times, and to dissociate themselves completely from all popular movements, and living as they did in the comparative comfort of an average annual income of £300, they were able to maintain that position.

The parish priests and curates were in a very different position. While the bishop depended on the priests for his income, and only indirectly on the people, the parish priests were nearly completely dependent on the people through dues and voluntary contributions. In good times they enjoyed an average income of £65 a year, which was supplemented by dining nearly half the year with their parishioners. However, in bad times this income would be considerably less.

Out of their £65, the parish priests gave their curates a horse, board and accommodation, and £10. There was a shortage of curates because of the closure of the continental Irish colleges in the wake of the French Revolution, and because of the poverty of the Irish people. Of the 1800 Catholic clergy, four hundred were Regulars, and it was generally considered that the democratic spirit was strongest among the Order priests. They had close ties with their continental brethren, and their consciousness of being members of an international community gave them a certain independence, but the Catholic bishops are careful to state that the 150

Regulars employed as parish priests and curates in the year 1800 are entirely subject to their respective bishops.[13]

Bishop Stock, Church of Ireland Bishop of Killala, wonders how Catholic priests could bring themselves to join a revolution which threatens to overthrow their church, and gives his own explanation for 'this mystery':

> The almost total dependence of the Romish clergy of Ireland upon their people for the means of subsistence is the cause, according to my best judgment, why upon every popular commotion many priests of that communion have been, and until measures of better policy are adopted, always will be found in the ranks of sedition and opposition to the established government. The peasant will love a revolution because he feels the weight of poverty and has not often the sense to perceive that a change of masters may render it heavier: the priest must follow the impulse of the popular wave, or be left behind on the beach to perish.[14]

This theory of Stock's had widespread support, and it was often suggested that the Catholic clergy should be paid out of public funds, and so be made independent of the people. The education of clerical students in continental Irish colleges was also held to have unfortunate effects on the loyalty of the young men involved, and had led to the foundation of St Patrick's College Maynooth in 1793, but this foundation had only opened its doors in 1795 and it can safely be said that none of the Connacht clergy at the time of Humbert's invasion could have had any connection with it.

No Catholic bishop had wittingly been involved in the insurrection, but loyalist suspicions were such that Archbishop Troy of Dublin, Bishop Caulfield of Ferns and Dr Dominick Bellew, Bishop of Killala, were widely held to be sympathetic towards the rebels. In the case of Doctor Bellew, it was sufficient for him to have been a brother of General Matthew Bellew, who was in command at Killala, and hanged there on 10 October 1798, for doubts to be thrown on his loyalty. He had been President of the Committee of Public Safety in Ballina while that town was under the control of the insurgents, and was known to have a fiery tem-

per, but the main accusations made against him were based on the
testimony of the Reverend Bernard Dease of Kilglass near Ballina,
who reported 'that Doctor Bellew told the priests to expect the
French' and made several other unfounded charges against him.
Eventually Dr Bellew 'appealed to the Dublin authorities for protection and directions were issued from there that he should not be
subjected to further harassment.'[15]

The prelates can fairly be said to have been above suspicion.
They were aware that the government counted on their support to
keep the country calm while war was being waged against France.
To secure their loyalty they had already been granted some relaxation of the Penal Code, and complete Catholic Emancipation was
being dangled before them in return for their support of the proposed Act of Union. But no such certainty existed where the loyalty
of the parish priests and curates was concerned.

The vast majority of the clergy did not openly support the rebellion, but silence cannot be equated with disapproval, and it is
likely that the poorer parish clergy would have had more sympathy
with their flocks and less with the civil authorities than did their
more affluent superiors. They had removed at an impressionable
age from the appalling poverty of rural Ireland to large continental
cities of affluence and culture, where modern political movements
and revolutionary ideas were in an advanced state of fermentation.
They could not fail to be caught up in the excitement of a brave
new world, and even the excesses of the French Revolution could
not dampen their zeal for change in the miserable conditions of
Irish life, where Catholics were deprived of equality and opportunity,
and were subject to rapacious landlords and brutal soldiery.

Connacht was intensely Catholic and Irish-speaking and had a
large rural population living in great poverty. There were still many
Catholic gentry families, some of whom were remnants of the old
proprietors and of more recent transplanters. Some of these had
lost their estates in the previous century and were waiting in hope
for the recovery of some or all of their property. In nearly all these
cases there was a special relationship between the heads of families
and their tenants, and between those dispossessed heads of families

of ancient lineage who lived among their fellow clansmen on what were formerly clan lands. These ties of loyalty were a source of power when it came to raising troops and procuring provisions for them. The local clergy had also ties of kinship in their neighbourhood which they found it impossible to resist. Their poets still spoke of help from across the sea, and when at last it materialised in the persons of Humbert and his men, the populace was to greet them with open arms.

The suddenness of the French arrival took the Connacht people by surprise. The rebellion had arrived on their doorstep without any preparations on their part, unlike the situation in Ulster and Leinster where the Unitedmen had made their plans and went out to rouse the people. The local people had never seen a large body of soldiery, and were utterly astonished when three large ships sailed into the bay, and one thousand Frenchmen came ashore wearing exotic uniforms and bearing with them all that was necessary to wage war on their behalf against their lords and masters. The tall, dark and handsome General Humbert had declared in his Proclamation that the French troops had come 'to support your courage, to share your dangers, to join their arms and to mix their blood with yours in the sacred cause of liberty'.[16] The French were equally astonished when they saw the people who were to be their comrades-in-arms 'in the sacred cause of liberty':

> We were astonished at the extreme poverty which met us on all sides from the moment we set foot in that region of Ireland. Never had we seen such a miserable country; the near-naked men, women and children have no other shelter than a small and wretched hovel which offers them no protection against the rigours of the seasons. And this wretched dwelling is shared with their farm animals! Their daily fare consists of potatoes and sour milk; they rarely eat meat and they scarcely ever eat bread. The misery of these people is due less to the barrenness of the soil than to the extreme ignorance and great laziness in which they wallow. Their lot would be more tolerable if they were more industrious, but they are so accustomed to their way of life that they do not notice their suffering. Nearly all these

semi-savages are Catholic and so utterly fanatical as to be pitiful. As we passed their disgusting cabins, which we entered only
for a quick glance such as one would throw at a repugnant object, they threw themselves before us, prostrated themselves at
our feet, and with their heads in the mud, said long prayers for
our success. All of them, men and women, wear hanging from
their necks, large, dirty, nasty scapulars, as well as chaplets or
rosary beads.[17]

These sentiments of Captain Jobit were shared by nearly all the
members of the French party. The hearts of those loyal sons of the
Revolution must indeed have quailed when, instead of the organised bodies of oath-bound Defenders and United Irishmen they
had been led to expect, they found themselves surrounded by totally
unsophisticated people whose only concern was where to find the
next bite to eat. However, the missing link between the French
strangers and the local populace was to be provided by the Irish
members of the party, Matthew Tone, Bartholomew Teeling and
above all, by the redoubtable Fr Henry O'Kane or O'Keon.[18]
Traditionally known as 'The Green Horseman', Fr O'Kane was
now a captain in the French army. A native of Tyrawley, Co Mayo,
he had studied for the priesthood in Nantes, but was forced by the
Revolution to join the French army. Dr Stock, who was quite taken
with him, describes him as 'a fat, jolly looking man, with a ruddy
countenance that carried nothing forbidding in it, except that his
black thick eyebrows ran into each other, as they often do in aborig-
inal Irish faces.' Whatever about his eyebrows, Fr O'Kane's knowledge of Irish, English and French enabled him to act as guide and
interpreter and as one of Humbert's aides-de-camp. He had exerted
himself to protect the loyalists from the local rebels, and this, together with the fact that he was a naturalised Frenchman, saved his
life at his court-martial in Castlebar. However, Stock became disillusioned with the 'quondam priest' and declared that 'the man was
deficient both in morals and common honesty'. He had, apparently,
'cheated the bishop of twelve guineas' and had 'carried off from
Dublin another man's wife'. But this charge of the bishop's can not
be substantiated. Miles Byrne knew O'Kane personally in Paris in

1803, and afterwards on campaign in Portugal in 1810 and 1811. He had served previously in Germany and Spain, and was among the first of his corps to be decorated with the cross of the Legion of Honour when that order was first instituted. Byrne writes that 'he was goodhumoured and generous to a degree' and 'was a true admirer of the hospitality of his ancestors'. He had written an account of the French campaign in Ireland which he had given to Dr MacNeven for publication, but the manuscript seems to have disappeared.[19]

One of the ironies of the conflict in Connacht is that Dr Joseph Stock, Church of Ireland Bishop of Killala and Achonry, was more closely involved with the entire chain of events in Killala from the arrival of the French troops on 22 August 1798 until the town was captured on 23 September, than any of the Irish rebel leaders, and his diary is our main source for what happened in that area. He lived there in considerable style with his eleven children and thirteen servants in his house or 'castle' on a large estate, thanks to a generous stipend. General Humbert and his staff officers joined the household from the time of the French landing until their departure for Castlebar, when they left Lieutenant-Colonel Charost in charge. The bishop got on well with his guests, since he knew sufficient of their language to be able to converse with them, and he appreciated the food and wine which the French troops commandeered from his Protestant neighbours. He knew he was dependent on his guests to preserve law and order in the neighbourhood and secure the safety of his large household from the menace of the insurgent mob which was gathered around the castle.

The bishop, while indulging in the usual categorisation of rebel leaders as 'drunkards', of priests as 'giddy', and the people as 'savages', could feel some empathy for the 'peasantry' when he wrote:

When the united weight of so many temptations is duly estimated, operating besides on a body of peasantry already estranged from their protestant neighbours by difference of religion, language, and education, it will rather be matter of surprise, that so little mischief was the result of the insurrection in Connaught, and that we had not the same horrid scenes of cruelty and religious intolerance to mourn over as had lately stamped indelible disgrace on the eastern province. It is a circumstance worthy of particular notice that during the whole time of this civil commotion, not a drop of blood was shed by the Connaught rebels, except in the field of war. It is true, the example and influence of the French went a great way to prevent sanguinary excesses. But it will not be deemed fair to ascribe to this cause alone the forebearance of which we were witnesses, when it is considered, what a range of country lay at the mercy of the rebels for several days after the French power was known to be at an end.[20]

The Rev James Little, Rector of Lackan, in the diocese of Killala, also writes of 'the mildness of spirit in the county of Mayo' in his diary which covers the first ten days after the landing of the French. He had been in the Killala diocese longer than his bishop, and shows a greater understanding of the people, but being unable to speak French, does not succeed in painting a pen-picture of the French that can compare with that of his superior. He was only one of several local Church of Ireland rectors and curates who, together with their wives and families, crowded into the Castle. They included Doctor Thomas Ellison of Castlebar; Dean Thomas Thompson of Killala, with his wife and two children, and his curate Robert Nixon; James Burrowes, private tutor to the bishop's family and Mr Marshall, Presbyterian minister of Multifarragh, near Ballina. As the Reverend Little remarks, this 'made the Castle very fully inhabited'. 'The whole house resounded like a bedlam,' writes Bishop Stock, 'with the loquacity of the Frenchmen below, and the shrieks and groans of the fugitives above.'[21]

Dean Thompson was to play an important role in the proceedings at Killala on 20 September, when he and Roger McGuire were sent to Castlebar with a letter from the bishop to the commanding officer there, 'setting forth our situation, and our hope that nothing will be done to the prisoners at Castlebar which may provoke reprisals on the protestants at Killalla'. Dr Stock was very satisfied with the results of this mission because Thompson managed to have a private conversation with General Trench, and impressed on him so strongly the 'desperate' situation of the loyalists at Killala, that the General decided to send his forces there two days sooner than he had intended.[22]

These men, who became involved in the rebellion, albeit unintentionally, were certainly loyalists to the core. The same cannot be said with certainty of those Catholic clerics who gave information against their fellow priests. They were probably opposed to the insurrection, but greed and personal spite may also have played a part. Fr Michael Conway was Parish Priest of Ardagh in the diocese of Killala and was paid £50 for information leading to the arrest of Fr Manus Sweeney, while Fr James Jennings of the Neale, near Ballinrobe, was one of those who had testified against George Chambers of Kilboyne near Castlebar and was rewarded with a like sum for his pains.[23]

Many priests felt that the insurgents had no chance of success, and felt it their duty to warn the people of the inevitable consequences of becoming involved in it by joining the French troops. Fr Bernard O'Grady of Kilfian in the Killala diocese is reported to have warned his parishioners from the altar of the dangers of joining in the rebellion, while Fr P. Flanagan of Kilbride in the same diocese, as reported by Little, had used 'some very unequivocal and pointed expressions of loyalty' to the rebel General Bellew, which much angered that gentleman.[24] The case of Dr Dominick Bellew, the Catholic Bishop of Killala, has already been stated. The principal evidence against him, that of Fr Bernard Dease, was not substantiated.

Rev Bernard Dease, parish priest of Kilglass near Ballina, had apparently been active in enlisting recruits for the French and was arrested early in September. In order to save his life, he made a statement to Lord Portarlington in Sligo incriminating among others, Dr Bellew and his brother Matthew, Fr James Conroy, Captain O'Dowd and Richard Burke. He wrote soon after to Edward Cooke, asking for his release on the grounds that four of the men mentioned in his statement 'have been sent to eternity'. These were the men mentioned above with the exception of the bishop.[25]

Fr James or Andrew Conroy, parish priest of Addergoole, near Kiltimagh, Co Mayo, was arrested and tried at Castlebar in

November, where he was accused of welcoming the French at Killala, and convincing them of the strategic advantage of taking the Barnageehy or mountain road from Crossmolina to Castlebar instead of the more usual Foxford road. He was charged with intercepting a courier named William Blake, who had been sent to inform General Hutchinson of the French change of plan, and was enrolled instead in the rebel army. The priest was also accused of having hospitably received the French and Irish officers at his house. The court-martial found him guilty and he was hanged from a tree on the Green at Castlebar opposite the Imperial Hotel. This tree existed until recently when it was uprooted by a storm. The priest's memory has remained alive in Mayo, and a memorial to him was erected in Lahardane in 1937.[26]

The second priest to be hanged for his part in the rising was Fr Manus Sweeney of Newport, whose memory has also remained very much alive in the county, but especially in the area from Newport to Achill. There is a great deal of folklore attached to the priest's story, more particularly during the period of nine months which elapsed from the time of his escape from Newport in September 1798 until he was hanged there in June 1799. A memorial cross was erected over his grave in the picturesque Burrishoole 'Abbey' in 1912, and a second monument was erected in 1944 on the site of his father's house at Dookinella, Achill Island.[27] The part played by these two priests in the 1798 rising can in no way be compared with that of the Wexford priest-leaders, but they were hanged rather to strike terror into the hearts of the people by executing those who were most revered in their community.

Bernard Dease mentions four priests in his testimony, and they are David Kelly of Ballysakeary, Thomas Munnelly of Backs, James Conroy of Addergoole and Owen Cowley of Castleconnor, all from the Killala diocese, Co Mayo. They are accused by him of being 'very active in bringing in men to the French from their several Parishes'. Fr Kelly was parish priest of Ballycroy in 1798 and 'successfully eluded his pursuers' according to Hayes. Fr Thomas Munnelly, C.C., Backs, had been brought to Waterford in November 1799, together with John Moore and others, for transportation 'from His Majesty's dominions'. Fr Munnelly went to the United States where he became pastor of a parish in Maryland.[28]

Fr James or Andrew Conroy of Addergoole has already been mentioned. The fourth priest on Bernard Dease's list is Owen Cowley, curate in Crossmolina, and he has also been the subject of much local tradition. Musgrave depicts this man as a fanatical bully when he had 120 Protestant prisoners at his mercy in Colonel Knox's house in Ballina. Only the intervention of the French commandant Truc and the rebel Colonel Patrick Barrett prevented him carrying out the fearsome threats he made daily to the hapless captives. Musgrave appends three sworn documents which testify that Robert Atkinson of Easky, Co Sligo, was struck with a stick across the head by him, but that appears to have been the extent of his physical abuse of the prisoners. After the rebellion there was a reward of £300 offered for his capture. He fled to Muingwar in Castleconnor parish, where he lived in a dugout and was looked after by the local people until he was found dead there in 1799. According to tradition, a beggar died the same night and was given a quiet burial, while the priest was given a public funeral under the name of the beggar. This may be the explanation behind Musgrave's statement that the priest was buried at midnight by a number of his colleagues who had been ordered to attend by Bishop Bellew.[29]

Fr McGowan was also in Crossmolina in 1798, where he may have been parish priest at that time. There are few hard facts relating to him. Musgrave relates that there had not been sufficient evidence to convict him for his part in the insurrection. However, soon after the battle of Ballinamuck he heard that the French had made another landing and he celebrated the good news so well that he fell from his horse and broke his neck. So that, 'though he escaped the gallows, justice overtook him in another way'. Monsignor MacHale discovered his gravestone in Kilmurry old graveyard near Crossmolina, and the much-weathered inscription seems to indicate that he died in April 1800. Perhaps MacHale misread the inscription, or Musgrave's 'soon after the surrender of the French at Ballinamuck' referred, in fact, to a much later date?[30]

Hayes is the only authority to give us information on Fr Brown of Foxford, when he writes that he was parish priest of Foxford, was imprisoned, escaped and was a fugitive for a long period. Also, according to Hayes, he was uncle of Admiral William Brown, the founder of the Argentine navy. Other shadowy figures are three Leitrim priests, Frs Ambrose Cassidy, Ford and O'Reilly, who were implicated in the rebellion, and are praised in an elegy in Irish by Theophilus O'Flynn which is preserved among the MSS in the Royal Irish Academy.[31]

Fr Paul Feighan, C.C., Newport, had been arrested and imprisoned by James Moore O'Donel, captain of the Newport-Pratt cavalry, early in 1798, 'for seditious conversation among the lower classes'. He was probably succeeded there by Fr Manus Sweeney. Little is known about Fr Daniel O'Donnell of Kilmacshalgan, Co Mayo, Fr Phelim McDonnell of Easky, Co Sligo or Fr Mangan, C.C., Dromore West, Co Sligo. Musgrave has several references to their anti-loyalist activity in the Ballina neighbourhood, and Hayes, without giving his sources, writes that O'Donnell and McDonnell successfully eluded their pursuers. It would appear that there was not sufficient evidence to justify the arrest of any of these priests.[32]

Fr Owen Killeen, a friar from Ballyovey in Co Galway, and Fr Michael Gannon of Castlebar, Co Mayo, were brought to Waterford in November 1799, together with John Moore and others, for transportation. Denis Browne, in a letter written in October 1799, describes Killeen as having surrendered under the proclamation. He writes further that 'the Priest did a great deal of mischief in Sligo previous to his coming to this country where he persisted in misleading the people. He swore in a whole side of a country to join the French when they should land.'[33]

Fr Gannon also surrendered under the proclamation. He was obviously considered more dangerous than Killeen, as he features among those proscribed by General Trench with a price of fifty pounds on his head. He had been chaplain to the Duc de Crillon in France, but returned to Ireland at the outbreak of the French Revolution, and it was doubtless his French connection which saved him from a death sentence. He acted as a commissary to the

French troops and was 'active and useful' to them according to Musgrave, who has left us a colourful picture of the priest wearing 'a large fierce cocked hat, à la militaire, and silk clothes made in a curious fashion, all the property of the late duke'. Miles Byrne writes that 'his appearance commanded respect, as he was tall and handsome with dignified, agreeable manners'.

Fr Gannon left Ireland for Lisbon, and from there wrote to Lucien Bonaparte, the French ambassador in Madrid, who invited him to that city. From there he proceeded to Paris, where in 1803 he was parish priest of a village near Saint-Germain-en-Laye. Miles Byrne writes that Mrs Thomas Addis Emmet told him 'how glad she always was to see Fr Gannan [sic] coming to the house, for her husband's spirits were always cheered by his visits and conversation, as he was never desponding about Ireland'. He later moved to a parish near Tours, and eventually became chaplain to a regiment at Lille where 'in this situation, half clerical, half military, he finished honourably his long career; but he was ever regretting his "sweet home"'.[34]

Fr Myles Prendergast, who was attached to Murrisk Augustinian Friary, near Westport, is one of those whose many years as a fugitive priest have survived in popular memory. He features on the list of those proscribed by General Trench with a price of fifty pounds on his head, and was forced to go 'on the run' in Connemara until he finally entered into negotiations for a pardon with Brigadier Major Marshall in November 1805. He was to be put on board an American vessel in Galway, when he would be given thirty guineas. According to a letter written by Myles Prendergast to Major Marshall on that date, a memorial and letter had been delivered to General Hill at Barna, the property of Marcus Lynch. 'A M. Boyde, whose Christian name I forget, land surveyor and projector, who came to Ballinakill in August 1804, was the person who encouraged me to write both the memorial and letter, as he said he had some interest with Lord Cathcart and General Hill.' He complains that he had been 'unjustly and unfairly' persecuted by the Westport Browne family fifteen months before the French invasion, that he had been obliged to live in the mountains 'and only by intervals used to lurk about home when said family would happen to be in Dublin or elsewhere from Westport.'[35]

Lord Sligo[36] had, indeed, been complaining bitterly to Alexander Marsden about the presence of Prendergast and other rebels in Connemara in 1802 and 1803, and seems to suspect that Richard Martin is not zealous enough in hunting them down. His brother, Denis Browne, is also critical of the situation in Connemara, and says that the interior is 'no more subject to the laws of Ireland than Iceland'. The government has received information that Prendergast 'is constantly concealed by Colonel Martin's tenantry, that he seldom remains more than a day and a night at any house. Further information sent on 1 June 1805 is to the effect that:

> The magistrates of the country do not wish to have anything to do with arresting John Gibbons, Prendergast, or such persons, as it would entail certain destruction on their familys for generations to come, particularly Prendergast, he being a priest.[37]

It is difficult to know what happened in Prendergast's case. He was forty-seven years of age at the time of his letter to Marshall in 1805, and it is said that he was over eighty years of age at the time of his death near Clifden. It is unlikely that he remained a fugitive for all that time. He may not have received a favourable answer to his memorial of 1805, but may have been pardoned subsequently, as it is said that both Richard Martin and Lord Mayo had interceded on his behalf. He remains a hero of the fugitive outlaw type so beloved of the popular imagination.[38]

In all, seventeen out of a total of 314 priests in the province of Connacht can be shown to have been favourably disposed towards the rebels, which gives us a figure of just under five and a half per cent.[39] This is considerably less than the twelve per cent involvement in Wexford and can be explained in various ways. The French invasion had exploded on to the Connacht scene before the more conservative elements of the population had time to determine their course of action. Some had been carried along headlong in the excitement, while others had hesitated until the excitement had passed them by. There had been considerably less politicisation in the province and few of the clergy had become involved in either Defenderism or the United Irish movement. In many cases the avowed anti-clericalism of the French far outweighed the liberal tendencies of the continental-educated clergy. A determining factor was the presence of professional leaders in the persons of the French and Irish staff officers, thus obviating the necessity for clerical participation at leadership level. But perhaps, above all, the paucity of hard fact overlaid by a superabundance of tradition in the stories of the Connacht priests leaves us a far from clear picture of the actual numbers involved.

Notes:

1   Stewart, A.T.Q., *The Narrow Ground, Aspects of Ulster, 1609-1969* (London, 1977), p. 102; Finlay Holmes, *Our Irish Presbyterian Heritage* (Presbyterian Church in Ireland, 1985), p. 86.

2   National Archives, Rebellion Papers, 620/26/184 (30 Dec 1796); 620/28/40 (4 Jan 1797); 620/28/67 (7 Jan 1797).

3   To Mr Pelham, Nat. Arch. Reb. Papers, 620/30/271 (31 May 1797).

4   To Pelham, Nat. Arch. Reb. Papers, 620/31/70 (10 June 1797).

5   To Altamont, Nat. Arch. Reb. Papers, 620/36/71 (24 Mar 1798).

6   To___, Nat. Arch. Reb. Papers, 620/37/240; 620/38/204 (17 June 1798).

7   *The United Irishmen, Popular Politics in Ulster and Dublin, 1791-1798* (Clarendon Press, Oxford, 1994), p. 127.

8   Barkley, 'Rev Principal John M., The Presbyterian Minister in Eighteenth Century Ireland', in *Challenge and Conflict: essays in Irish Presbyterian History and Doctrine* (1981), p. 58, 62.

9   Curtin, loc. cit.

10 Keogh, Dáire, *The French Disease, The Catholic Church and Irish Radicalism, 1790-1800* (Four Courts Press, 1993), pp. 131, 175.

11 Whelan, Kevin, 'The Role of the Catholic Priest in the 1798 Rebellion in County Wexford', in Kevin Whelan (ed.), *Wexford History and Society* (Dublin, 1987), p. 296.

12 Hayes, Richard, 'Priests in the Independence Movement of '98' in *Irish Ecclesiastical Record* (October 1945), pp. 258-9.

13 Vane, Charles, Marquess of Londonderry (ed), *Memoirs and Correspondence of Viscount Castlereagh, second Marquess of Londonderry,* Vol. IV (London, 1850), pp. 99-101.

14 *Bishop Stock's 'Narrative' of the Year of the French: 1798,* (ed.) Grattan Freyer (Irish Humanities Centre, 1982), pp. 64-5.

15 Nat. Arch. Reb. Papers, 620/40/28; Rev E. MacHale, 'Some Mayo Priests of 1798', in *North Mayo Historical Journal,* Vol. II, No. 5 (1991-92), pp. 9-10; Keogh, *French Disease,* p. 152.

16 Hayes, Richard, *The Last Invasion of Ireland* (Dublin, 1979), p. 22.

17 Costello, Nuala (ed), 'Jobit's Journal of the French Expedition, 1798', in *Analecta Hibernica,* No. 11 (July 1941), pp. 15-16.

18 Henry O'Kane's surname presents something of a problem, as
    contemporaries also write O'Keon and O'Kean. On balance O'Kane would
    appear to be the better choice. His military rank is also very uncertain. He is
    generally referred to as Captain O'Kane, but he was a Major of Grenadiers in
    the French army, and is described as Colonel O'Kane in his commission to
    serve in Ireland (Hayes, *Last Invasion*, pp. 205-6).

19 *Bishop Stock's Narrative*, pp. 47-8; Fanny Byrne (ed), *Memoirs of Miles Byrne*
    (Irish University Press, 1972), Vol. III, pp. 62-3.

20 *Bishop Stock's Narrative*, pp. 19-20.

21 Costello, Nuala (ed), 'Little's Diary of the French Landing in 1798' in
    Anal. Hib., No. 11 (July 1941), pp. 104, 134; Stock, p. 13. There were 'not
    fewer than fourscore' refugees there when Killala was recaptured (Stock,
    p. 86).

22 Stock, pp. 79, 86.

23 Nat. Arch. State of the Country Papers, 1018/16, Earl of Altamont to___
    (15 June 1799).

24 MacHale, 'Some Mayo Priests', p. 10; Costello, 'Little's Diary', p. 128.

25 Musgrave, *Irish Rebellion*, p. 569; Nat. Arch. Reb. Papers, 620/40/58 (15
    Sept 1798); 620/117/6.

26 MacHale, 'Some Mayo Priests', pp. 11-12.

27 For more information on Fr Sweeney, see S. Mulloy, 'Father Manus Sweeney
    (1763-1799), in *Cathair na Mart*, No. 14 (1994), pp. 27-38; Pádraig Ó
    Móghráin, 'Gearr-Chunntas ar an Athair Mánus Mac Suibhne', *Béaloideas*,
    XVII (1947), pp. 3-57.

28 Nat. Arch. Reb. Papers, 620/40/58 (15 Sept 1798); Hayes, *Last Invasion*,
    p. 197; MacHale, 'Some Mayo Priests', p. 17.

29 Musgrave, *Irish Rebellion*, pp. 548-50, 824-6; MacHale, 'Some Mayo
    Priests', pp. 14-16.

30 MacHale, 'Some Irish Priests', p. 16; Musgrave, *Irish Rebellion*, p. 552.

31 Hayes, *Last Invasion*, pp. 197, 251.

32 *Proceedings of a Court of Inquiry at Castlebar, the 1st of December, 1800*
    (Dublin, 1801), p. 26; Musgrave, *Irish Rebellion*, pp. 532, 567-8, 580;
    Hayes, *Last Invasion*, p. 197.

33 MacHale, 'Some Irish Priests', p. 17; to William Marsden, Nat. Arch. Reb.
    Papers, 620/56/48 (19 Oct 1799).

34 Nat. Arch. State Prisoners, Carton 20; Musgrave, *Irish Rebellion*, p. 563;
    Memoirs of Miles Byrne, Vol. III, pp. 62-3.

35 R. Marshall to Alex Marsden, Nat. Arch. State of the Country Papers, 3732
    (28 Apr 1806); Myles Prendergast to R. Marshall, loc. cit., (25 Nov 1805).

36 The former Earl of Altamont. He had been created First Marquess of Sligo as
    a result of the passing of the Act of Union.

37 Denis Browne to the Lord Lieutenant, Nat. Arch. State of the Country
    Papers, 1023/5 (30 Oct 1803).

38 Lavelle, Rory, 'The Mayo rebels of '98 in Connemara', in *Connemara,
    Journal of the Clifden and Connemara Heritage Group*, Vol. 1, No. 1 (August
    1993), pp. 70-5.

39 If we include Fr Bernard Dease, the figure would be six per cent.

The Politics of Clerical Radicalism in the 1790s

L. M. Cullen

I

One of the many striking things about 1798 is the prominence of clergymen from all three major religious groupings, Anglican, Presbyterian and Catholic in the events of the year, and of the preceding and following years. This of course reflected the prominence of clergymen in society. This activism has been played down somewhat in later analysis. In the case of Anglican clergymen, for instance, the fact that they can be found on both sides of the political divide has been largely overlooked: the reality of course is that the role of Anglican clergymen is more complicated than has been usually assumed. They are often seen as uniformly loyalist, and hence as part of a political background which does not itself require interrogation. If the Anglican clergy are examined more closely, it will be seen that some of them form part of the explicit opposition to political and security policies alike in the 1790s, and that they played a role on both sides of a polarised society. Unfortunately, history has been bedevilled by the concept of *Protestant ascendancy*. Some Anglicans were part of the opposition to Protestant ascendancy. To a certain extent current interpretation draws on assumptions of the nineteenth century when the Established Church became firmly committed to defence against encroachment on its interests, and it became more uniformly identified also with a political position shared with a threatened landed class and with the Castle. The spread of evangelicalism of course reinforced this. It was widespread and influential even at the level of the hierarchy. While not all clergymen were evangelicals, it certainly created the public image, and more particularly provoked the increasingly angry response of Catholics. Thus issues like Protestant proselytising missions in the west of Ireland, the rivalry of chaplains to baptise orphans in the poor houses, and the Protestant rescue societies alike reflected and contributed to divides and tensions which ran deep even in the society of the very end of the nineteenth century.

In the case of Presbyterian and Catholic clergymen, their role has been analysed to a greater degree and is therefore better known; and it was of course a political issue at the time or later. Those that took the field in 1798 or, in the case of Presbyterians, had intended to do so, are easily identified. The tendency overall in the case of both sects has been to play down the numbers, or the significance of what it implied: the small numbers in relation to the total clergy are stressed. In the case of Catholics, while one article in modern times, by Richard Hayes in the *Irish Ecclesiastical Record*[1] sought to stress how widespread the rebel priests were, the more common view, even when the activism of individuals has been stressed, has been that they were a small minority. Quigley's radicalism and membership of the United Irishmen was only reluctantly conceded in Fr Brendan McAvoy's study in *Seanchas Ardmhacha*, for instance.[2] However, this poses real problems, as it is not clear that loyalty or disloyalty at large can be easily established on the base of the known cases, and that the rest of the clergymen were in some predictable way loyal. For instance, as David Miller pointed out, Presbyterian radicals were from all theological leanings, hence not as argued in the past from those of a single theological side.[3] In the case of Catholics, in addition to clergymen implicated in the rebellion, there were others of radical sympathies. The subscribers to the volume of Corry's radical verse published in Newry 1797, drawn from Kildare and from the Ulster border regions, included 16 Presbyterian and 11 Catholic clergymen.[4] Some of these have documented careers; others are unknown.

The direction of study has been to assume that those clergymen whose political views are not documented had different views from those who became politically notorious, and hence that it is legitimate to stress the fewness of the radicals or the radical leanings among the clergy. This, however, involves easy acceptance of the arguments made by contemporaries in the Catholic Church who wanted to play down the numbers or by those in the Presbyterian Church who wanted to discredit the New Light movement, and hence ignored the awkward fact that Presbyterian churchmen at large had a record of political dissent and activity. The ultimate answer is that we do not know the views of the others: at best we can only guess that they covered a spectrum of views. It is precisely the same problem as arises in relation to magistrates. Magistrates are seen as supporters of government. Yet the fact is that in many counties they were not (and that the government and zealot local magistrates did not see them as such): they opposed in east Down; in Kildare and in Wexford and Wicklow they were divided between an identifiable small group of loyalist activists and a large group prompted by motives which were variously liberal or radical. The dialectic of magistrate opinion is best illustrated in the correspondence from John Edwards in Bray to the Castle: it is a view similar to that held by many magistrates.[5]

II

There are two problems in relation to the clergy. The first is that the quantity of contemporary information is small, and that inevitably they and their defenders had no interest in developing the theme after the rebellion. A book such as Steel Dickson's is unusual precisely because it is an account by a man who had been an activist and later a political victim. Indeed, the conflict between Steel Dickson and Robert Black, agent on behalf of Castlereagh to the Presbyterian Synod, illustrates two facets of that church, and emphasises the primacy of politics. The politics of the late 1790s and early 1800s show very clearly that the Synod was politically divided, and that Castlereagh and the government feared the Presbyterian clergy. Ironically, Castlereagh's much-disliked man of general political business was an Anglican clergymen, Cleland, and Robert Black's role as a political manager of the Presbyterian Synod was a difficult and complex one.[6]

In the case of Catholic clergy the only apologia by an individual clergyman is Quigley's,[7] and that was tampered with, if Madden's suggestion is correct, to play down his radical credentials. For others we have none by the clergymen themselves, unless we include the self-serving accounts put together by Caulfield, the Bishop of Ferns, or promoted by him and by Troy, his metropolitan. Moreover, and it has not been sufficiently recognised, these writings were not intended to vindicate either individual clergymen or rebels, or even the interest of Catholics at large. Their purpose was to preserve the institutional interests of the church. In the wake of the rebellion, the church was not, despite the burning of church buildings in south Leinster and at least one post-rebellion murder of a Catholic clergyman and violent attacks on several clergymen, seriously threatened. The large correspondence by Archbishop Troy was concerned exclusively with ecclesiastical issues: the interests of the laity almost never obtrude in it, and even correspondence with Catholic figures does not loom large except where, as in the case of figures like Plowden, engaged to write on the events of the times, they were expressly defenders of the church's image. What was threatened in 1798 was its prospects of institutional advantages in the form of preservation of its new Maynooth college or of gaining state subsidisation or maintenance of clergymen. The first open vindication of the Wexford clergy rebels was by Miles Byrne in 1863.[8] All other writers, including Catholic ones, whether of highly compromised background like Edward Hay or like Cloney, a former active rebel, were at one in distancing themselves from defence of the role of churchmen. Troy and Caulfield disliked Hay: Caulfield regarded his intervention as unhelpful even before his book had appeared, and the dislike of Hay comes up repeatedly in the correspondence between the two ecclesiastics. Miles Byrne's account, as published in 1863, which with favourable comments cast the clergy in a positive subversive role, itself led to quick clerical reaction, including the creation of the preposterous John Murphy legend.

In the case of Anglicanism, we are better served, in part because the clergy were in a position of authority. However, explicit writings by individual clergymen are few. On the clerical magistrate side, there is a remarkable document, by Thomas Handcock,[9] a man who has to be taken seriously, to a degree respected as a clear-sighted realist, and who later made a scholarly contribution to the history of the county. There are in fact a larger number of liberal writings, either published or unpublished, than of loyalist clerical ones. They have never been looked at as a corpus. They have been used as the isolated sources by individuals who were witnesses to events, and whose self-evident fairness gives them some authority as independent observers. Yet they point to a different thing: the existence of a liberal wing in the Established Church. It had its antecedents in the two Synges and in Bishop Clayton, and arguably came of age with Thomas Leland, the Trinity College divine and college fellow, friend of Edmund Burke. This interest was well-defined in the 1780s; it could be seen even in the internal politics of a county as committed to the interests of the Established Church as Cork, with one clergyman on the fringes of the county engaged in the pamphlet controversy against Bishop Woodward of Cloyne;[10] and in the late 1790s it offered public backing to Cornwallis' enlightened policy. The true status of Gordon's *History of Ireland* in 1805, which repeats much of what was said in his earlier and more directly controversial work, is seen in the list of subscribers: it has few loyalists, many Catholics and rebels and no less a figure than Edward Fitzgerald in exile in Hamburg. Of course, the authors wrote as churchmen, and hence they reflect fashionable intellectual views, a somewhat patronising view of the Catholic Church, and, despite their very genuine liberalism, some real fears of Romanism and what they saw as its intolerance. Modern Irish nationalist Catholic writers have overreacted to these views, which were commonplace ones for their times. Hayes disregarded both Stock and Gordon, and the animus in his remarks in his book, *The Last Invasion of Ireland*, betrays on his part his own violent and unqualified partisanship. In fact his article on the clergy in its title refers to the priests in the 'Independence Movement', which is of course language of the twentieth century. Charles Dickson, author of modern histories of the rebellion in Antrim and Wexford, likewise regarded them as loyalists. W. H. Maxwell can be added to this collection of liberal clergymen, though of course not as a directly contemporary witness to '98 itself. His novel *O'Hara* in 1825 has strong United

Irishman sympathies, and his *Wild sports of the west* has a remarkable chapter which is illuminating on Denis Browne's underrated political role in Co Mayo; his *History of the rebellion*, prompted by the new interest in the rebellion in the 1840s, is a much fairer account than it has been given credit for.

That many clergymen were tolerant should not surprise us. They were among the educated people of the age. This was true of clergymen at large, whether of the Established Church, or of the Catholic and Presbyterian ones. The consequence was that there was a tradition of clerical prominence in politics: de Bernis was foreign minister in France as late as 1758, Terray *controleur* general in 1769, and de Brienne chief minister in 1787, and both Boulter and Stone as primates were leaders of the Irish administration in the 18-month intervals between Irish parliaments. However, bishops were ceasing to be central political actors. Thus, in France, while bishops remained politically important as did Archbishop Dillon of Toulouse, a successor, de Brienne, as a minister in 1787 was already an anachronism. In England their decline had begun somewhat earlier, quickened by the fact that bishops had more difficulty, in an age when the divine right of kings still had force as political doctrine, than lay figures in making the transition from loyalty to the Stuart kings to a new figure on the throne. In Ireland, where Protestants could not afford the luxury of a backward glance, the change was less evident than in England, and Boulter and Stone were already anachronisms by English standards. Indeed, they were also the last of the great Irish political bishops, though Archbishop Agar of Cashel was a major political figure in the Irish Council as late as the 1790s, and Woodward, as an ally of John Foster, created a conservative political interest in the Dublin Society in the late 1770s and, as a bishop in the mid-1780s, was the national literary spokesman for the conservative interest. The Bishop of Londonderry, Hervey, Earl of Bristol, attempted a political role in the 1780s, though as a maverick outsider, on the left side of the political spectrum. It failed, and most conspicuously in his own diocese, his illusory political strength lying in his appeal to a diffuse network of advanced radicals in Dublin and in east Ulster.

Precisely because clergymen were educated, and prepared to debate political as well as economic issues, they inevitably expressed views on the major questions of the age. Clergymen wrote many books on secular subjects, a fact which lasted well beyond the decline of their direct role in politics. This was true in Europe, but it was equally true in England. John Smith's *Memoirs of wool* in 1747 is an instance as, even later, is Dean Tucker in his writing on economic subjects. A significant amount of writing in Ireland was by clergymen. Some were works on economic matters, such as Madden's *Reflections and resolutions* in 1738 or Bishop Berkeley's *Querist* in 1735, and they inevitably wrote on political issues as well. Swift is the best example. He was an accomplished writer in the new school of writing in English politics, polarised as they were in 1710, and his abilities were later evident in Ireland, especially in the 1720s and nowhere more than in the *Modest Proposal*, arguably the greatest political pamphlet of the age (and central to understanding the significant parliamentary session of 1729-30), rivalled only in its century in France by the best of Voltaire's essays. The Synges and Clayton had set the wheels in motion on the question of tolerance; Thomas Leland pursued the same issues in the 1760s and 1770s, and his *History of Ireland* in 1773 was non-partisan and liberal in intent. Bishop Woodward's incursion in 1786 on the conservative side started an avalanche of writing, some of it on both sides by co-religionist clergymen, and some in opposition by Catholic and especially Presbyterian clerics.

Married clergymen in their family circle created a milieu with a taste or respect for learning, and it was they and their offspring, female as well as male, rather than the gentry as such who provided the backing for learning. In Burke's small circle of six fellow students in the famous club of 1747 to debate public issues, two of the members were to take holy orders, a reminder that clergymen should not be seen as they have been as a bastion of the establishment. After all, after the 1798 rebellion, it was not only graduates of the college, but clerical graduates of the college who were the most outspoken supporters of the policy of conciliating rebels by Cornwallis, the Chesterfield of a second troubled year in Irish history. They include Bishop Stock of Killala, a humane and gifted fellow, Joseph Gordon curate in Wexford, and James Little, the scholarly rector at Lackan, whose account of the rebellion took long to write because his house had been wrecked but which he had started with the intention of publication.[11] All three had an interesting profile. They were literary figures. Stock was a literary bishop; Little was a scholar and member of the Royal Irish Academy; and Gordon was the quintessential scholarly clergymen, writing a number of books.

If Bishop Woodward set the pace in the political pamphleteering of 1786-8, it was less as churchman than as a supporter of Lord Shannon in the politics of Co Cork. However, he has to be seen as a representative of one of two wings within the church. There was in fact a clash within the church between its hard-line bishops such as Agar, and others like O'Beirne and Stock. Their public profile, not a shortage of lay magistrate figures, explains the role played also by clergymen as magistrates. About 10 per cent of the magistrates were clergymen, much the same proportion as in England, and their role did not in fact derive, as often suggested, from a shortage of lay figures for office. Some were highly prominent as conservative figures in their areas: that accounts for the assassination of the Rev Butler in Meath in 1793, the Rev Knipe in the same county in 1797, and the Rev Hamilton in Donegal in the same year. Some were the political managers of their area, as Neligan was in Ballina (and Stock's 1800 pamphlet is in some degree a reply to Neligan's role). Maunsell in Portadown was one of the catalysts of support for the Orange Order; Dean Warburton was increasingly a backer of the conservatives in Armagh (deviating progressively over time from the pro-Charlemont role of clergymen like the Anglican Edward Hudson or Presbyterian Campbell); and the Rev Cleland was a key figure in Down, where he was land and political agent for Castlereagh and from 1797, the contact man with the spy Nicholas Magin, the best placed and arguably only informer at a really high level within the councils of the United Irishmen. Among Wexford magistrates, Roger Owen, who was later ill-treated by the rebels, had taken his duties very officiously. The account by his sister of Wexford events in 1798 concedes implicitly that he was an Orangeman (if so he would have been one of the first Orangemen in the county). Barrington, who knew Wexford well and was critical of clerical justices, recorded of parson Owen that 'as he looked for church preferment and was of course in the neighbourhood of Wexford a violent, indeed an outrageous royalist... he was not over-popular in *quiet* days'.[12]

Presbyterian clergy were no different in the fact of their local political importance. They were leaders in their society. Indeed, as there was virtually no Presbyterian gentry (except in east Down, where, as in the case of the true religious affiliation of Catholic gentry in Ireland at large, there arises the problem of deciding whether they were Anglican or attached to their original church and when they ceased in spirit to be so attached), they found themselves not only identified with their communities but, to a greater degree even than Anglican clergymen, in the absence of a numerous Presbyterian gentry, were cast in the role of political spokesmen of their communities. Inevitably, that meant that in rural areas they were chaplains, even captains, of Volunteer corps. They had a much closer, and more willing, involvement in the Volunteers than the clergymen of Anglican communities. That led in turn to a transition into United Irishman politics; Dickson, Ledlie Birch, and Porter in particular were saturated in the politics of radical thought and action, and Samuel Barber is the most arresting example, the author of the two most radical pamphlets in the writing of 1786-88 and in 1792 a central figure in the story of the attempts from both sides to determine the politics of the Rathfriland Volunteers. The moderatorship of the Synod is a complex affair because it was elective, but the election of Dickson for 1793 illustrates how far the majority were prepared to go in support of men of known radical views. Barber's place in Down politics in 1792, and Dickson's prominence in 1793, point to the scale of politicisation; even clergymen who did not become politicised in a radical sense, like William Campbell, represented a strong commitment to Charlemontite thought and action.

The place of clergymen in public life was evident among

Catholics as well, though as Catholic education was less effective, incomes smaller and many educated Catholic clergymen, seeking advancement on the continent, opted not to return to Ireland, it was slower to develop. However, a clerical role in lay life clearly existed. It can be seen in the poetic circle in Munster poetry (including the praise poems of clergymen by lay members); Carpenter as Archbishop of Dublin represented the role eminently (before Troy, as his successor, began the process of putting church interests as the single-minded object of policy); and Bishop Murphy of Cork in the early nineteenth century commissioned Gaelic manuscripts and was a book collector on a grand scale. In a political context Catholic clergymen were not different from others, though, given the political disadvantages of the Catholic Church, they were less prominent. However, they had a role. The first interesting example is that of Carpenter in Dublin, and his successor Troy was of course to have close links with the Castle. The tensions over the loyalty oath of 1774, which superficially seem labyrinthine and absurd, revolved essentially around a political issue: the gallican versus ultramontane view of the place of the church in society. Archbishop Butler of Cashel represented the gallican view, Troy as Bishop of Ossory represented the ultramontane view. The underlying political issue explains why the divide was so sharp, why laymen preceded churchmen in taking the oath outside Munster, and why Carpenter's achievement was considerable in winding down the issue in the late 1770s. Troy from 1786 represented the rise of a member of the ultramontane faction to the politically most sensitive post in the Irish Catholic Church, the ascendant role of the Rome-oriented interest, and its effort to subordinate all issues to the institutional advance of the church.

Edmund Burke, who knew Ireland and its Catholics well, thought that the political power of Catholic clergy was small. This was correct (though anti-Catholic zealots thought otherwise, and used the danger of clerical power as an argument against political rights for Catholics). The 1798 rebellion is important in the discussion of this issue, as it raises the question, which has never been quite resolved, of the role and motives of Catholic clergy, especially those who became participants, and the degree to which their actions or outlook was representative of thinking within their church.

III

If the radicals are easy to identify, we can not assume that they were the exception and that others were untouched by new ideas. Ironically the same methodology is not applied to Anglican clergymen. The known hard-line ones are taken to represent the views of the clergymen at large. That contrasts with the conclusion adopted in the case of the other two churches: the disloyal clergymen, if Catholic, are claimed to have been few in Wexford or in Mayo, and, if Presbyterians, to be confined mainly to those with New Light views. In fact the contrast in treatment between established and non-established clergy arises from politics. Both the Catholic and Presbyterian churches, for rather different reasons, massaged the truth, and wanted to play down involvement. On the other hand, later writers with a liberal agenda, who could be sparing in regard to those on their own political side, could afford to be sweeping in their views of Anglican clergymen. Thus, judge Fletcher in 1814, a former radical whig MP of the 1790s and an intimate of the Wexford Grogan and Colclough interests, launched into a startling invective on clerical magistrates, declaring that:

> Some clergymen there may have been, who in a period of distraction, perusing the Old Testament with more attention than the New, and admiring the glories of Joshua, (the son of Nun) fancied they perceived in the Catholics, the Canaanites of old; and, at the head of militia and armed yeomanry, wished to conquer from them the promised glebe. Such men, I hope, are not now to be found in that most respectable order; and, if they are, I need scarcely add, they should no longer remain in the commission.[13]

The same view, largely with parson Owen in mind, had of course been made also by Barrington, who, married to a daughter of a brother of the Wexford Grogans, had an impeccable knowledge of the county, and spoke with more truth of it than he did of other aspects of Irish life.[14] There is no reason why the same method should not be followed in both cases. In the case of the Anglican clergy, the story of politically active clergymen should not be allowed to determine the conclusion about the outlook of the remainder of members of the their church.

In the Catholic Church, Troy represented the advent of the ultramontane view, and the Bishop of Ferns, Caulfield, was a faithful and timid acolyte. He was a shallow, narrow-minded and ineffective person, dependent on and influenced by Troy. It is not surprising that James Gordon is somewhat uncomfortable about him: despite Gordon's vigorous commitment to the defence of Catholics, he found himself unable to avoid the admission that he had difficulty in understanding Caulfield's explanation of his failure to account fully for his action – or inaction – on the day of the massacres on Wexford Bridge. The purpose of the Catholic clerical interest was essentially one of protecting the interests of the church, and they had far less in common with Irish lay society than is usually assumed (a divide that surfaces in the unease by both Caulfield and Troy about Edward Hay's readiness to enter the lists in literary defence of Catholics, undirected by them). They were also in the political sense apologists, unscrupulous in making a case or at least not really interested in looking at it with independent eyes. Troy's closeness to Plowden, author of works which in effect pleaded the clerical case, is an illustration of the propaganda role, and of their closeness to a political interest in England.

It seems surprising that their arguments have been accepted as readily as they have since they were essentially open apologists for the church's position. They represented in their outlook and writing an obsession with clerical interests, a total lack of concern about matters of lay import, and a startling assumption that ecclesiastical and lay Catholic interests converge. In a mixed society, they reflected a narrow point of view certain to give offence even to moderate Protestants. Hussey's indiscreet pastoral in 1797 reflected this attitude; it represented the view of Rome (his views on education in particular gave offence, and in Irish circumstances and especially those of 1797, at best they lacked tact). In fact they were not only violently attacked, but were viewed with disfavour by Hussey's friend, Burke.

Caulfield's singleminded obsessions, and his readiness to formulate views without a foundation, is revealed in his initial belief that church burnings in Wexford were conducted by rebels who were anxious to damage the credibility of the yeomanry.[15] His lack of ready knowledge of the views of his own clergy is revealed also in his inclusion of Fr John Redmond of Camolin in the initial list of 9 disloyal clergymen which he provided at the outset of September at the behest of Troy. Redmond was only later excluded from the listing: the list itself, even with the exclusion of Redmond, however, had grown in the meantime from 9 to 11.[16] The disregard for truth is blatant in relation to Michael Murphy: one of the pamphlets in 1799, prepared with the connivance of Caulfield and Troy, defending the Catholic position denied that he had held a curacy at all: according to it 'he was never called to a curacy on account of his incapacity and riotous temper'.[17] The handling of Michael Murphy is interesting: his name was not included in the first list; it appears in the 1799 list, with the phrase 'not empl' [not employed] added in another hand. Omitted from Caulfield's first list of clerical rebels, he not only enters later lists and accounts – inevitably given his notoriety – but features as a clergyman deprived of his functions. If he had been suspended or under suspicion, Caulfield should have been aware in 1798 of Murphy's record, and it would have helped his purpose in fact to refer to the case. The 1799 pamphlet was compiled by Clinch of Maynooth, and Clinch was in touch with Troy throughout 1799, and at one stage had sent through Troy a list of queries for Caulfield to answer. The figures cited in the pamphlet *The state of his majesty's subjects professing the Roman Catholic religion*, for instance, are figures that on Corrin's authority Caulfield had supplied to Troy: what is said in the pamphlet in regard to Murphy is in contradiction with the evidence published in the Dublin newspapers of Murphy's exercise of his function as curate in 1797-8, and according to Hay's account, Murphy was present on one occasion with Mountnorris and Hay when the signatures of parishioners were being secured. Caulfield was at first reluctant to get involved in public controversy, and he was drawn into it by Troy who himself was acting in concert with Erskine, the papal representative for the British Isles, who wanted public statements rebutting the charges against the clergy, and who at one point argued that it should be claimed that Protestants had been as involved as Catholics. None of Caulfield's letters, written at the behest of Troy, who was conducting a national campaign rather than a local Wexford one, is a disinterested statement of Wexford events.

IV

If clergymen were involved so closely, that raises questions about sectarianism in society. From one point of view that already existed, and it is not necessary to adduce the role of clergymen in the 1790s to account either for its character or progress. From another point of view, not only political agitation at large, but the views supported by the Orange Order and the United Irishman propaganda, all irresponsibly gave sectarian fears a new currency. Clergymen were not responsible for them. It is necessary, however, to draw a line between clergymen in general and clergymen who were activist magistrates like Cleland in Newtownards, or like Maunsell in Portadown and Neligan at Ballina, both of whom had a hand in the spread of the Orange Order, or Roger Owen in north Wexford, who was almost certainly one of the early Orangemen in Wexford. Both Fletcher (who through his Colclough associations in the 1790s had a good knowledge of Wexford conditions), addressing the Wexford grand jury in 1814, and Barrington (married to a Wexford Grogan lady and a frequent visitor to the county in the 1790s), writing around 1830, regarded in recollection the role of clerical magistrates as damaging factors in Wexford.

If some Anglican clergymen were either activist magistrates or abettors of the Orange Order, the counterpart on the Catholic side was open involvement in radical causes or even in the United Irishmen. Were Catholic clergymen officers? It is hard to avoid the belief that in some cases they were. There is also a divide between individual clergymen in terms of sectarian outlook. One can draw a distinction between individual Anglican clergymen in Wexford: say Gordon and Owen, who were poles apart. As for Catholic clergymen, Gordon, for instance, had little time for John Murphy whom he saw as a shallow fanatic; on the other hand, he spoke well on this front of Philip Roche. Thus there were divides among the clergymen of each religion. Inevitably they reflected the divides in local lay society, respectively Catholic and Anglican.

The role as such of the clergy is one thing. The question of sectarianism, which could affect individuals whether lay or clerical as one of several possible responses to the complex challenge all faced, is another issue. Inevitably, they overlapped, and especially where massacre could be alleged, it was tempting to argue a clerical involvement or responsibility. Thus, extreme apologists for the loyalist view wanted to involve them, and Musgrave represents this at its most consummate or blatant. In the case of massacre, not only was the argument useful ammunition, but it provided the opportunity of suggesting that clergymen not simply failed to intervene but participated directly in one form or other. Musgrave went so far as suggesting, though making clear that he had the information on hearsay, that Bishop Caulfield had blessed the executioners. The Catholic clergymen and their bishop never explained satisfactorily why their intervention was limited and so late on 20 June, and Gordon in his writing made clear that Caulfield's account had not convinced him. Significantly, Caulfield's own public response was unconvincing. Embarrassed by Gordon's account 'from whom I would expect a more candid and fair mode of reasoning', his lame statement that he was in his house from 11 or 12 to 8 pm left everything unexplained.[18]

The truth may well be of course that, for reasons that do not flatter him, Caulfield's account has a large element of truth. He was deeply unpopular, and as the rebels were themselves divided into two camps, one more extreme than the other, he carried little weight (a point which in effect he and his apologists later stressed). Caulfield was not only a loyalist, but an obsessively strong one, as early as 1792, and surprisingly forthright in his hostility to the laity. Moreover, he later suffered by his identity with the Mountnorris camp, which in the wake of the 1797 election became the focus of the divide among Catholics. Thus, one of his closest associates was Thomas Richards, who was one of the few liberal Protestants to the south of the town who was not a Grogan supporter. He was as were the Richards very close to the Talbots, with their strong Mountnorris associations, and in the wake of the rebellion, almost the sole lay person for whom Caulfield expressed concern was Mrs Talbot (one of the accusations that he had to deny was that he was dining at her house on 20 June). Inevitably Caulfield must have had no friends among the rebels, and his own narrow and timorous mentality can only have added to his political problems during the occupation of the town. A letter by Caulfield in July 1798 brings out the extent of his isolation: referring to 20 June, he said that 'Mr Corrin dined with me (for my cry to the clergy was that we should keep together living and dying)': in contrast Hay stated that 'The Rev Mr Corrin, who had been absent from the town the whole of the day on parochial duty had but just returned'.[19] Caulfield in a private letter may be regarded as more reliable than Hay: however, the variety of contrasting explanations can only have added to the doubts of un- involved parties about the conflicting versions of events. Caulfield's explanation could be put in a different light as that of a man of lit- tle courage and who, not for lack of knowledge, but through his isolation and fear, took no risks on 20 June. His explanations and those in the pamphlets he promoted do not carry conviction to the reader, and one is left with the uncomfortable suspicion that there is more to be said, and that he did not choose to say it. His argu- ment, and that in some of the pamphlets, that the mobs were un- manageable may be first and foremost a product of their personal fear at the time, not an objective and disinterested assessment of the situation

We have from successive sources, different accounts of interven- tion on Wexford Bridge on 20 June by Corrin, Roche, Kyan and Richard Monaghan.[20] All the accounts imply slightly different cir- cumstances. The extreme case is that of Edward Hay which com- bined virtually all the then-extant accounts. Having cited Corrin as having saved 'the lives of several who had just been ordered to the bridge', Kyan as saving two named prisoners 'with some others', Edward Roche who 'snatched Mr James Goodall and others from the jaws of death', Hay noted that 'different other persons of inferior note, and some even of the lower class, interposed so as to save one or other of their neighbours; and at length it pleased God that this horrid butchery ceased'.[21] Hay's account makes it possible to reconstruct, though of course on the basis of the evidence of a man who was unreliable, some of the time sequences of the day. It starts with events early in the day, and then 'some time after'. Four hours then elapsed before Hay, who in the interval left the town in great trepidation, returned; and of the later hours of the day he suggests that he was in danger from 'the inclination of many of whom I had now thwarted for hours'.[22] However, Caulfield reported in 1799 on the authority of the friars that 'one of them saw Mr Edward Hay that day of the massacre, in the forenoon and that by chance in the street, and without any application whatever [from him]'.[23] This seems to contrast with the alarm and fear for the safety of the prisoners which his own words claim to have been motivating him from early morning. Conveniently for his evasive account, and indeed the very basis of his evasions, is his claim that he retired at this stage, and later in the sequence of events which he relates, he 'burst into tears, and sunk into a state of insensibility'. The first news to Bishop Caulfield came in a plea to Corrin who was at dinner with him, in a message from Kellet, one of the prisoners awaiting execution: it occurred towards the end of dinner.[24] This would put it probably early to mid afternoon. Corrin proceeded to the bridge: Caulfield did not do so. The picture in Hay's account, and to a lesser extent in Caulfield's accounts, of mobs coming in or a remorseless build-up of fury from a mob is not well-documented. The ease with which one potential victim was saved by a clergyman is borne out in a letter from Caulfield in 1799: this occurred in the morning, and does not seem to have resulted in any general clergy alert. If this was the case, and bearing in mind that Hay's evasive explanations stir up rather than allay suspicion, the cumulative condemnation is even worse. There was, if we accept Hay's argument, a number of interventions, each of them severely limited in scale: Caulfield's letter provides the brief account, already referred to, of one Protestant rescued in the morning by a clergyman who secured the intervention of a pikeman to carry him away. If so many intervened and they all saved some individuals, why was intervention not more general, why was it not earlier, and why were not more saved on each occasion? In this context, the inadequacies of Caulfield's apologia become all the more evident, and Gordon's observation seems the most prudent, indeed, the only prudent one that can be made. At the time, the only logical resolution to the uncomfortable dilemma created by persistence in maintaining this stance, was to reduce the numbers said to have been massacred. Thus, while the number is given in several accounts as near 100, Hay and the Catholic writers opted for figures which were at the lowest 35 or 36, as if mere arithmetics either reduced the horrors of the happening or removed the need for a fuller and dispassionate account. Corrin also emerges as opting for the lower figures for victims both on the Bridge and earlier in the month at Scullabogue barn.[25]

The involvement of the clergy in the massacres, *pace* Musgrave and others, has no known historical basis; at worst their culpability (and presumably that of some lay figures as well) lay in failure to intervene; loyalist criticism of the clergy also implied the suggestion that they had more powers than they had (and the recitals of Catholic rebel clergy claiming miraculous powers for themselves all originated in loyalist accounts). Despite many insinuations of the contrary, they can not be identified with murders on the Bridge, at Scullabogue or on Vinegar Hill. In regard to clergymen as opposed to Catholic rebels at large, what is more arresting is the case of the forced baptisms, because here clergymen actively participated. The case is made at some length by Musgrave. In other accounts it is not much mentioned, and it was rather quickly dropped from the debate. Gordon refers to it incidentally, but simply in relation to two clergymen far away from the real centre of the troubles, and, according to Gordon, acting from laudable motives. Hay disposes of the issue by being vague in detail, but suggesting that Protestants demanded to be baptised, and were present in the chapels in numbers in order to advertise their new-found loyalties.

His words are worth quoting. Referring to 'the absurdity of fear on this account alone, and to undeceive the numbers of sudden converts who were applying to the Catholic priests to be baptised, beseeching in the most earnest manner to be thus received into the bosom of the Catholic church, from an idea that it was then the only plan of safety', he went on to say that

so persevering were the generality in their piteous entreaties, that the Catholic clergy found themselves very distressingly circumstanced; for should they refuse to comply with the wishes and earnest solicitations of such Protestants as offered themselves in this way, they perceived that they would be subject to the most violent animadversions for any fatal accident that might befall any of them ... Their alarms, however, worked so strongly on the minds of the affected converts, that all arguments, exerted to dispel their fears generally proved ineffectual, as they would still persist in most earnest solicitation for admission. Some clergymen, however, in this dilemma, positively refused baptising Protestant converts, but then they took a far better and consistent mode of quieting alarms. They gave the strongest assurances to such as applied to them, that the Catholic church does not deem it necessary to rebaptise any denomination of Christians otherwise than conditionally, as the existence of any previous baptisms whatever, and attendance on divine duties and divine service, was sufficient conformity, ... A curious circumstance, however occurred in Wexford at this time which eventually produced a great number of conditional baptisms. A young lady who on first application failed of persuading a Catholic priest to confer on her the favour of baptism, had the diligence and address afterwards to discover that the Protestant minister who had undertaken to perform that ceremony in her infancy, had only filliped or sprinkled the water at her with his finger, and so it was within the limits of probability that a drop might not have reached her head so as to form an ablution. Being very ingenious and persevering in her arguments, so as to appear capable of puzzling the nicest casuist, she at last made out her own a doubtful case, and was accordingly quieted by conditional baptism. When the particulars of this transaction got abroad, the solicitations to the Catholic clergy for the boon of conditional baptism became considerably more frequent ... It must be remarked, however, that the place itself suffered not the smallest indignity during the whole period of the insurrection, except in the instance of the abandonment of their usual place of worship by the Protestants, of whom great numbers flocked in the most public conspicuous manner to the Catholic chapel, where they affected the greatest piety and devotion. The epithet of 'craw-thumpers' opprobriously applied to Catholics for contritely striking their breasts at their devotions, was never more strongly exemplified than by these *converts.*[26]

Here, as in the case of the Wexford Bridge massacres, there is manipulation of numbers. On the Bridge, numbers have to be reduced; in terms of baptism, the demand for the sacrament has to be multiplied, eagerness to receive baptism has to be stressed, and a mass demand for baptism dilutes any responsibility by Catholics, lay and clerical, for promoting it. It is avoided in the correspondence between Caulfield and Troy, and is not dwelt on in Caulfield's account. The issue surfaces on a sole occasion when Caulfield mentioned that 'some overcome by fear affected to become Catholics and to join the insurgents, to save their liberty and lives'.[27] This theme, and from this source, is repeated in *The state of his majesty's subjects in Ireland professing the Roman Catholic religion* published in 1799.

However, the issue comes up in what must be regarded as the least politicised sources of all, the memoirs of several Protestant women. It occurs on a minor scale in the account by Mrs Adams (sister of the Rev Roger Owen) which was published by Crofton Croker in 1824.[28] The diary of Elizabeth Richards is even more to the point. Her father, Thomas Richards, was a friend of Caulfield and he and the bishop were both together, having travelled in one another's company from Dublin, in Oulart on the morning of 26 May exhorting people to be loyal. In this case there were pressures on her as on others to conform, and also evidence of resistance to the proposal.

In Mrs Adams' and Richards' accounts, the most arresting feature is that the pressure to conform came from lay friends or acquaintances of the narrators. According to Jane Adams, the proposal came from, or was carried, by her servant Alley. When the question arose more directly in the priest's presence, his response was, as reported by Mrs Adams:

> 'Madam, that is between you and your God; I should be sorry to influence any one, though many have come to me for that purpose.' I said I was sure he would have but a bad opinion of any one who could so suddenly, and through fear, change their religion. I gave him great credit for his answer to me.[29]

The earlier reference to Alley broaching baptism does not clarify whether the proposal originated with her or whether she was acting at the behest of others. In Jane Adams' account of what the priest said, the future argument that people sought baptism is hinted at. However, the hard fact is that, in the accounts by individuals we have, some Protestants refused to be baptised. The limited direct evidence we have, and other evidence has to be regarded with deep scepticism, provides no clear instances of Protestants *demanding* baptism. It does, however, provide, notably in Elizabeth Richards' diary, evidence of pressures from their friends, and of resistance in the response by some Protestants to the suggestion. We also have to make a distinction between baptism, and attendance, under some duress, at Catholic services (though Hay represents attendance at church services as a consequence of baptism). Elizabeth Richards held out against baptism. It is not clear that her mother was baptised: in fact her mother attended Catholic service on the first Sunday of the rebel occupation of the county town; none of the family attended on the two subsequent Sundays. Hay makes the damaging admission of a number of clergymen baptising Protestants, who, of course, on his account through fear, demanded baptism. A number of Catholic clergymen are said to have administered baptism. The unnamed clergyman in Mrs Adams' account, however, seems to come out of the story rather well, and Elizabeth Richards' diary also seems to give a favourable account of the role of Fr Corrin, the parish priest of Wexford. However, she also gives an account of seeing a large number of gloomy and frightened Protestants in the convent. According to Caulfield, at the outset of the occupation Protestants took refuge in his house, in Corrin's house and in the convent 'as a place of safety, begging and imploring protection; that those houses were constantly thronged with the Protestants of the neighbourhood ...'[30] If Elizabeth Richards' account is correct, the convent, probably larger than the residences of either Caulfield or Corrin, may have been a central refuge. On her account, an atmosphere of fear existed in it. The balance of probability is that there were pressures on Protestants from laity to be baptised, that some priests did not resist the movement or even welcomed it, and that the argument that Protestants *demanded* baptism was already a fiction to justify the procedure, and to avoid conceding that there were pressures on them to conform.

We know very little about the inner thoughts of people, whether on baptism or on massacre. Even in the case of the Scullabogue massacre, for instance, detail of the precise relationship between the actual event and the battle in Ross, and the timing of the massacre in relation to the battle, are too thin to warrant too confident an explanation either by way of apologia or inculpation. One can construct some of the events as Daniel Gahan has done:[31] beyond that, as to motive and numbers, it is foolish to go. The argument that the killing was conducted by rebels fleeing from New Ross and in response to a specific atrocity by loyalist forces there (the setting fire to a rebel hospital for their wounded) is not well-documented and seems rather facile. Admittedly a sort of reciprocating logic between loyalist atrocities before the rebellion and rebel actions in the rebellion, and between the behaviour on both sides during the rebellion, seems to exist. However, Catholic or nationalist apologetics, or on the other side Musgrave-style representation of massacre as part of the inner logic of rebellion, are both out of place.

v

What is puzzling in Wexford in the last analysis is less the sectarian themes than the prominence of clergymen in active rebellion. This has parallels elsewhere, for instance the role of Catholic clergymen in Mayo (who seem in some instances to have moved to the site of the action rather than to have been overwhelmed by it in their own parishes), or Presbyterian clergymen in Co Down, where their ab-

sence from the field in the final denouement of the story is mainly
due to their arrest beforehand. Barber was one of the few radical
clergymen still at liberty. Hailed by the young Charles Teeling as
the 'first in command', his reply was that 'I am not fitted for the active duties of the field, but I will aid you with my counsel, and second you with my arm, and what a man of sixty years of age can do,
I pledge myself to perform'.[32]

The real problem, north and south, Presbyterian as well as
Catholic, is less that of accounting for the involvement of clergy
than for their absence in neighbouring areas. Wexford clergymen
embroiled in the rebellion came predominantly from a swathe east
of the Slaney corresponding to the Mountnorris estate and beyond
it to the estates of the liberal Whigs just north of Wexford town,
and from west of the Slaney in the region running parallel to the
Blackstairs mountains. Similarly involved clergy are largely absent
in the rest of the county. Likewise, involvement of clergymen in Co
Down contrasts with a comparative absence of direct involvement
by Presbyterian clergymen in radical causes in Antrim, politically
the most radical region in Ulster. Any satisfying explanation of the
reasons for the involvement of clergymen must account for these
contrasts both in Leinster and in Ulster.

The idea of priests being leaders of the people comes up in
Musgrave and other sources, and this was, for rather different reasons, the case argued by the Catholic clergyman Kavanagh in his
writings from 1870 and by the rhetoric of spokesmen in the 1898
celebrations in which clergymen, or at least one of them, John
Murphy, is transformed into a heroic or Moses-like figure leading
his people to safety, or at least attempting to protect them from oppression (itself progressively ever more exaggerated in the telling as
we move from post-rebellion apologetics – themselves suspect – to
the highly synthetic late nineteenth-century accounts). Though
both Edward Hay and Bishop Caulfield pointed out that only curates were involved in rebellion, the degree of involvement, if measured statistically, is quite meaningful in terms of the numbers of
clergy involved within these two well-defined regions, one in the
east the earliest centre of popular activism in Wexford, the other,

west Wexford, the source of the most dedicated forces in the field in the actual rebellion. This raises issues which are eliminated if statistical study is pitched at county level when clerical participation becomes diluted by non-involvement in the south of the county.

Both Stock and Gordon, liberals though they were, distrusted the loyalty of the Catholic clergy. In Stock's case, and he was influenced implicitly by the role of clergymen in Mayo, his view was that they depended for their income on their parishioners and the advantage of state pensions would be that it would end dependence by the clergymen on their community and hence the danger of contamination by its political views. There is a striking contrast in his book between his reluctance to give any details of the role of clergy (in line with the liberal approach of playing down culpability) and the underlying stress on the doubtful loyalty created by their dependence for their income on their flocks. The attitudes of clergy were, however, probably far more complex than the mere fact of a financial dependence on their parishioners. The areas in which clergymen were involved were areas of intense politicisation prior to the rebellion. The point may be inescapable that some of them were variously early United Irishman leaders, or were recruited at a later stage when organisation began to escalate from April 1798. As May was the month of the regular three-month United Irish elections to all offices, the officer status of some clergy (excluding some clergy who were likely United Irishmen already), if officers they were, could only have come into existence in that month.

Elsewhere, in Leinster, while clergymen with radical or suspected radical views existed, few activists in the field can be found. They were singularly lacking in Kildare or in Wicklow despite local United Irishman strength and ultimate action in the field. The reasons would seem to spring from contrasts in local politicisation. Wicklow, and even more Kildare, had a large liberal political establishment, and county opposition to the government did not fracture in 1797 and early 1798. The point may be that political pressure on Catholic clergy originated less from the political divide between loyalists and radicals, than from intense politicisation within their own communities when a divide took shape between radicals and more moderate liberals. Such an internal divide existed in Wexford; it did not have parallels in Wicklow, Kildare and even in Carlow.

Mayo may fit into the same pattern. There was a sharp divide between pro- and anti-Catholic wings in north Connacht Protestant society, and one of the features of Mayo is the somewhat unusual role of Denis Browne, the political manager of the county who combined a firm opposition to radicalism with strong sympathies in favour of Catholic political rights. Hence internal politicisation among Catholics was already a factor, logically a follow-on to the near successful attempt by Browne (though a friend of the Catholics) – Mayo was the last county to declare attendance – to prevent the county's Catholics from supporting the 1792 convention. Many years later, W. H. Maxwell, in a not unsympathetic analysis, re-called Browne as a bullyboy whose methods were already in his own time becoming outmoded.

The two areas within Co Wexford where recruitment was wide-spread were centres of real tensions, even if the local circumstances differed between west Wexford (to which Philip Roche was trans-ferred because his political role in east Wexford had given offence to his bishop, and in which Kearns, who had earlier served in Kildare, was present before the rebellion), and east Wexford. In 1797 the central political issue in both areas was the role of Mountnorris in running his son-in-law for the county. East Wexford had a distinct political profile, and was ahead in political activism. This was the great centre of gentry sympathies in favour of Catholics. Though Mountnorris presented himself as friend of the Catholics (his step-father was Matthew Talbot, in his lifetime the county's premier Catholic gentleman), his involvement in the election on behalf of his son-in-law, Maxwell Barry, caused an up-heaval. The powerful radical interest of the Grogans and Colcloughs followed the main Whig interest (the national Whig interest at large divided) in withdrawing from the general election. Withdrawal from the election had originally been proposed by the United Irishmen, and the radical Whig decision, which the Grogans and Colcloughs dutifully followed, was inevitably backed by rank-and-file United Irishmen, precociously present in east Wexford and organised by the dedicated, left-wing Francis-Street emissaries along the main road leading to Dublin through Oulart and Castlebridge to Wexford town. However, the real base of Grogan and Colclough support was south of the Slaney. North of the Slaney the sympathetic gentry were Whigs rather than radicals, and seem to have been swept into support of the Mountnorris campaign. The axis of local political conflict thus revolved around the Mountnorris interest, opposed by some liberals (in the Grogan's case, when they decided not to participate, they gave their interest for what it was worth to Ely, thus ditching Mountnorris), and supported by others who dissented from the decision to withdraw from politics. The area to the east of the Slaney was thus deeply divided, with radicals or liberals involved on behalf of Maxwell Barry, or, if they followed the Grogan line, opposed violently to his candidature. However, few gentry seem to have taken the pro-Grogan line in this region, and the anti-Mountnorris interest there seems to have relied on the lower-order United Irishmen, who mirrored also a divide between the Wexford United Irish leaders, seeking to create for their own advancement a United Irishman Society from the top down, and others connected to the democratic Francis-Street interest in Dublin, concentrating on building organisation from the bottom up. Inevitably frictions sharpened. Catholics on the east bank of the Slaney were divided between Edward Fitzgerald and Edward Hay, who supported the Mountnorris campaign, and others, including Edward Hay's brother John Hay and Thomas Dixon, apparently on the other side. So bad were relations between the two sides that John Hay and Edward Fitzgerald fought a duel. With Edward Hay and John Hay, Bishop Caulfield and Thomas Richards, all present in Oulart and its fringes on 26 May 1798, the day of the outbreak of the rebellion in Wexford, it is remarkable how many people of consequence on both sides of the political divide were present on that day and by choice at that location.

Hay's later account maintained that the troubles during the three-week rebel occupation of the town of Wexford were caused by bad people from the north of the county. However, they were from close at hand from districts just north of the estuary of the

Slaney, and they corresponded to one of two factions which already existed locally before the rebellion. It was from here that the politics of Co Wexford were imported into the town. Le Hunte of Artramont (singled out by Thomas Dixon in his vendetta), was probably already perceived by some as an enemy because he may have backed the Mountnorris campaign. He was certainly not in the Grogan camp, and the divide seems to have gone back as far as the 1776 town mayoral election, when Le Hunte took a different view from the Grogan interest. Le Hunte was no bigot: the Catholic members of his yeomanry corps were part of his force to the day the rebellion broke out, when they went over *en masse* to the rebels, one of them, Edward Roche, as a leader. The reasons for the arrest of Le Hunte were on all counts preposterous: according to Elizabeth Richards on 15 June 'the people say that Colonel Hunte was the chief of that society [the Orange Order] and that their meetings were held in a room in his house'. His arrest also contrasts with tolerance for others, notably the town's Protestant mayor Jacob and William Hatton and with the active presence of Protestants even in the leadership. The theme that comes out in the apologia of Edward Hay and others, that they could not control the people, reflects less a lack of control over a mob as such than an acute hostility between two radical factions. However, the Protestant United Irishman leaders were all without exception from south of the Slaney, conspicuously part of the Grogan-Colclough mafia in politics (excepting Perry in the north, who, however, was married to a Catholic, and would seem to have formed part of the Fitzgerald-Edward Hay axis in the complex local politics of 1797-8). It was from the south of the town that the Grogan interest in the well-documented and bitterly contested mayoral election of 1776 was drawn.[33]

West of the Slaney, where a Grogan-style radical gentry interest did not exist (though a moderate one of the Phaires, Alcocks and Carews did), Catholics participated enthusiastically in the 1797 election. Maxwell Barry was, of course, from his speeches in the Irish parliament, a known bigot, and some reluctance to respond to earnest canvassing on his behalf must have existed. It was in this region too that from across the border in Carlow Colonel John Staunton Rochefort ran as a candidate in Wexford, and that from January 1798 onwards the Orange Order began to appear. In fact, while Ogle withdrew from the election in 1797, he seems to have participated in the campaign (from Thomas Cloney's account, Cloney, an active canvasser for Maxwell Barry, refused to drink Ogle's health at a subsequent dinner), and Cloney had a high profile in the politics of 1797. He was not yet a United Irishman, and John Kelly, who was one in June 1797, withdrew at the request of Caesar Colclough, whose contacts with the Castle, though moderate (and in a personal sense self-seeking), were in contrast with the hostility of the Colclough-Grogan interest at large. Opposition by Ogle to Mountnorris's candidate hardly of itself turned Maxwell Barry into a candidate who could command willing consent by all, and this point cannot have been lost on some of the voters and political managers on the ground. Hence, the strong liberal partisanship on behalf of Maxwell Barry in west Wexford may itself have led to resentments by some, doubly so as the United Irishmen were beginning to appear in the region, and the determined Francis-Street faction, not the anaemic east Wexford leadership group, set the pace. Thus both east and west of the Slaney, despite different contexts, tensions existed. It is likely that it was this intense politicisation that drew clergymen into politics either as supporters of the more radical faction or as part of an opposing group to the unholy alliance in west Wexford. South Wexford was free of these tensions because the Grogan interest effectively represented all the local opposition interest to government and kept out of active involvement in the election: the consequent lack of electoral conflict may have slowed the spread of politicisation and equally, as a concomitant factor, the drawing of clergymen into public political stances.

Neighbouring Wicklow, Carlow and above all Kildare presented less of a problem for clergy. The local political establishment in Wicklow and especially Kildare was benign; Catholics were not pressurised into taking well-defined positions as they were in north Wexford on both banks of the Slaney. In both Wicklow and

Kildare, and in Carlow, electoral politics did not loom large among
Catholics: in contrast in Wexford there was a divide between, on
the one hand, the Grogan Whigs and the radical United Irishmen
with much in common and, on the other hand, a more moderate
faction, seduced by Mountnorris's politics, who like some of the
less radical Whigs nationally were prepared opportunistically, against
the policy of the Whig leaders, to participate in the 1797 election.

The 1797 election may well have been the defining factor in
local life, producing friction not only within the opposition but on
the government side, with the emergence of an overt Orange faction
in opposition at the time at any rate to the more orthodox Ely support of government (beneficiaries also in the style of eighteenth-
century politics in 1797 of the Grogan 'interest' and hence subtly
constrained to be more moderate, as indeed Ely's contacts with
Catholics in 1799 were to prove). Ogle's withdrawal from politics
had not been from public life (he was elected for Dublin in 1798).
He seems, despite a very public retirement, to have remained politically active in 1797. The fact that Colonel Rochefort (a man also
with many contacts in Queen's county, itself a county to the right
of centre in 1797), who was responsible for establishing the Orange
Order in Carlow, and had some months earlier run as a candidate
in Wexford, may have fitted into a pattern of creating an activist
loyalist force in south Leinster. Ogle's stance during the election in
Wexford and his later advent to Dublin politics may have been fitted into a pattern of introducing a more activist loyalist force than
the orthodox one of Lord Ely. On the Union itself, Ogle, consistent
with his Orange credentials, opposed; Ely ultimately supported.
Indeed, the introduction to Wexford of Kingsborough's North
Cork Militia in April 1798 would seem more the result of lobbying
by Ogle than anything else (a response secured by Ogle to Mountnorris's campaign to prevent armed forces being sent to Wexford),
and would fit into the pattern of a growing Orange presence in
north Wexford, small to start with but growing rapidly in the
spring. The Orange Order at its advent seems very much to have
been imposed from the top down rather than to have been a response to pressures on the ground. This itself may help to account

for the fact that, in many narratives from both sides, there are accounts of kindness across the political divides, which suggests that local polarisation and the depth of bitterness varied a good deal from place to place and from family to family. The spread of the Orange Order in south Leinster is related to this political context and its ramifications across several counties. In the wake of the rebellion, the burning of Catholic chapels (involving over 40 chapels and government compensation in Ferns of £5500), largely a phenomenon of the compact territory of north Wexford, south Wicklow and adjacent Carlow, seems to have been an orchestrated affair in the hands of activist loyalist yeomanry, and offers in a crude fashion a rough guide to the frontiers of this region. Obsessions with Orangemen before the rebellion were by no means a figment of the imagination, and were all the more effective because United Irishman propaganda had been summoning them out of the air even before they had become a real force on the ground.

A community bitterly divided on political grounds does not of itself generate sectarian feeling, but Ogle's image and the fact that the North Cork militia, who arrived in the county in April 1798, were commanded by his friend Kingsborough did not help. Ogle and Kingsborough had been always among the first speakers and the most vehement in anti-Catholic rhetoric in parliamentary debate. The Orange sentiments of his regiment, which Kingsborough and his men did not attempt to conceal, and which was closely linked to the political stance of Ogle, also made the Orange issue a local public one: it was less at first a case of what the regiment did militarily (it did nothing of consequence in its first weeks) than of the propaganda value it presented to United Irishmen of stressing both its Orange profile and its Ogle associations.

As to what the views of the clergy were, we can not with confidence say, though Gordon's unflattering description of Murphy should not be lightly discarded. His political views, however, he shared with others, and they should be seen less as those of a spontaneous leader than of a participant in politicised society (in the parish where he was curate, despite the pressures from Mountnorris, there was opposition to a declaration of loyalty in yet another

Mountnorris campaign in April 1798). Miles Byrne speaks very well of him; he tends to be unduly favourable in his views of prominent rebels (though he was writing at a much later stage in life than other actual participants, and inevitably that produced errors and rosy hues), but his point may well be correct that Murphy was committed by conviction or ideals to the cause and had a measure of leadership ability. It is by no means impossible to reconcile the views of Gordon and Byrne. If so, Murphy would in fact simply reflect some of the features we see from other evidence: the Slaney region was organised, linked to the radical wing of the United Irishmen, and certainly had some, although not necessarily all, fanatical followers. A sudden acceleration of United Irishman recruitment from April and the now-public presence of the Orange Order both added to tensions, and especially to mutual fears of intended massacre. The fact that both rebels and the yeoman cavalry units engaged in widespread house burning at the outset of the rebellion is also symptomatic of a breakdown of community relations. In fact, this was less a universal feature of the county than one which existed in particular districts. It was evident to the immediate west of Enniscorthy. Jane Barber's account is a useful non-political measure of their existence there, and in a later account Barbara Lett noted 'that I returned to the country with these humble women who, a short time before, entered the town decked with Orange lilies, the insignia of the Order, which they now hastily removed upon hearing the rebels were returning to destroy them'.[34] The interesting feature here is less their fears than their use of Orange insignia. The same climate could be found in the vicinity of Gorey (and Hunter Gowan's and Roger Owen's activities accounted for their presence in this region). The murder of the rector Samuel Heyden may have been in part accounted for by the fact that he was the agent for the Wexford lands of Lord Monck, a very high profile loyalist politician in Dublin and Wicklow. Immediately north of Wexford, the Castlebridge-Kilcormick district represented a similar pattern. Thomas Dixon was to give it later notoriety. The murder at Kyle of Burrowes, rector of Kilmuckridge, in the opening hours of the rebellion, is interesting. One of Luke Cullen's sources suggests some unease at the fact that he was killed, and speculated as to whether it was necessary that it should happen thus.

The sense of menace in local communities not only also existed but was fomented by partisans on both sides. Thus, on Miles Byrne's chilling account, the United Irishmen rode through one village in the north of the county calling out to each other the names of 'the well-know chiefs of the Orange party', so that by morning people were in no doubt of the purpose of their opponents.[35] While the magistrates assembled in Wexford, given the powerful liberal element among them, decided on 23 May to defer for a further fortnight the taking of more drastic measures, some magistrates, as far as can be judged in the troubled northern districts, went beyond legality in the week preceding the final outbreak of the rebellion on 26 May.

Ulster raises some of the same issues. There the contrast is superficially between the Belfast region and the rest of Ulster. Charles Teeling saw all the Presbyterians as coming from within a close radius of Belfast, stressing that they dwelt 'within the compass of a limited district; and from a central point, the residence of the most distant was not many miles, with the exception of the Rev Mr Smyth, who was stationed in a contiguous quarter of the county of Derry – all were of Antrim or of Down'.[36] More directly, however, it is the contrast between Down and Antrim. The reason seems fairly clear cut and similar to that accounting for contrasts among Catholic clergy in Leinster. In Antrim, the gentry were either sympathetic or, in the case of the Donegall family, largely absentee. Hence, society had a degree of consensus in public support of opposition and of the radical Presbyterian stance. Elections in particular did not fundamentally polarise society. In Down, on the other hand, from their base in the west of the county the Downshire family sought to undermine radical support in the county at large. Hence all Down elections were bitter affairs, and in particular there was massive involvement, intended to throw back the encroachments of Downshire influence, in the general election of 1790, the most famous and protracted election in Irish history. The bitterness it engendered was added to when young Robert Stewart, who had been elected by radical support in 1790, betrayed his new trust as a radical, as began to become very clear from as early as 1792; and the great Presbyterian heartland of east Down became on that account more than very worked up. Inevitably, clergymen were involved, and James Porter's famous *Billy Bluff,* which first appeared in the pages of the *Northern Star* and afterwards as a separate pamphlet with immense popularity, had as its thinly disguised targets both Robert Stewart's father and his agent Cleland.

Catholic curates came from prominent local families, and thus often reflected the political views of the lay members of the family (or like the several Dixon families at Castlebridge in Wexford producing both a politically unaffiliated clergyman and a clergyman who with two brothers were United). Inevitably this drew some clergymen, by virtue of family ties and local pressures, into taking sides and into United Irishman involvement. The same pattern can be detected in the north. Although Antrim was unquestionably the most committed United Irishman county in the north and, with east Down, one of the two most Presbyterian regions in the north, activists among its Presbyterian clergymen are hard to find. On the other hand, they were numerous in Down including figures such as Barber at Rathfriland, Dickson at Portaferry, Ledlie Birch at Saintfield, Porter at Greyabbey, McMahon at Holywood, Sinclair and Simpson at Newtownards, Bailie Warden at Bangor, and Samspon and William Warwick not yet affiliated to a congregation. The reason seems clear: Down was a county with a strong Anglican gentry presence: community resistance to political pressures by Anglican gentry in Presbyterian districts inevitably drew clergymen into committed opposition in unison with their congregations.

The question is less one of drawing a simple black-and-white line between loyalist and subversive clergymen, than of explaining why radical sympathies in some regions converted clergymen into militant activists, and in other districts failed to draw them into a like scale of public commitment. Whether these inactive clergymen shared fully the political views widespread around them, we can not say. Even in the baptism issue, what is interesting is that the pressures came from lay Catholics. Clergymen were conforming either weakly or out of conviction to what was either a wider intolerance, or an urge to remake society: they were not leading society, they were flowing with it. In a sense this seems to vindicate the view of Burke, as far back as 1792, on the weak or ineffective role of the Catholic clergy. In Presbyterian communities, with their long story of opposition between clergy and Anglican gentry, the political activism of Presbyterian clergy seems to have been greatest in districts where they found themselves faced with an overbearing Anglican gentry force, and thus found themselves once more cast in what in essence had been the traditional role they had exercised of opposing Anglican landlord, parson and parson-magistrate. In this sense the activism may be said to have been caused by the policies of Downshire and perhaps even more by the betrayal of the Presbyterian political cause by Robert Stewart. However, even these thoughts have to be regarded as speculative. What this paper is intended to do is to suggest that our knowledge is limited, (and while it will be added to as time goes by) that we must steer clear of contemporary apologetics and equally the propaganda, often false, which provoked the apologetics, and that we must, in looking at the rebellion, avoid getting involved in a new form of apologetics which too simplistically either eliminates sectarianism (there are signs of this in current debate), or alternatively makes it into the driving force (that too, emptied out of old bottles, is present afresh in the new historiography).

Notes:

1   Hayes, R., 'Priests in the Independence movement of '98', *Irish Ecclesiastical Record*, 5th series, vol. LXVII (Oct 1945), pp. 258-70.
2   McEvoy, Brendan, 'Father James Quigley', *Seanchas Ard Mhacha*, vol. 5, no.
2   (1970),pp. 247-268.
3   Miller, D.W., 'Presbyterianism and modernisation in Ulster', *Past and present*, no. 80 (August 1978), pp. 66-90.
4   Cullen, L.M., 'Political structures of the Defenders' in *Ireland and the French Revolution*, (ed) H. Gough and D. Dickson, Dublin 1990, pp. 130-1.

5   On Edwards, see L.M. Cullen, 'Politics and rebellion: Wicklow in the
    1790s', in *Wicklow: history and society*, K. Hannigan and W. Nolan,
    (eds), Dublin 1994, pp. 414, 423-4, 431, 465-6, 475-6.

6   See *Memoirs and correspondence of viscount Castlereagh*, 4 vols., London,
    1848, Charles Vane, (ed), Marquess of Londonderry.

7   Coigley(Quigley), James, *Life of the Rev James Quigley*, London, 1798

8   Byrne, Miles, *Memoirs*, Paris, 1863.

9   Anon. (ed), 'Reminiscences of a fugitive loyalist in 1798', in *English historical
    Review*, vol. 1 (1886), pp. 536-544.

10 Luke Godfrey of Kenmare, Co Kerry.

11 Stock, Joseph, *A narrative of what passed at Killala... during the summer of
    1798 by an eye-witness*, Dublin, 1800, (there were many editions of this pam-
    phlet); James Gordon, *History of the rebellion in Ireland* (London, 1801,
    1803); James Littlle, 'An unpublished diary of the French invasion', edited
    by N. Costello in *Analecta Hibernica*, vol. II, pp. 59-174.

12 Barrington, Sir Jonah, *Personal sketches and recollections of his own time*, vol.
    3, London, 183, p. 279, (see also pp. 276, 286).

13 *Charge of the Hon. Justice Fletcher to the grand jury of the county of Wexford at
    the summer assizes of 1814.*

14 Barrington, op. cit., vol. 2, p. 276.

15 Dublin Diocesan Archives, Archbishop's house (D.D.A.), AB2/116/7, no. 83,
    3 Nov, 1798, Caulfield to Troy.

16 D.D.A. , AB2/116/7, no. 75, 2 Sept 1798, Caulfield to Troy; AB2/116/7, no. 134,
    21 May 1799, Caulfield to Troy. The changes may have been noted by
    Clinch, a lay professor at Maynooth with whom Troy had much contact. A
    note by Troy on 11 Oct 1799 to Clinch said that he had sent on Clinch's
    queries to Caulfield. D.D.A., AB2/116/7, no. 138.

17 *The state of his majesty's subjects in Ireland professing the Roman Catholic reli-
    gion containing an account of the conduct of the Roman Catholic clergy in
    Wexford during the rebellion of 1798, and the refutation of a pamphlet signed
    Veridicus (1799).*

18 *The reply of the Right Hon. Dr Caulfield and of the Roman Catholic clergy of
    Wexford to the misrepresentations of Sir Richard Musgrave* (Dublin,
    1801), p. 13.

19 D.D.A. AB2/116/7, no. 73, Caulfield to Troy, 31 July 1798; Edward Hay, *History
    of the Irish insurrection of 1803* (Boston edition, n.d.), p. 266.

20 Some details of Corrin's role are also furnished by Caulfield, D.D.A., no. 73,
    31 July 1798; no. 74, 31 Aug 1798.

21 Hay, Edward, op. cit., pp. 265-6.

22 Hay, op. cit., pp. 254, 257, 261.

23 D.D.A., AB2/116/7, no. 165, 3 Nov 1799.

24 D.D.A., AB2/116/7, no. 165, 3 Nov 1799.

25 D.D.A., AB2/116/7, no. 135, 24 May 1799.

26 Hay, op. cit., 190-192.

27 D.D.A., AB2/116/7, no. 76, 4 Sept 1798.

28 Crofton Croker, T., *Researches in the south of Ireland...(with an appendice con-
    taining a private narrative of the rebellion of 1798*, London, 1824, pp. 347-385.

29 Crofton Croker, op. cit., pp. 369-70.

30 D.D.A., AB2/116/7, no. 74, 31 Aug 1798.

31 Gahan, D., 'The Scullabogue massacre 1798' in *History Ireland*, vol. 4, no.
    3 (Autumn 1996), pp. 27-31.

32   Teeling, C.H., *Sequel to the personal narrative of the Irish rebellion* (Glasgow edition of 1976, reprinted Irish University Press, 1969) p. 202 .
33   Goodall, D., 'The freemen of Wexford in 1776', *Irish genealogist*, vol. 5, no. 1 (Nov 1974), pp. 103-121, no. 3, (Nov 76), pp. 314-334; vol. 5, no. 4 (Nov 1977), pp. 448-463.
34   Ranson, Joseph, 'A '98 diary by Mrs Barbara Newton Lett, Killaligan, Enniscorthy', *The past*, vol. v (1949), p. 142.
35   Byrne, op. cit., vol. 1, pp. 14-15.
36   Teeling, op. cit., p. 208.

Index